PATTERNS OF CHANGE

Patterns of Change

*Intensive Analysis of
Psychotherapy Process*

Edited by
LAURA N. RICE
York University
LESLIE S. GREENBERG
University of British Columbia

THE GUILFORD PRESS
New York   London

© 1984 The Guilford Press

A Division of Guilford Publications, Inc.

200 Park Avenue South, New York, N.Y. 10003

Printed in the United States of America

Library of Congress Cataloging in Publication Data
Main entry under title:

Patterns of change.

   Bibliography: p.
   Includes indexes.
   1. Psychotherapy—Research. 2. Personality change—
Research. I. Rice, Laura North, 1920-
II. Greenberg, Leslie S.
RC337.P37   1984   616.89'14   82-15535
ISBN 0-89862-624-2

CONTRIBUTORS

MARJORIE COHEN, PhD, Department of Psychiatry, Hospital of the University of Pennsylvania, Philadelphia, Pennsylvania

PAUL CRITS-CHRISTOPH, MA, Department of Psychology, Yale University, New Haven, Connecticut

ROBERT ELLIOTT, PhD, Department of Psychology, University of Toledo, Toledo, Ohio

LESLIE S. GREENBERG, PhD, Department of Counselling Psychology, Faculty of Education, University of British Columbia, Vancouver, British Columbia, Canada

JOHN HARTKE, PhD, The Fairmount Institute, Philadelphia, Pennsylvania

MARDI J. HOROWITZ, MD, Department of Psychiatry, School of Medicine, University of California–San Francisco, and Center for the Study of Neuroses, Langley Porter Psychiatric Institute, San Francisco, California

MARJORIE H. KLEIN, PhD, Department of Psychiatry, Center for Health Sciences, University of Wisconsin, Madison, Wisconsin

LESTER LUBORSKY, PhD, Department of Psychiatry, Hospital of the University of Pennsylvania, Philadelphia, Pennsylvania

CHARLES R. MARMAR, MD, Department of Psychiatry, School of Medicine, University of California–San Francisco, and Center for the Study of Neuroses, Langley Porter Psychiatric Institute, San Francisco, California

PHILIPPA MATHIEU-COUGHLAN, PhD, Office of Student Mental Health, Wesleyan University, Middletown, Connecticut

LAURA N. RICE, PhD, Department of Psychology, York University, Downsview, Ontario, Canada

EVA PILA SAPERIA, MEd, Ontario Institute for Studies in Education, Toronto, Ontario, Canada. Current affiliation: University of Toronto, Toronto, Ontario, Canada

BARTON SINGER, PhD, Department of Psychiatry, UMDNJ—Rutgers Medical School, Piscataway, New Jersey

NANCY WILNER, MA, Department of Psychiatry, School of Medicine, University of California–San Francisco, and Center for the Study of Neuroses, Langley Porter Psychiatric Institute, San Francisco, California

PREFACE

In our day-to-day practice as therapists we have been continually fascinated by the compelling but elusive patterns in the series of interactions that form a psychotherapy, trying to sort out and maximize the truly active ingredients. As psychologists engaged in psychotherapy research our central goal has been to understand and construct models of the underlying mechanisms that make therapeutic change possible. The present volume represents a merging of these two directions in a new research strategy for studying patterns of change in psychotherapy.

It was apparent to us at the end of the '60s that fine-grained analyses of statement-by-statement client–therapist interactions could identify some of the essential elements of therapeutic change and that without this knowledge outcome studies would yield little information on which to build a science of psychotherapy. However, there were formidable methodological problems in finding meaningful patterns in such overwhelming quantities of complex material. After reviewing existing methods and trying out some of them on our data, we concluded that the best instrument for pattern identification was the "human integrator," who in psychotherapy research would be the disciplined clinical observer. The human ability to identify complex performance patterns and their changes at an appropriate level of subtlety seemed to be far superior to any preexisting combination of category measures and computational tools. We decided, therefore, to draw on clinical observation to help identify change phenomena which appeared to recur both within and across clients and then to study rigorously the moment-by-moment process that characterizes these phenomena.

Rice, in her work on the evocative function of the therapist, had begun to identify a recurrent and seemingly potent event in the context of client-centered therapy, a point at which clients were able to resolve some of their own problematic reactions. Discussion of this work led us to a formal definition of a unit called an "event," which we thought could be profitably identified by clinicians for more detailed research. The event consisted of a client "marker" of an opportunity for change, a series of therapist interventions designed to promote change at this marker, and the ensuing client process leading to resolution of the affective problem. Greenberg, in applying this perspective to the identification of a recurrent potent event from the practice of Gestalt therapy, showed that it could profitably be used to isolate and describe an event in which intrapersonal conflicts were resolved.

An important influence on our thinking at this stage came from our introduction by Dr. Juan Pascual-Leone to the methods of task analysis used by Piagetians and developed by neo-Piagetians to study the moment-by-moment performances of children solving cognitive problems. The juxtaposition of the two points of view—one, that it was profitable for process researchers to study potent therapeutic events, and two, that it was possible to study complex human problem-solving performances by means of task analysis—led to the application of task analysis to the study of therapeutic events. It also became clear to us that a naturalistic observation approach alone was not an adequate research strategy. Although naturalistic observation was useful in initially observing and identifying events, an investigative approach in which one begins to experiment with ways of making the event occur more fully more often was far more productive than waiting for the occurrence of good, pure samples. Task analysis embodied this type of investigative strategy, enabling one to study client task performance in the context of therapist-provided task conditions. We found that the application of this approach to the study of the events we had chosen from client-centered and Gestalt therapy was so revealing and helpful to practice, teaching, and supervision that we began to consider the potential usefulness of this approach to the field as a whole.

During the period 1974 to 1980, we regularly presented the results of this work at the annual meetings of the Society for Psychotherapy Research and were encouraged by the response to our work. A number of participants appeared to share our views on the potential value of process research and also agreed on the need to reexamine the goals and methods in general use. Although we were aware of the work of Lester Luborsky and his colleagues on the symptom-context method, of Mardi Horowitz and his group on state analysis, of Marjorie Klein and Philippa Mathieu-Coughlan on the Experiencing Scale, and of Robert Elliott on the use of interpersonal process recall, it was from the series of presentations and discussions at the Society's meetings that we became aware of how much we all shared common goals and believed in the importance of discovery-oriented, intensive analysis of therapeutic phenomena.

In deciding to put this volume together, we were keenly aware of the need for demonstrating the diversity across orientations and types of issues studied of observationally based, discovery-oriented approaches to the study of change. We therefore asked the authors previously mentioned to contribute chapters to this book in the hope that viewing all the approaches together would provide a stronger understanding than any one alone of the viability of a new research strategy for studying change episodes.

A cornerstone of this new style of research is the rigorous use of clinical method to study change. Therefore, chapters in this book should be of interest to both researchers and clinicians involved in the process of change in psychotherapy. The approach presented in this book, based as it is on the intensive and rigorous observation of clinically significant change episodes in psychotherapy, will, we hope, lead to advances in both research and practice.

Laura N. Rice
Leslie S. Greenberg

CONTENTS

Introduction

LAURA N. RICE
York University

LESLIE S. GREENBERG
University of British Columbia

Why is it that some people change or resolve particular affective problems in psychotherapy, while others do not change or even get worse? Without answers to this basic question we cannot have a true science of psychotherapy. Our success rates will probably not improve substantially, and practicing clinicians will continue to rely on theoretical and personal preferences rather than research evidence. There is a wealth of general theoretical explanations of therapeutic change, but little research evidence at a level that could guide treatment selection and improve practice. We need to identify moments of change and study them systematically and in detail. It is the identification of recurrent observable change phenomena and the discerning of patterns among variables that describe these phenomena that could lead to the establishment of a research-based science of psychotherapy.

Psychotherapy research has increased in sophistication over the last two decades and has clarified a number of the questions that need to be asked. Great advances have not taken place, however, in explaining how psychotherapy brings about change. Seemingly hopeful directions such as differential treatment and "core conditions" research have proved disappointing. The field is looking for new approaches.

A discovery approach to understanding the mechanisms of change has been proposed in a number of reviews of the status of the field. The problem has been one of developing research strategies that are at the same time creative–inductive, discovery-oriented approaches and yet characterized by the use of disciplined methods. What is needed is a research approach that, rather than relegating discovery to the subjective domain, focuses on discovery as part of the research activity. This approach must provide a set of systematic and rigorous procedures which follow in a logical order, have built-in checks that ensure consensual agreement, and result in reliable findings that can be shared by the community of experts in the field. In this book we propose a research approach with a rigorous methodology for identifying and investigating change episodes based on

1

the intensive analysis of recurring patterns of client performance. Examples of a number of different approaches demonstrating this style of research have been collected in this volume in order to provide a perspective on the breadth and possible applications of such an approach to the study of change. In addition to demonstrating the features of a discovery-oriented approach, we will show how this style of research can greatly enhance the more traditional hypotheticodeductive approaches currently used in the field.

The research approaches illustrated in this volume all share the common goals of describing recurring patterns of client process and understanding essential mechanisms of client change. They also share some common methodological features and underlying assumptions which set them apart from most of the psychotherapy research that has been done. Although a number of researchers are moving in the direction of more intensive observation of process in context, little has been written on systematic procedures for doing this type of research. In the first section of the book, Rice and Greenberg consider the need for discovery-oriented, intensive analyses and discuss some underlying assumptions and necessary features of a new paradigm of psychotherapy research designed to discover mechanisms of client change.

The second section of the book covers the application of some of the intuitions and methods of task analysis to the study of classes of therapeutic change events. Two examples of the use of task analytic methods in analyzing the performance of clients successfully resolving affective tasks in psychotherapy are presented. In Chapter 2, Rice and Saperia report on an analysis of client performances in the successful resolution of "problematic reactions," with therapists using "systematic evocative unfolding" within a client-centered mode. In Chapter 3, Greenberg reports on studies of successful client resolution of intrapersonal conflict through the use of a two-chair intervention in the Gestalt mode. These studies yield an understanding of the paths followed by clients who achieve successful resolution and of some mechanisms of client change in psychotherapy.

In Chapter 4, Greenberg surveys task analytic approaches to the study of problem solving and suggests applications of this approach to the study of psychotherapeutic events. He discusses ways in which task analysis has been used productively in such fields as cognitive development and human problem solving to identify the components of competent performance, and he shows how psychotherapy can be viewed as containing affective task performances that can be studied by task analysis.

In the third section of the book, four distinctive approaches to the description of recurring patterns of client process are presented. For some years, Luborsky and his associates have been developing an approach they call the "symptom-context method," which they have applied to momentary forgetting, stomach pain, migraine headache, and other symptoms with identifiable onset during therapy sessions. The symptom-context method involves first identifying the onset points of some recurrent symptom and then making detailed and rigorous observations of the context (both client and therapist statements) just before, during, and after the appearance of the symptoms. In Chapter 5, Luborsky, Singer, Hartke, Crits-Christoph, and Cohen describe their analysis of abrupt increases and decreases in depression for a single patient over the course of therapy. Further, they make an initial test of certain theories of depression formation and suggest a number of productive avenues for further research.

Horowitz and his associates have developed a method for making rigorous intensive analyses of "states of mind" of clients during therapy sessions, beginning with certain problem states, then mapping other characteristic states, and finally examining the transitions between states. They have concluded that this is one of the most productive ways of conceptualizing a client's functioning at a clinically meaningful level. In Chapter 6, Marmar, Wilner, and Horowitz report on a study of the use of states in segmenting and analyzing a therapy. Their studies contain a number of significant implications for understanding moments of client change, as well as suggestive implications for the nature of productive therapist interventions.

Mathieu-Coughlan and Klein have for some years been developing and testing the Patient Experiencing Scale, a measure designed to tap the different levels of experiencing that have been hypothesized by Gendlin and Rogers as crucially related to therapeutic change. The Experiencing Scale has been widely used as a predictor of outcome in client-centered and experiential psychotherapy. In Chapter 7, the authors tackle the new and provocative question of how clients change from one level of experiencing to a higher level. Integrating theory and detailed observation, they have attempted to understand how such decisive shifts upward are possible. They illustrate and describe ways in which client transition points are influenced by levels of therapist functioning, using results obtained from the newly constructed Therapist Experiencing Scale.

In Chapter 8, Elliott approaches the analysis of change episodes from quite a different direction. Using an adaptation of interpersonal process recall (IPR) to isolate points at which clients perceive a therapist operation to have been especially helpful, he then proceeds to identify by means of process measures the qualities of the interaction that have made it a decisive point for these clients. He discusses a number of issues regarding the use of the IPR techniques to bring the client's and therapist's perspectives on moment-to-moment events into a productive comparison with process descriptions of the same events.

In the final section, Rice and Greenberg suggest a three-stage research program for identifying, explicating, and verifying client performance patterns and underlying mechanisms of change from a variety of orientations. The suggested program emphasizes the importance of bridging the gap between researchers and clinicians. It is hoped that this book will help provide avenues for the kind of collaboration that is needed.

ISSUES IN PSYCHOTHERAPY RESEARCH

1

The New Research Paradigm

LAURA N. RICE
York University

LESLIE S. GREENBERG
University of British Columbia

INTRODUCTION

A central goal of both clinicians and researchers is to make sense out of
the complex transactions of therapy, yet both are dissatisfied with the
degree to which research findings actually have impact on the conduct of
psychotherapy and counseling. Thoughtful clinicians are strongly motivated by the need to understand the process of psychotherapy. They are
constantly making observations about the kinds of therapeutic process
that seem to accompany client change and speculating about the underlying mechanisms of change. As therapy supervisors they feel that they have
deepened their understanding of the process of psychotherapy and that
this wisdom is worth passing on to those whom they supervise. At the
same time, these clinicians are keenly aware of the many pitfalls of
unverified clinical observation and the tendency to construct hypotheses
on the basis of one or two exceptional clients. What is needed is a research
method that can tap the rich clinical experience of skilled therapists in a
way that will also push them to explicate what they know, yielding a
rigorous description of the important regularities they have observed.

A number of surveys have concluded that psychotherapists seem to
be moving away from rigid adherence to "schools" toward a willingness to
incorporate promising therapeutic interventions from other orientations
(Garfield & Kurtz, 1976; Goldfried, 1980; Kelly, Goldberg, Fiske, &
Kilkowski, 1978). Although this is a stimulating and hopeful development,
the move away from schools and the comforting guidelines they entail
makes even more urgent the need to understand the ways in which
the interactions of therapy can become the vehicles of therapeutic change.
Each established therapy orientation has its own internal consistencies
which provide a kind of matrix of interpersonal expectations within
which the client and therapist operate. Without these constraints and
guidelines it becomes doubly crucial that the ongoing process of a more
eclectic therapy should be guided by an empirically grounded understanding of the important classes of events that may be encountered. Further-

7

more, it is becoming apparent that even the basic questions concerning therapy outcome, such as the question of the effectiveness of particular treatments, cannot be adequately answered until clearer description and understanding of what actually happens between client and therapist in different "treatments" is obtained.

In spite of a large and increasingly sophisticated research literature on the process and outcome of psychotherapy (Orlinsky & Howard, 1978; Parloff, Waskow, & Wolfe, 1978), the search for real understanding seems to be frustratingly delayed. Clinicians have become increasingly aware of how little of the research literature, even the process research, really increases their understanding of the interactions of therapy in a way that can be fed back into practice (Barlow, 1981). The empirical research designed to test hypothesized relationships between process measures and some external variable such as outcome sometimes yields suggestive findings, but it is by its very nature dealing in probabilities across individuals and is always subject to a welter of alternative hypotheses. Perhaps most serious of all, the grain of the research is too coarse and the variables inspected too few to provide an adequate description and understanding of what is actually occurring in therapy.

Our conviction is that a new style of research paradigm is called for, one that will make use of intensive analysis for discovering the internal structure of the interactions of therapy while using some more extensive method for verification of some of the basic processes of therapeutic change. We urgently need strategies that will help us to understand how and why psychotherapeutic change takes place. Process research is crucial to the endeavor to understand the workings of therapy, but our conventional external variable research methodologies, which relate single variables without attention to internal relationships among them, must be replaced. We need rational–empirical strategies which, by definition, use both across-situation theoretical models and rigorous observation of specific in-situation performances (Pascual-Leone, 1976, 1978) as well as making use of both the clinician's map or tacit knowledge (Polanyi, 1966) and the rigorous observations of the empiricist.

The purpose of this book is to describe and illustrate a general investigative strategy focusing on the important phenomena of psychotherapy by studying process within its in-session context. Recently a number of different approaches to the intensive analysis of psychotherapeutic process have been developed. Although these various approaches have arisen from different theoretical backgrounds and differ in focus, they share some basic aims and assumptions and represent a new approach to the investigation of psychotherapy. Drawing on these approaches, we will discuss in detail some of the fundamental principles that characterize this new investigative strategy for studying process in context. These principles constitute the underlying assumptions of a new paradigm.

Later each of the different approaches will be presented by its originators and its use in psychotherapy research illustrated by concrete examples. Despite their differences, these illustrative studies are united by the intensive analysis of certain identifiable and recurring moments of change in the psychotherapy process. They focus at a clinically meaningful level on the description and understanding of the emergence of these change points, while also making use of rigorous observation strategies that permit replicable confirmation or disconfirmation. Thus, each of these approaches requires the use of rigorous research operations in both the discovery and verification phases of the research.

The present chapter will first briefly look back at the psychotherapy process research literature and the differential treatment literature in order to isolate some of the problems that have impeded the search for understanding. The remainder of the chapter will discuss the importance of research on mechanisms of change and then explicate the principles of an investigative strategy for doing such research.

PSYCHOTHERAPY PROCESS RESEARCH

Research on the process of psychotherapy has yielded some interesting and useful findings, but has not led to the kind of understanding for which the field had hoped. Client process variables applied to pretherapy or early therapy samples do sometimes yield significant relationships with a variety of measure of outcome, thus improving the prediction that is possible from actuarial variables or diagnostic classifications. However, as Orlinsky and Howard (1978) have commented about such findings, "The latter is certainly useful knowledge but it falls far short of the desired conclusion that certain features of process are productive of good or poor outcome" (p. 320).

Research on the variables derived from Rogerian theory—accurate empathy, genuineness, and nonpossessive warmth—seemed at one time to hold considerable promise for understanding and improving psychotherapy. The findings from more recent studies, however, have often yielded inconclusive and conflicting results. In their comprehensive review of this literature, Lambert, Dejulio, and Stein (1978) concluded that methodologically improved studies of these variables should be continued, but that at this time the verdict concerning their effectiveness is still in doubt. Mitchell, Bozarth, and Krauft (1977), in another comprehensive review of this literature, have concluded that relationships with outcome are probably much more complex than was anticipated.

A basic difficulty with most of the process research that has been done is the underlying assumption of homogeneity of process. The typical approach has been to select samples from one or more sessions for rating, and to summarize ratings across samples for a single session, or even across sessions. Even when the samples are of adequate length and frequency, this aggregate approach can yield only limited understanding of the kind that could guide clinical practice. Gurman (1973) has shown that rated levels of therapist empathy varied considerably during the hour and over sessions. Clearly, process varies over time and different processes have different meanings in different contexts. Aggregating process as though all process during therapy is the same involves a uniformity myth from which psychotherapy research has been suffering. All process in a psychotherapy is not the same, just as all clients, all treatments, and all therapists are not the same (Kiesler, 1966). Different processes occur at different times in therapy and have different meanings in different contexts. It is more the pattern of variables than their simple occurrence that indicates the therapeutic significance of what is happening in therapy.

Gottman and Markman (1978), in their review of research methodologies, have pointed out the inappropriateness of attempting to draw conclusions on direction in influence from such findings as significant positive correlations between therapist empathy and level of client self-exploration across client–therapist dyads. The correlation tells us nothing about the ways in which these client and therapist behaviors are distributed throughout the hour. Thus with this approach there can be no evidence that client exploration immediately follows empathy. They make the important point that it is not *rates* but *patterns* that we should be studying. "Do rates adequately capture the process equation? Do we really presume that simply the more frequently a client self-discloses the better?" (Gottman & Markman, 1978, p. 28).

An underlying assumption of aggregate designs is that a given client or therapist behavior is either "good" or "bad" without regard to the context in which it appears. This fits poorly with the observation of experienced therapists that a given kind of therapist response or client performance seems to be crucial at one point and irrelevant or even detrimental at another. For instance, just after a client has disclosed some embarrassing or frightening feeling, a supportive and empathic response containing a high degree of acceptance seems clearly preferable to an expressive response that pushes for exploration. At a later point in the hour the reverse may be true. A client disagreement with a therapist's statement may be seen as resistance at one point and a prelude to creative exploration at another. Depending on the context, a client's expression of vulnerability may be the sign of greater self-acceptance and increased awareness or could be the sign of feelings of increased dependency and an inability to mobilize resources.

It seems probable that some of the equivocal findings concerning the empathy, warmth, and genuineness triad may be due not only to general design problems but to a disregard for the role of the context in which these characteristics would be most crucial. In fact, Lambert *et al.* (1978),

Mitchell *et al.* (1977), and Gottman and Markman (1978) have suggested that these variables might be most profitably studied at particular points in the therapy interaction. The recommendation of Lambert *et al.* (1978) for increased specification of context is especially relevant here:

> This would enable researchers to examine more closely the nature of client behavior and to refine their judgments about the process of effective therapy beyond the level of merely assigning a numeral to a complex interaction that surely deserves more refined assessment. In this regard the random sampling of therapy sessions might become a thing of the past, one of those interesting but crude first steps toward a more complete understanding of human behavior. (p. 484)

It seems probable that we have clung to the aggregate procedure, with its attendant uniformity myth, because we have felt the need for some kind of simplifying assumptions to help us to deal with the enormous volume and complexity of psychotherapy interaction. The investigative approaches to be described and illustrated in the present volume use a very different kind of simplification strategy, one geared to the goal of understanding. Rather than assuming a given kind of process to have equal significance at any point in therapy, this new approach relies on the segmentation of therapy into different episodes or events in order to understand process in the context of these clinically meaningful units. This approach of breaking therapy down into classes of recurring events prevents one from being swamped by the data through a selective focus on those episodes in the therapeutic interaction that hold promise of illuminating the change process.

DIFFERENTIAL TREATMENT RESEARCH

Research on differential treatment effects has failed to yield conclusive results: No one therapy has been shown to be significantly superior to any other for any particular set of problems, especially after long-term follow-up (Frank, 1979). At present there is therefore little research evidence available to guide the clinician in differential treatment application. One possible interpretation of these results is that nonspecific relationship factors account for all the therapeutic change. An alternative view would suggest that the lack of demonstrated differential effects is due to the fact that the present level of understanding of the active components of change within these different approaches is still too imprecise to produce differential effects on a consistent basis. This latter view implies that therapeutic success in any orientation would be vastly improved by greater understanding and specification of productive client performances and the interventions that have facilitated them. Furthermore, this kind of understanding would enable us to focus on some of the classes of events in different approaches that are uniquely valuable for different clients at particular points in therapy.

Research on differential treatment effects has recently taken a step forward by ensuring that the treatments being compared have actually been administered. This involves both specification of the kinds of therapist behaviors that constitute the "treatment" and monitoring tapes of therapy sessions to check on the actual occurrence of these behaviors. A major weakness in these designs remains, however: They have still not confronted the problem of specifying client behavior. It seems to be assumed that the specified treatment variable, when administered to a group of clients homogeneous on some individual difference variable, will "take" in a similar fashion with most of the clients, resulting in a relatively homogeneous client response to treatment. The assumption that people similar on some individual difference variable will react to specific treatments in a somewhat uniform fashion is contrary to clinical experience and has received little research confirmation. Attempts to link client traits or diagnostic categories to therapy outcome have yielded disappointing and oddly inconsistent findings (cf. Garfield, 1978).

Viewing psychotherapy as an interaction between an experimentally administered fixed treatment and some trait or diagnostic variable, and assuming that this will produce relatively homogeneous client performances involves one more example of the uniformity myth concerning process. This assumption has lead to both statistical and conceptual problems. The major statistical problem is the large client variance characteristically found in differential treatment designs. In comparing samples with large performance variance, the statistical power of one's tests, that is, the ability to detect true differences, is decreased and the experimenter is unlikely to be able to detect when something of interest is present. Controlled experiments involving extremely variable material require many observations to obtain a satisfactory degree of statistical power, a condition very difficult to achieve in psychotherapy research.

The conceptual or strategy problem is similar to the one that has plagued the field of personality measurement. As Mischel (1973) has pointed out in the domain of personality, human beings are just too good at making discriminations to be treated as fixed variables in a person-situation interaction, and thus the research focus must shift from "attempting to compare and generalize about what different individuals are like to an assessment of what they do behaviorally and cognitively in relation to the psychological conditions in which they do it" (p. 265). Cronbach, the original proponent of the rapprochement between the experimental and correlational camps embedded in the differential treatment design, has more recently discussed the difficulties in studies using the proposed interactional designs (Cronbach, 1975). He points out that the scientific observation of human behavior has often been neglected in favor of hypothesis testing and that this bias needs to be redressed by increased use of intensive local observation.

Clearly, people in therapy are goal-setting beings who actively construe the task and situation and act in terms of their goals and construals. Clients will respond differentially to the same interventions depending on how they perceive the situation and in terms of their own goals and intentions; yet, as Orlinsky and Howard (1978) have noted, there is a surprising dearth of studies of interactive behavior in therapy, considered in terms of strategic exchange.

We are suggesting that rather than grouping people together on some individual difference variable, the criterion for forming samples to be studied should be some observable "marker" that indicates that the person is at that moment in a particular state or problem space (Simon & Newell, 1970). In other words, the groups to be studied are not groups of people, but rather groups of episodes of therapeutic interaction in which the clients are engaged in person–situation interactions that have important commonalities.

If particular client performances in particular in-session contexts are found to be related to successful outcome and can be shown to be brought about differentially by specific therapeutic methods, it may yet prove possible to demonstrate clear differential treatment effects. The proposed new investigative strategy, in which process is studied in the context of strategic interactions, could help to illuminate the differential effects question by specifying what client performance strategies are set in motion by what therapist interventions at what particular points in therapy.

MECHANISMS OF CHANGE: THE COMMON GOAL

The approach we are suggesting in this book involves the intense scrutiny of particular classes of recurrent change episodes in psychotherapy, making fine-grained descriptions of these moments of change together with the patterns of client–therapist interactions that form their context. At this point one might well ask how this fine-grained, almost microscopic level of understanding could possibly have a substantial impact on the broad, strategic issues that currently confront the field. How could it help to provide direction for the increasing move toward eclecticism? What answers could it provide for questions concerning the efficacy of different treatments for different kinds of people or problems? How could it help to increase the productive flow of information between clinicians and researchers?

Our reply to these questions is that the goal of this new paradigm is to understand the essential mechanisms of client change. What is most needed in the field is the identification and specification of mechanisms of client change at a level that transcends the particular situation in which they are initially recognized and studied. These are the essential elements that must be understood in order to deal with the pressing issues in the field. It is our conviction that a research approach that focuses on fine-grained process description of patterns in recurrent change episodes within specific contexts can enable us to grasp the essential nature of the mechanisms leading to change, and thus to illuminate change across different therapeutic situations.

A number of points require clarification here. The first point is the importance of focusing on client change mechanisms. Such terms as therapeutic "technique" or "strategy," common in the field, emphasize the therapist and seem to imply something done by the therapist alone. Preoccupation with the role of the therapist and the theoretical orientation used have led investigators to lose sight of the mechanisms of change within the client, and yet it is these that we need to understand. It is the client who changes.

The second point is what is meant by client mechanisms of change. It is apparent from examining the intensive analyses in this volume that there are at least three levels of abstraction at which one might attempt to understand what the client needs to do in therapy in order to achieve change. The first level, which we shall refer to as client *process*, concerns the manifest client performance in the session. The second level, which we designate as client *operations*, concerns the client's internal mental operations. The elementary *information-processing operations* of cognitive psychology constitute the third level (Posner & McLeod, 1982). Specification of client operations involves drawing an inference from the observable process about the internal operation the client is actually carrying out.

The following example may help to clarify the relationship between the levels. A client may manifest a process that would be rated on the basis of verbal output as Stage 4 on the Experiencing Scale (Mathieu-Coughlan & Klein, Chapter 7) and a vocal quality that would be rated as "focused" on Client Vocal Quality (Rice & Saperia, Chapter 2). On the level of client operations one might infer that the client was engaged in *inner tracking* in order to *symbolize* an inner referent. At the third and most fundamental level, elementary cognitive–affective information-processing operations underlying the client operations would be specified, for example, shifting attentional focus and comparing two symbols. At the moment, there is no definition of what constitutes an elementary mental operation (Chase, 1978), but it is hoped that the detailed study of human performance in specific task situations will lead to the identification of fundamental operations that can be used to characterize the functioning of the human mind (Posner & McLeod, 1982).

Of these three levels for understanding mechanisms of change, it is the level of client operations that currently promises to be the most transferable level of understanding across orientations. Eventually we may be able to describe phenomena much more precisely at the third level, thus being able to tap research findings from other areas of psychology. At this point it seems more possible to use client operations or series of operations as the transferable entity. In other words, one or more client operations found to be important in moving the client to a new state of cognitive–affective awareness could be transferred and applied beyond the context in which it was discovered and explicated.

An example of a series of operations identified in cognitive therapy may clarify this level we are calling "operations." One approach extensively used by Meichenbaum (1977) and other cognitive-behavior modification therapists is to train clients to substitute positive self-statements or task-relevant coping statements for negative self-statements. The internal operations of the client could be identified roughly as follows: (1) *Focus* on internal dialogue, (2) *recognize* negative self-statement, (3) *stop* the negative self-statement, (4) *construct* a relevant positive self-statement or coping statement, and (5) *explicitly repeat* this latter statement. Closer observation would be needed to determine if this sequence is correct and if additional operations need to be identified between those already specified. As shown in this example, one is usually trying to understand a series of operations rather than a single one. Such a series of operations can be transferred and used in the context of a very different therapeutic orientation.

Another point to be clarified concerning the issue of transferability is the role of therapist interventions. Clearly, the essential client operations take place in an interactional context in which client operations are shaped by specific therapist interventions, and their essential nature must be grasped in this context. Our contention is, however, that once these internal client operations are understood in one context they can be transferred to other contexts, because they are the essential ingredients of change. The idea of transferability of client operations may be clarified by some examples taken from the research programs described in Sections II and III.

In Chapter 7, Mathieu-Coughlan and Klein describe four "processes that must take place in the client's phenomenology if good experiential therapy is to occur" (p. 223). The most basic one, identified on the process level as a shift from Stage 3 to Stage 4 on the Experiencing Scale, is the operation of *referring inward* and thus being able to speak from one's own experiencing. The authors show various ways in which the therapist can facilitate the appearance of this process through his or her responding or by means of explicit focusing instructions. They consider this experiential shift the basic client step, without which the other crucial experiential steps are impossible. This move from speaking about oneself to speaking directly from a "felt referent" is one that therapists from many different orientations would recognize as a turning point in therapeutic work. As Mathieu-Coughlan and Klein point out, this client operation, identified and explicated in the context of client-centered therapy, can be facilitated by therapists in many different ways.

In Greenberg's chapter on resolving intrapersonal conflicts (Chapter 3), one of the essential client steps in moving from self-criticism to self-acceptance is found to involve having the client in the role of harsh critic, taking responsibility for stating exactly how he or she would like the "experiencing" part of the self to change. The operation of selecting attributes to criticize enables the client to enage in a second, associated operation of *realizing that the locus of the criticism is internal.* This sets in motion the operation of *differentiating out* his or her own values and standards, which in turn allows the client to engage in the operation of *explicit reevaluation of the values and standards.* This series of client operations, shaped in different ways by other therapists, could be useful in a variety of therapeutic situations involving the need to differentiate basic values from automatic self-critical thoughts.

In Rice and Saperia's research, reported in Chapter 2, on the unfolding of the clients' experience of "problematic reaction points" (points at which their own reactions were felt to be problematic), one of the key client operations that seemed to move clients to a new cognitive–affective awareness was *recognizing salience* in the stimulus, that is, recognizing what it was in the original stimulus situation that had felt salient. This was shaped by the therapist in two steps. First, the therapist attempted to utilize vivid reflections and reflective questions to evoke in the client a vivid sensory feel for the stimulus situation at the time of the problematic reaction. Then, in the context of this reexperiencing of the situation, the client was encouraged to *scan the situation* for the aspect that had felt salient. *Identification* of this salient feature or quality seemed to position the client to begin the operation of differentiating out his or her own subjective construal of the situation. This kind of shift from an external description of a situation to a fresh awareness of one's own idiosyncratic construal of the situation involves a series of client operations that could profitably take place in a variety of orientations.

IMPLICATIONS OF THE FOCUS ON CLIENT OPERATIONS

ECLECTICISM

Two major ways in which research yielding an understanding of recurrent client operations could contribute to the development of a scientifically based eclecticism are apparent. The first type of eclecticism would involve the therapist's operating primarily within a chosen orientation, but, in addition, making use of clusters of client operations together with the therapist interventions by which they were originally shaped. For instance, a client-centered therapist might make use of the two-chair approach for resolving the type of intrapersonal conflicts described in Chapter 3, while a psychoanalytically oriented therapist might use focusing instructions to help the client to attain a more experiential stance. This transfer of clusters of operations and interventions could be especially useful when the necessary client operations seemed not to be achievable within the primary orientation for some clients. The only restriction on such transfers would be that the nature of the therapist interactions should not be inconsistent with the kind of primary relationship climate one is trying to maintain. This approach would be essentially a kind of technical eclecticism (Prochaska, 1979).

In the second type of eclecticism the therapist would first gain a basic understanding of change-producing client operations drawn from a variety of orientations; this understanding would transcend the particular orientations in which the operations were originally identified and studied. One would thus become aware of some clusters of client operations that seem to be essential or recur frequently in a variety of orientations, though shaped by rather different therapist interventions in each orientation. For instance, the operations of referring inward or reevaluating might be found to be universal at some point in any therapy. One would also become aware of effective client operations that were identified only in the context of one particular orientation, and thus could make a unique contribution to the treasury of operations. The final goal would be a synthesis into a new unifying theoretical structure of a broad range of common and unique transferable client operations with demonstrated effectiveness for change (Goldfried, 1980).

DIFFERENTIAL EFFECTIVENESS OF TREATMENTS

An understanding of the client operations underlying particular change phenomena could also have implications for predicting the differential effectiveness of treatments. Whether one remains within a general orientation or adopts either of the two forms of eclecticism, it would still be important to be able to predict in advance the general kinds of therapist interventions that are likely to be maximally effective for a given client. The key to this prediction lies in the kinds of client operations that will be commonly required in therapy as practiced by a given therapist or orientation. An example is the client operation of differentiating out new facets of inner awareness using an internal referent. In client-centered therapy this is an essential operation at many points in the therapy. Some clients seem able to do this fairly easily under the right conditions, while others find it alien. Rather than attempting to retrain clients to engage in this operation, it might be more congruent with the client's goal as well as more cost-effective to refer him or her to a cognitive–behavioral therapist. An approach to the problem of predicting in advance a client's ability to perform different operations is described in Chapter 9.

RELATIONSHIP FACTORS

This emphasis on the study of mechanisms of change in specific situations is not intended to imply that the more general relationship factors are not important in achieving therapeutic change. The general relationship factors, in addition to their own curative powers, interact with the more specific factors in two important ways. First, specific interventions intended to facilitate particular client mechanisms of change only work in relationship climates that are conducive to the type of client performances required to set these mechanisms in motion. Second, and possibly of greater importance, clients do not perceive general and specific factors as independent entities. The clients' evaluations of the quality of their alliance with their therapists depends upon, among other things, the clients' perception of the relevance of the specific tasks in which they are engaged in therapy (Bordin, 1979; Horvath, 1981). If what they are actually doing in therapy is making sense to them they form a stronger alliance and perceive the overall relationship as empathic and helpful (Horvath, 1981).

PRINCIPLES OF THE NEW INVESTIGATIVE STRATEGY

A cluster of interrelated methodological decisions underlies the different approaches to the discovery of process patterns and the understanding of change mechanisms that are included in this volume. Some of the decisions are relatively more important in one study than in another, but the principles underlying these decisions are relevant to all of the studies. These principles are the following:

FOCUS ON RECURRENT PHENOMENA

We have discussed the fallacy of assuming homogeneous process throughout the therapy hour. However, a rejection of aggregate external variable designs need not leave us in the position of dealing with an infinite series of idiosyncratic interchanges. There are episodes or events in therapy that are similar to each other in some important ways: Although not exact repetitions of each other, often dealing with quite different specific content, they do have some clearly identifiable structural similarities. They recur sufficiently often within and across clients to permit a systematic focus on their commonality. Thus the first strategy decision is that rather than sampling randomly we anchor the segments to be studied at points in the hour at which a particular kind of event is taking place, and study the process in the context of these events. There are many different ways in which such recurring episodes could be selected, but probably the most promising phenomena to select for study are points in the process at which some particular kind of client change is taking place. These are the points at which theoretical issues often come into focus. And clearly these are the points that are likely to be most crucial to the eventual outcome of therapy.

IMPLICIT THEORY

The investigator selects a particular kind of recurring event for intensive analysis on the basis of both theory and observation. Indeed the two are often closely related since rather different phenomena may be salient in different orientations, that is, one's general theory of therapy and personality change will guide one's selection of phenomena and inform one's thinking about them. Nevertheless, in some basic sense the results of this kind of intensive analysis are not theory bound. Since each class of change episodes is structurally homogeneous and the intensive analysis involves reliable process ratings at a descriptive level, this kind of investigative strategy yields a basic description or map from which one might eventually construct models of human functioning and change that could encompass the active ingredients of a variety of different orientations.

RATIONAL–EMPIRICAL METHOD

The central strategy of the new paradigm can perhaps best be labeled a "rational–empirical" approach (Lewin, 1951; Pascual-Leone, 1976, 1978; Pascual-Leone & Sparkman, 1978; Piaget, 1970). The basic rationalist supposition that guides the approach is that, for a person of a given type, there exist invariances in the organization of his or her inner processes which apply across situations to generate the person's performance. The rational–empirical approach takes seriously the invariance across situations of internal processing characteristics, but also stresses the importance of the performance demands of the class of situations. The theory-building efforts in a rational–empirical approach therefore combine these two perspectives by assuming internal processing invariances in a particular class of situations. This perspective provides for the study of specific performances in concrete situations in order to discover empirically grounded patterns in a particular class of situations. It is from these invariances in a specific class of situations that processing characteristics that hold across situations can be inferred for a person of a particular type.

Using this approach one starts with a clinical notion of what is important. This implicit or tacit knowledge is explicated as best one can and an initial model of the phenomenon is constructed on the basis of the regularities perceived across people and across situations of a particular class. Guided by this initial construction, which represents the rational aspect of the analysis, the primary investigative tool used is rigorous observation and induction, the empirical aspect of the approach. The empirical aspect is, however, informed by the clinician's experience as represented in the model. One looks intensively at a series of examples of a particular kind of change episode drawn from the same client or from different clients and tries to isolate the essential patterns that form the structure of this kind of change episode. An organized series of such empirical trials is made, each one enriching and clarifying one's understanding of the essential pattern. The tool of clinical observation and induction is used in a rigorous and additive fashion. One's emerging descriptions of the invariant structure of these events, based on the intensive study of each single case and described on reliable measuring instruments, are checked against the actual behavior of the next ones studied. Finally, from the refined descriptions of in-situation performances, models of the person's internal operations are constructed, which are held to apply across different instances of the situation studied and across people of a given type.

PATTERNS

The change phenomena are studied in terms of sequences and patterns that have unfolded over time. The particular segments are selected for intensive analysis because a certain kind of change has or has not taken place. The analysis focuses on the patterning of behavior before, during, and after the change event under study. Thus, in selecting segments, it is not the *amount* of a given client process during the episode that is important but the *pattern* of the client process that is under study.

DESCRIPTIVE OBSERVATION

The analysis depends heavily on detailed descriptions of the processes engaged in by the client throughout the change episode and is a fine-grained one, allowing for as much complexity as is consistent with the reduction of observed behaviors to meaningful and identifiable classes. In other words, if patterns are to be clearly identified, some reduction of complexity must take place. However, the observational categories should be, as far as possible, at a descriptive level rather than at an inferential level combining a hodgepodge of behaviors presumed to be conceptually related. Furthermore, there must be evidence for the interrater reliability of these observational categories as well as evidence for their conceptual relevance.

FOCUS ON THE CLIENT

The central focus in the new paradigm is on the client rather than the therapist. It is the client who changes, and we are trying to understand how that change comes about. The influence of the therapist is not ignored: We are interested in the whole sequence of transactions before, during, and after the change point. The therapist behavior is clearly specified and is regarded as part of the context of the event. Focusing on the client during the event is a simplification strategy which enables us to look first at patterns of client behavior and then to view the therapist as one important source of influence on the client at that point. As one learns more and more about the ways in which the event unfolds over time, the effects of certain interventions can themselves become objects of study.

INDIVIDUAL DIFFERENCE VARIABLE

The focus of the methods presented is on studying target performances that are similar as performances. They are initially collected without regard for the type of person producing the performance. The individual difference variable is used more as an exploratory variable than a classification category: Rather than being used as a form of control of client variability, the individual difference variable is seen as one of the many possible constructs that might help explain client performance. There are several ways in which individual differences could be addressed. On the simplest level it is clear that for some clients a given change phenomenon will be rare or nonexistent, while for others it may be a frequent occurrence. It may be that the therapist is not providing the context for its occurrence, or a basic individual difference may account for its occurrence or absence. The individual difference variable can also be used to help explain client performance differences in similar in-therapy contexts.

PROCESS IN CONTEXT

The client process is studied in context in order to permit a fuller understanding of the clinical meaning of the client behavior. Studying process in the context of targeted phenomena can be thought of as a method using process rating in a two-tiered or hierarchical fashion. First one applies categories for objectively identifying the target phenomena, and then one rates the moment-by-moment behaviors on more refined systems that constitute or surround the phenomena. Thus, the target behavior is described in reliable categories and then takes on added meaning by being defined in terms of its particular function in a particular context.

PLACE OF VERIFICATION

One final common feature that distinguishes research programs in the new paradigm from the traditional research approach is that, rather than beginning with the formulation and testing of hypotheses, these programs build toward hypothesis testing as the final step of a rigorous program of discovery and understanding. Hypothesis testing provides evidence of the generalizability and utility of the discoveries made to that point. Some preliminary evaluation of the therapeutic potency or relevance to change of the client performances to be studied is, of course, called for in the early stages of the research program. Investigators need to assure themselves that particular client performances are associated with change before they plunge into the intensive study of these performances. Elaborate verification studies, however, come at the end of the program, when a deeper understanding of the mechanisms of change affords much greater control over the sources of variance affecting outcome.

CONTRIBUTIONS OF THIS APPROACH TO THE STUDY OF PSYCHOTHERAPY

The primary yield of the new paradigm is an understanding of particular classes of change phenomena and the client mechanisms underlying the change. First, on the process-descriptive level the change episode and its surrounding context are mapped out with a good deal of precision and replicability. The question "What actually takes place in this class of change phenomena?" can be clearly answered. On an inferential level one can begin to construct a model of the series of client operations that are essential components of this class of phenomena. Eventually it may be possible to construct theoretical models stated in terms of the cognitive–affective information-processing mechanisms that underlie the phenomena. These specific theories can then be integrated into our more general theories of human functioning and change.

Second, process can be related to outcome in a more systematic and satisfying way. Once a change event has been described and understood, its relevance to particular kinds of outcome can be tested. Relationships to outcome may be very complex, in some cases necessitating the establishment of a number of theoretical connections. In other research programs the outcome questions to be asked are fairly clear ones: "Do clients for whom a successful performance on a particular change event is clearly documented tend to have a more successful eventual outcome on certain change measures than do others?" Whether the connections are simple or complex, it is apparent in each of the studies that understanding the particular change phenomena can move us one step closer to understanding that complex event called outcome.

Third, appropriate therapist interventions can be selected from a more informed position. In each of the approaches described in the following chapters the *client* is the focus. The client is the one in whom change takes place; the therapist's job is to facilitate the process of client change. If we can isolate and understand the client operations essential for a favorable client change process, then criteria for evaluating a particular therapist intervention become much clearer. We will no longer be summing across interviews therapist behavior that is considered "good" or "bad" without regard to context, in an attempt to find a simple relationship to outcome. We will ask the more appropriate question concerning which therapist interventions facilitate the appearance of the necessary components of a successful client performance. This approach should also provide information relevant to some important issues in therapist training and supervision.

Finally, one more kind of yield should be mentioned, one that is seldom discussed in connection with research. An important gain for the investigator from this kind of study is a deeper clinical understanding of the therapy process. Excitement is generated as the investigators and their students listen to tapes and speculate from their own clinical experience, posing questions and thinking theoretically in new ways. They look at the interactions in the kind of fine-grained way that can be so productive in the context of therapy supervision, but in this approach these speculations are continually being checked against a series of actual performances that are objectively rated on descriptive process systems. This in turn leads to new, provocative questions. Each of the separate studies in Chapters 2–8 will illustrate something of this stimulating clinical thinking, as verbatim material is analyzed and discussed. In fact, one of the underlying goals of this book is to stimulate more "thoughtful clinicians" to undertake research, and thus to make use of the wealth of creative clinical thinking that is potentially available.

REFERENCES

Barlow, D. H. On the relation of clinical research to clinical practice: Current issues, new directions. *Journal of Consulting and Clinical Psychology*, 1981, *49*, 147–155.

Bordin, E. The generalizability of the psychoanalytic concept of the working alliance. *Psychotherapy: Theory, Research and Practice*, 1979, *16*, 252–260.

Chase, W. G. Elementary information processes. In W. K. Estes (Ed.), *Handbook of learning and cognitive processes*. Hillsdale, N.J.: Erlbaum, 1978.

Cronbach, L. J. Beyond the two disciplines of scientific psychology. *American Psychologist*, 1975, *30*, 116–127.

Frank, J. D. The present status of outcome studies. *Journal of Consulting and Clinical Psychology*, 1979, *47*, 310–316.

Garfield, S. L. Research on client variables in psychotherapy. In D. L. Garfield & A. E. Bergin (Eds.), *Handbook of psychotherapy and behavior change*. New York: Wiley, 1978.

Garfield, S. L., & Kurtz, R. Clinical psychologists in the 1970s. *American Psychologist*, 1976, *31*, 1–9.

Goldfried, M. R. Toward the delineation of therapeutic change principles. *American Psychologist*, 1980, *35*, 991–999.

Gottman, J., & Markman, H. J. Experimental designs in psychotherapy research. In S. L. Garfield & A. E. Bergin (Eds.), *Handbook of psychotherapy and behavior change*. New York: Wiley, 1978.

Gurman, A. S. Instability of therapeutic conditions in psychotherapy. *Journal of Counseling Psychology*, 1973, *20*, 16–24.

Horvath, A. *An exploratory study of the concept of the therapeutic alliance and its measurement*. Unpublished doctoral dissertation, University of British Columbia, 1981.

Kelly, E. L., Goldberg, L. R., Fiske, D. W., & Kilkowski, J. M. Twenty-five years later: A follow-up study of the graduate students in psychology assessed in the VA selection research project. *American Psychologist*, 1978, *33*, 746–755.

Kiesler, D. J. Some myths of psychotherapy research and the search for a paradigm. *Psychological Bulletin*, 1966, *65*, 110–136.

Lambert, M. J., Dejulio, S. J., & Stein, D. M. Therapist interpersonal skills: Process, outcome, methodological considerations, and recommendations for future research. *Psychological Bulletin*, 1978, *85*, 467–489.

Lewin, D. *Field theory in social science*. New York: Harper & Row, 1951.

Meichenbaum, D. *Cognitive behavior modification*. New York: Plenum Press, 1977.

Mischel, W. Toward a cognitive social learning reconceptualization of personality. *Psychological Review*, 1973, *80*, 252–283.

Mitchell, K. M., Bozarth, J. D., & Krauft, C. D. A reappraisal of the therapeutic effectiveness of accurate empathy, nonpossessive warmth, and genuineness. In A. S. Gurman & A. M. Razin (Eds.), *The therapist's contributions to effective psychotherapy: An empirical assessment*. New York: Pergamon Press, 1977.

Orlinsky, D. E., & Howard, K. I. The relation of process to outcome in psychotherapy. In S. L. Garfield & A. E. Bergin (Eds.), *Handbook of psychotherapy and behavior change*. New York: Wiley, 1978.

Parloff, M., Waskow, I., & Wolfe, B. Research on therapist variables in relation to process and outcome. In S. L. Garfield & A. E. Bergin (Eds.), *Handbook of psychotherapy and behavior change*. New York: Wiley, 1978.

Pascual-Leone, J. A view of cognition from a formalist's perspective. In K. F. Riegel & J. Meacham (Eds.), *The developing individual in a changing world* (Vol. 1). The Hague: Mouton, 1976.

Pascual-Leone, J. Compounds, confounds, and models in development information processing: A reply to Trabasso and Foellinger. *Journal of Experimental Child Psychology*, 1978, *26*, 18–40.

Pascual-Leone, J., & Sparkman, E. The dialectics of empiricism and rationalism: A last methodological reply to Trabasso. *Journal of Experimental Child Psychology*, 1978, *26*, 46–54.

Piaget, J. *Structuralism*. New York: Basic Books, 1970.

Polanyi, M., *Tacit knowledge*. Chicago: University of Chicago Press, 1966.

Posner, M., & McLeod, P. Information processing models—in search of elementary operations. *Annual Review of Psychology*, 1982, *33*, 477–514.

Prochaska, J. O. *Systems of psychotherapy: A transtheoretical analysis*. Homewood, Ill.: Dorsey Press, 1979.

Simon, H., & Newell, A. Human problem solving. *American Psychologist*, 1970, *25*, 48–59.

SECTION TWO

TASK ANALYSIS

The three chapters in Section 2 present different aspects of a task analytic approach. In a task analysis, components of a successful performance are identified in order to understand how different kinds of problems are solved. The ultimate goal is to construct a specific model that would account for the problem-solving performance. The application of a task analytic approach to two classes of change "events" is examined in this section in order to gain an understanding of how the resolution of affective tasks can come about. A therapeutic event is defined as being constituted by a client "marker" of an opportunity for change, a series of therapist interventions, an ensuing client performance, and, in successful performances, an affective resolution.

In Chapter 2 the task analytic approach is used to gain an understanding of the mechanisms of change in the resolution of "problematic reactions," a class of change event drawn from the practice of client-centered therapy. The emphasis is placed on describing and illustrating the early stages of the analysis. In Chapter 3 task analytic procedures are used to understand client mechanisms of change in a class of events drawn from the practice of Gestalt therapy, and the emphasis is placed on the later stages of the analysis. Together, these two chapters should provide an understanding of the procedures for conducting a rational–empirical analysis of the essential steps in the resolution of affective problems. It is hoped that clinicians reading this section will attempt to identify from their own clinical experience "markers" of potential change events that might productively be analyzed.

In Chapter 4 the task analytic approach is discussed more broadly, and the rationale for conducting a rational–empirical task analysis of therapeutic change events is discussed in depth. Although some of the concepts used in Chapters 2 and 3 are discussed here, those chapters can be read first without loss of understanding.

2

Task Analysis of the Resolution of Problematic Reactions

LAURA N. RICE
York University

EVA PILA SAPERIA
Ontario Institute for Studies in Education

INTRODUCTION

Successful psychotherapy can be viewed as involving the resolution of a series of affective tasks. A good therapy, of course, has a wholeness and continuity that makes it a unique experience for each client–therapist pair. And yet within this continuity one can recognize a series of events, a set of interactions between client and therapist having a discernible beginning, a particular structure, and a conclusion, which in successful resolutions involves a sense of completion and relief, an implicit sense that something has changed. One of the things that distinguishes the experienced therapist from the beginner is the ability to recognize certain kinds of client statements as "markers" signifying that there is an affective task that needs to be worked on and that the client is ready to work on it. Experienced therapists also have some general, often implicit, guidelines, derived from theory and extensive clinical observation, for working with different kinds of affective tasks.

The application of task analysis to the study of such classes of recurring events in therapy is an attempt to tap into some of this clinical wisdom and to increase and refine our understanding of the active ingredients of change involved. Such a task analysis can have at least three kinds of yield. In the first place it yields a detailed performance model of the processes that must be engaged in by the client in order to achieve successful resolution of this class of affective tasks. Second, it can yield greatly increased knowledge of the ways in which a therapist may best facilitate the client process at each stage. Thus the research can have immediate implications for conducting therapy and training therapists. The third kind of yield can be improved theory: One can use the detailed performance model to begin to construct a theoretical model of the underlying mechanisms of change in this class of events.

A rational-empirical task analysis typically contains four steps:

1. Selection and description of the task and task environment, and explication of the general theory of human functioning that forms the context for study of this task.
2. Rational analysis leading to an "idealized" performance model.
3. Detailed moment-by-moment descriptions of a series of actual client performances.
4. Comparison of each of the actual client performances with the idealized model, leading to successive revisions of the performance model.

Task analysis is a method that can be used in a variety of research programs. The research program described here contains, in addition to these basic steps, a number of other steps required by the particular goals of the research or by the complexity of the psychotherapy process. Because of the tremendous complexity of therapeutic interaction it is crucially important to build in a series of verification steps along the way. Therefore in the program reported here there is a kind of alternation between steps involving creative clinical thinking and steps involving rigorous verification.

The event analyzed and illustrated in the present chapter was chosen from the practice of client-centered therapy. One of the fundamental assumptions of client-centered therapy is that human beings are basically motivated to seek out and engage in growth-producing experiences (Rogers, 1959). Thus the notion of the client as engaging in affective tasks involving exploration and search and leading to resolution is wholly consistent with client-centered theory. It is also consistent to view the therapist as a crucial part of the "task environment," establishing optimal conditions for the search. It is not as obviously consistent to think of these optimal conditions as involving "task instructions," since Rogers was clearly spelling out the attitudes of the therapist and not specific interventions for particular purposes. A number of neo-Rogerians, however, have pointed out that one function of these Rogerian attitudes is to establish optimal working conditions for clients to engage in the kinds of processes assumed to lead to positive change and have tried to spell out more precisely what the client needs to do and experience on such a search (Gendlin, 1964, 1981; Rice, 1974; Wexler, 1974). They have also suggested ways in which the therapist may best facilitate the search at certain points by preventing deflections, encouraging the focus on inner awareness, or stimulating the emergence of new facets of inner experience. One such formulation by the present author (Rice, 1974) provided some of the theoretical rationale for the unfolding and resolution of "problematic reaction points."

This chapter describes in detail some of the steps in a research program involving a rational–empirical task analysis of the resolution of "problematic reactions" and seeks to convey a feel for each step, leading to an understanding of the client operations essential to the resolution of the task. Therefore each step in the process of exploration and discovery is described in some detail in the place in the sequence in which it occurred. An attempt is made to show the importance of the alternation between rational and empirical steps, and the way in which the process of cycling through these steps enables one to engage in a productive kind of intensive analysis in which more and more is learned about a class of events that was at first only vaguely recognized.

SELECTION AND DESCRIPTION OF
THE TASK AND TASK ENVIRONMENT

Theory can play an important role in a rational–empirical task analysis (Pascual-Leone, 1976). The investigator may begin with an explicit general theory of therapy and personality development, as well as a kind of implicit clinician's cognitive map concerning the important interactions of therapy. In other words, one approaches the study of therapeutic events with a great deal of clinical wisdom based on theory and observation.

On the other hand, the findings of a task analysis of therapeutic events can have implications that go beyond a particular theoretical orientation. In the first place, an intensive analysis that yields a fine-grained performance model of the path(s) to resolution can force correction or extention of the theory rather than being constrained by it. In the second place, one can use the fine-grained performance diagram to develop a theoretical model of the mechanisms that underlie this kind of therapeutic change. The development of several such models from a number of different classes of events drawn from a variety of orientations may well be the best route to an integration or synthesis of different therapy orientations.

The General Theory

In the present study the underlying general theory of human functioning is client-centered theory, somewhat reconceptualized in cognitive, information-processing terms. Some client-centered assumptions that are especially relevant to the present study follow:

1. Human beings have an inherent actualizing tendency, a push toward growth, differentiation, and autonomy. They will engage

in creative new experiences even though these experiences may increase tension (Butler & Rice, 1963; Rogers, 1959).

2. Under the right conditions clients are able to become aware of all inner experiences that are potentially available to awareness, even those that have previously been distorted or denied to awareness because of threatened incongruence with the self-concept (Rogers, 1959). Thus no interpretation from outside is necessary.

3. These experiences, newly symbolized in awareness, force reorganization of the self-concept; under the right therapeutic conditions, the new organizations are more veridical and integrated ones (Rogers, 1959).

4. Individuals act in the world on the basis of their perceptions of the world and of self. If these perceptions change, then an individual's behavior and inner reactions change (Rogers, 1959).

The following assumptions seem to be implied in, or at least consistent with, the Rogerian formulations, but they have more explicit implications for therapy when conceptualized in cognitive, information-processing terms (Rice, 1974).

5. People continue to experience troubling and maladaptive reactions in certain classes of situations because their more or less enduring conceptualizations lead them to make distorted construals of such classes of situations.

6. A client's awareness and description of such troubling experiences tends to be highly condensed, often involving only a reference to the general stimulus situation and some response that took place. Our assumption is that a complex series of events actually intervenes between the appearance of the stimulus situation and the response that the client considers to be problematic, involving scanning and rescanning the stimulus situation and assimilating the input, which in turn may lead to retrieval and/or further output in the form of images or affect, followed finally by organization of output. It is assumed further that much of this intervening process is potentially available to awareness and can be recaptured in therapy.

7. The classes of situations in which such distorted construals are made are idiosyncratically organized. In other words, the enduring conceptualizations that would apply to any particular situation are not predictable in advance and must be discovered by the client.

8. If clients can vividly reexperience, unfold, and reprocess any one member of such a class they can become aware of their own construals and their idiosyncratic meanings. This awareness will not only lead to more satisfying reactions to such situations, but

the understanding thus gained can be generalized to a broad range of related situations.

9. Unfolding and exploring any one such situation will be as profitable as any other, provided that it still has some liveness and poignancy to the client. The crucial thing is that this single experience should be reprocessed in all its idiosyncratic vividness. Attempts to seek patterns or compare and contrast with other situations during the early exploratory stage will lead to a higher level of abstraction and away from the crucial new discoveries.

THE TASK

As client-centered therapists we had observed that clients often described incidents in which they had found themselves reacting in ways that seemed to them to be strange, inappropriate, exaggerated, or problematic in some other way. Sometimes these incidents seemed immediately relevant to the themes being dealt with in therapy, but often they were seemingly trivial incidents from the immediate or remoter past that the client just seemed to want to recount at that point. We had found that helping the client to explore such incidents in a vivid way sometimes led not only to a sense of resolution concerning that particular episode but also to new perspectives in other important areas. This result seemed consistent with the theoretical assumptions previously listed, especially the seventh and eighth. Unfolding this one incident did seem to tap into issues that were important to the client. Furthermore, this seemed to be a time of readiness for the client, involving a recognition of something puzzling going on and a willingness to explore it. It seemed clear that such episodes sometimes did lead to therapeutic change, but we were only vaguely and intuitively aware of how such change took place and how a therapist might best facilitate it.

Thus, this seemed like a class of events that would merit intensive analysis. The events occurred frequently with some clients and occasionally with almost all clients, and the frequency could easily be increased by suggesting that the client attend to such episodes. Further, the resolution of these episodes often did seem to lead to favorable change as perceived by both client and therapist. Finally, an understanding of the mechanisms whereby such productive shifts took place could well have implications for a broader range of therapeutic episodes in which crucial shifts in perception of self or environment seemed to result from reprocessing key experiences.

The event begins with a client's statement of a problematic reaction point (PRP), so named because it is a point at which the client recognizes that his or her own reaction to a particular situation is problematic in some way. This is the "marker" by which the therapist recognizes the beginning of this event. The definition of a problematic reaction point is a structural one; it could include a variety of content. A PRP task marker must contain three elements:

1. A particular stimulus situation.
2. A reaction that may involve feeling or behavior or both.
3. An indication that the client finds his or her *own* reaction problematic in some way.

Two examples may help to clarify this definition: first ("When he said that about [1] the schools at dinner the other night,) (I felt [2] very upset.) (I knew he didn't really [3] know anything about it but all evening I just couldn't shake off the bad feelings."), and second (I was hunting for Lawn Street [1] and when I slowed down to read the street sign, the guy behind me blasted me with his horn.) (I forgot all about my street and followed [2] him all the way up Yonge Street blowing my horn.) (That [3] was crazy.) Each of these examples has the three necessary elements, although in the first example the client is talking about an inner feeling reaction and in the second about a behavioral reaction. It has been found that these markers can be identified with high reliability by judges.

The client's task at such a marker is to explore and unfold the complex inner reactions and construals that intervene between the stimulus and situation and the observed reaction. The client needs to reexperience and reprocess the episode in a way that leads to resolution. One way in which the resolution of an affective task is different from the solution of most cognitive tasks is that there is no solution specified or predicted in advance. However, resolutions can be recognized by the client's implicit sense of completion and relief. It is almost as if the client "possesses a tacit test of when the answer to the problem has been found" (Greenberg, Chapter 4).

THE TASK ENVIRONMENT

On the basis of the general theory, and informal observation, listening to tapes, and trial runs by the research team, it was determined that the most effective task environment (i.e., therapist intervention) at a PRP would be "systematic evocative unfolding" (Rice, 1974). Evocative unfolding is designed to evoke the original stimulus situation vividly and to stimulate clients to reexperience and explore their own inner reactions and subjective construals of relevant aspects of that situation. The therapist uses this evocation systematically to focus and refocus clients on their internal experience during the problematic incident. The therapist must try to evoke the client's *own* idiosyncratic experience in this one particular situation and resist any temptation to identify patterns, compare with other situations, or otherwise move to a higher level of generalization or abstraction. In the method of systematic evocative unfolding the therapist is nondirective with respect to content but is highly directive with respect to process. A condensed version of the manual used for training therapists for the evaluation study reported in the next section follows.

1. After the PRP is stated the therapist actively tries to get a vivid feel for the scene in order to increase the immediacy with which the scene is experienced by the client.
2. There are two edges to the client's unfolding awareness of the problematic experience, each of which needs a separate and different focus of attentional energy:
   a. First try to help the client get in touch with a differentiated awareness of his or her own feelings and other inner reactions evoked by the stimulus situation. Use vivid fragments of the stimulus situation to reevoke the inner reaction, but leave the focus (open edge) on the inner reaction side. The focus continues on this side until the exploration peters out or until the client spontaneously switches his or her focus.
   b. Next focus vividly on the stimulus side, on how it seemed and what stood out. Even though the content of the exploration is the outside situation, remember to keep an inside focus on the client's subjective awareness and construal of the stimulus rather than on just external description. Continue to focus on the stimulus side until it peters out or until the client spontaneously switches to the other side.
3. There will be some switching back and forth between the two sides before resolution is reached. The therapist should freely switch to the side that seems live to the client at any given moment, but should always reflect with a focus (open edge) on one side or the other. Trying to focus on both sides at once seems to lead to a cognitive packaging of the experience rather than to the unfolding of new facets of it.
4. Continue until resolution is reached. This will be indicated by client relief and some sense of understanding of how the reaction fits the stimulus construal.

EVALUATION OF THE POTENCY
AND UNIQUENESS OF THE EVENT

The question that arose at this stage of the research was whether or not the task environment that had been selected would indeed enable clients presenting a PRP marker to achieve resolution of this affective task more successfully than would a nonspecific client-centered task environment.

This question could not yet be fully answered. Although we had some theory and informal observations to draw upon in writing a training manual for the therapists involved in the study, the event was only partially understood at this point. The manual, presented in condensed form in the previous section, represented an initial attempt to make explicit our implicit cognitive map concerning the best ways of facilitating resolution. After the event had been intensively studied, it was possible to write a far better manual.

This step had two purposes. The first was to generate examples of successful resolution to be used in the task analysis. The second was to test whether the event beginning with a PRP marker and involving a task environment designed to facilitate the evocative reprocessing of the situation would lead to more successful resolution than an event beginning with a PRP marker followed by a nonspecific client-centered task environment. In other words, we were asking if the event we were proposing to study had sufficient uniqueness and potency to be worth analyzing intensively.

The clients studied were not in ongoing therapy, but were recruited from upper-level undergraduate psychology courses. Volunteers were told that we were interested in studying different therapeutic approaches and that they would have two interviews, a week apart, with the same experienced therapist as well as being asked to fill in some questionnaires at the close of each session. An investigator then explained how to recognize a PRP and gave some examples of them. The volunteers were asked to bring a PRP to each interview.

Twelve clients were seen by three experienced, client-centered therapists. Each session began with a client describing a PRP, but in one session with each client the therapist used systematic evocative unfolding and in the other session the therapist used a nonspecific client-centered approach. The order of the two treatments was counterbalanced. After each session the client met with a research assistant and was asked to indicate on a 5-point scale how productive the interview had been in leading to new perspectives. Clients were also asked to rate the applicable items from the Therapist Empathy and Therapist Level of Regard scales from the Barrett-Lennard Relationship Inventory (Barrett-Lennard, 1962).

The client ratings of productivity on the 5-point scale were significantly higher for the sessions involving systematic evocative unfolding than for the sessions involving nonspecific client-centered responding. On the Wilcoxen matched-pairs signed-ranks test, the difference was significant beyond the .05 level. The difference in favor of the evocative interviews was of approximately equal magnitude for the clients of each of the three therapists. The scales from the Barrett-Lennard Relationship Inventory had been administered as a check on the level of therapist involvement and empathy in the two treatment conditions. The difference between the two kinds of interviews was not significant for either Therapist Empathy or

Therapist Level of Regard, although there was a slight trend in favor of the nonspecific client-centered interviews. We concluded that the higher productivity ratings for the evocative interviews were not confounded by degree of therapist involvement or enthusiasm in the two approaches. The results of this study lent confirmation to the expectation that the event consisting of a PRP and a task environment involving systematic evocative unfolding did more frequently lead to resolution than did a less specific but equally empathic and caring client-centered approach and was therefore worth studying intensively.

Although this procedure would be classified as an analogue approach, there is considerable evidence that the volunteer clients regarded it as a real therapeutic experience. The ratings of productivity for both kinds of interviews were mostly at the higher end of the scale, and spontaneous comments to the research assistant were very positive. In fact, several of the students asked for a referral either to a counselor at the student counseling center or an outside therapist because they had found it such a productive experience that they wanted to continue their personal exploration.

THE RATIONAL ANALYSIS: DESCRIPTION OF AN IDEALIZED CLIENT PERFORMANCE

On the basis of our general theory and our clinical knowledge of the task we engaged in a kind of "thought experiment" performed on the "idealized" case (Husserl, 1939/1973). One mentally tries out different approaches to the task, attempting to identify those that might lead toward resolution and those that are probably deflections or blind alleys. This step may also involve informal listening to therapy tapes and discussion with a research team. In doing this one always keeps in mind the particular task environment, which will structure to some extent the client's approach to the task. One asks oneself these questions: "What are some of the possible components of performances that lead to resolution?" and "What series of processes does the client need to go through in order to reach resolution?" This rational analysis provides a framework for looking at the actual performances of a series of clients. Each client performance is highly complex, involving different content and personal style; beginning with a tentative rational model enables one to process this complexity. Any behavior in an actual client performance becomes interesting as it fits, fails to fit, or enriches the rational performance model.

Figure 2-1 shows the first tentative model derived from rational analysis of the idealized client. The numbers in Figure 2-1 indicate the sequence of different performances in which the client needs to engage:

1. The client states the PRP, usually with some description and elaboration of the whole situation, including his or her own reaction, which may involve behavior or feelings or both.

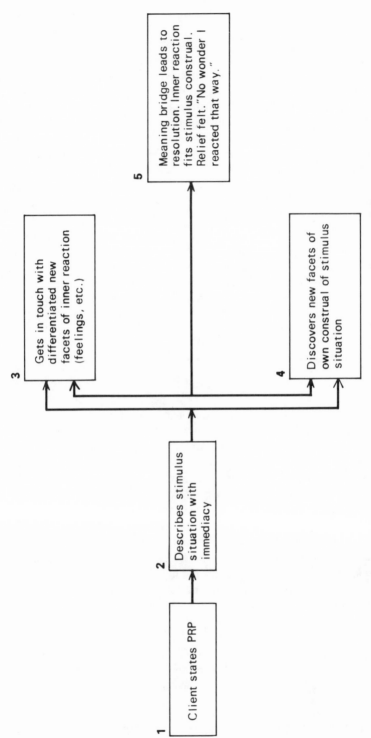

1 Client states PRP

2 Describes stimulus situation with immediacy

3 Gets in touch with differentiated new facets of inner reaction (feelings, etc.)

4 Discovers new facets of own construal of stimulus situation

5 Meaning bridge leads to resolution. Inner reaction fits stimulus construal. Relief felt. "No wonder I reacted that way."

FIGURE 2-1. RATIONAL PERFORMANCE MODEL BASED ON "IDEALIZED" CLIENT.

2. Next the client describes the stimulus situation in more detail while the therapist tries to get a vivid feel for it. If this step is successful the client will be "back in" the situation with considerable immediacy.
3. The client then gets in touch with his or her inner reaction, differentiating out new facets of feelings.
4. The client discovers new facets of his or her own construal of the situation, differentiating out new facets of it. There will be movement back and forth between Steps 3 and 4 until resolution is reached.
5. A meaning bridge, that is, a client awareness that the inner reaction, however problematic-seeming, fits the stimulus as construed, leads to resolution.

EXAMINATION OF ACTUAL PERFORMANCES AND COMPARISON WITH THE RATIONAL MODEL

Using tape recordings as well as transcribed protocols, the research team made a detailed step-by-step description of each of the six most successful resolutions obtained from the study previously described, endeavoring to specify the process in which the client was engaged at each step. An attempt was made to develop an increasingly precise set of descriptive labels or molar codes with which to classify each unit of client performance. Although these categories were initially suggested by the first rational model, they were reexamined and revised as each new client interview was examined, in a successive series of attempts to catch what was important in the phenomena. New codes were added for processes that had not been anticipated but that seemed to be potentially important. In other cases, categories suggested by the rational model did not prove to make interesting distinctions and had to be reformulated. Sometimes a code that had been assigned to a particular client segment in a previous transcript was found to be too specific to that client and had to be redefined in a more general way to encompass examples of the same process in other clients.

This continuing process of generating the descriptive codes served a double purpose. In the first place, it sharpened our thinking about the ways in which these actual performances did indeed confirm or change the tentative rational model. Second, it yielded a set of categories generated by the data, which thus had particular relevance to the task being studied. This approach seems to have some of the advantages of conjoint measurement (Krantz & Tversky, 1971), since both the models and the measures are developed and evaluated at the same time.

Each coded interview was then compared with the rational performance model. The examination of each actual client performance led to a revised rational model, and this model in turn was used for comparison with the next actual client performance examined. For the sake of clarity we will oversimplify this iterative process of single-case comparisons and describe first the discoveries and modifications resulting from study of the first three interviews and then the revised model resulting from the discoveries in the next three interviews.

DISCOVERIES FROM THE FIRST THREE ACTUAL PERFORMANCES

The revised performance model resulting from study of the first three client performances is shown in Figure 2-2. The intensive empirical analysis of these first three cases provided some confirmation of the rational analysis, but revealed some necessary intervening steps, as well as an alternate path to successful resolution. In addition the analysis revealed several kinds of client performance that seemed to deflect the client from more productive tasks. A discussion of a few of the things learned at this stage of the analysis follows.

One of the commonest deflections was the tendency of clients to react to their own reaction and focus on how irrational or undesirable it had been, expanding on their own childishness or irrationality or on the undesirable consequences. If the therapist focused on this secondary reaction rather than refocusing the client on the primary one, the problematic reaction itself was sealed off from further exploration and unfolding. The dotted lines in Figure 2-2 between Steps 1 and 2 indicate this deflection and refocusing.

One assumption of the rational analysis that was strongly confirmed was the importance of the client's maintaining a vivid and concrete reexperiencing of the stimulus situation. Although this was particularly crucial in Step 3 (see Figure 2-2), it was an important ingredient throughout the unfolding. When the exploration of either the stimulus side or the reaction side seemed to be going stale or getting deflected, if the therapist vividly refocused the client on the experience of the stimulus situation as it was just at the time when the reaction was triggered, the search seemed to come alive again. For instance, Client J's problematic reaction point involved being so bothered one day by cars behind him that he turned up his rear-view mirror and left it that way for 2 weeks. His exploration remained literal and repetitive as he concluded, "Well, I just turned the rear-view mirror up so I wouldn't have to look at anybody any more but to just focus straight ahead." The therapist's response and the ensuing dialogue follow.

T: I have a picture of you sitting in your car and there are all those other cars out there behind you and maybe one roaring up *right* behind you. . . ?

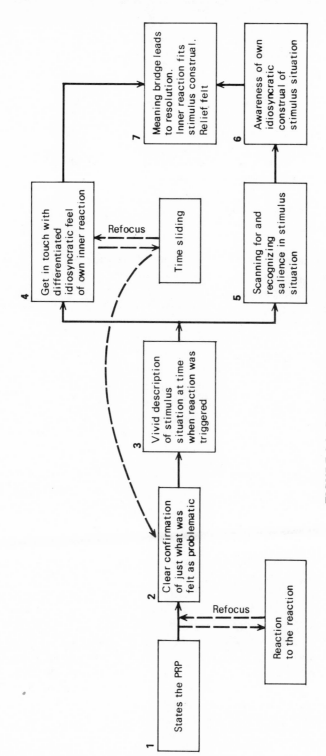

FIGURE 2-2. REVISED PERFORMANCE MODEL.

41

C: Yeah. They seem to come up from behind me and put the pressure on me to do something.

T: Oh, I see.

C: What do I have to do now? Because he's there I have to *do* something.

T: I get an image of you going along, and there was someone pushing you, prodding you—"Move! Move! Get going!"

C: Yeah. It's like they want you to get going an awful lot of the time.

T: Yeah. Sort of—"John, get going! Move! Move faster! Do what I want!"

C: Yeah. (*long pause*) The way you said that there sounds just like a parent, you know?

An important intervening step not included in Figure 2-1, but added to Figure 2-2 as Step 5, concerned the stimulus side of the exploration. There seemed to be an important step between the initial description of the stimulus situation and the client's awareness of subjective construal, a step involving a search for what was felt as salient in the situation. Saliency was not a matter of cognitive judgment, but more an affective recognition (Zajonc, 1980). The therapist would say something like "There was just something that got to you, something about his face, or the way he said it—? I don't know—." Sometimes the client would know instantly. At other times it would start the client on a self-directed search for salience. The clients seemed able to scan for and recognize salience fairly easily, especially if the stimulus situation was being evoked in a vivid fashion. And once they became aware of the salient aspect, it became a powerful evocator of their own subjective construal of crucial aspects of the situation.

An alternate path to resolution discovered in our analysis was the phenomenon we came to call "time-sliding." Two of the three clients, while exploring new facets of their own feelings, had a sudden, very live memory of an earlier situation in which they had experienced that same feeling. It was clearly not an intellectual search for similarities but a spontaneous vivid memory. The therapists had been instructed to stay with the idiosyncratic qualities of a single episode rather than encouraging the client to seek patterns or generalize. Thus, the therapist was forced to make a choice. In one case the therapist made a brief reflection of the remembered experience and then followed that by refocusing on the original situation. In the other case the remembered situation seemed to be much more alive for the client than the one originally brought in. Therefore, the therapist switched the focus to the remembered situation, returning to Step 2, (shown in Figure 2-2 by dotted line from Step 4 to Step 2) and continued with the new PRP until successful resolution was reached.

DISCOVERIES FROM THE NEXT THREE ACTUAL PERFORMANCES

Analysis of the second set of three client protocols led to some discoveries that forced us to rethink the previous rational model, and to go back and reexamine the first group of cases. The refined model resulting from these discoveries is shown as Figure 2-3. The first three stages are fairly similar to those in Figure 2-2, but the later stages are new. The discoveries involved sections that had previously been classified during our examinations under the rather general code "broadening out" (not shown in Figure 2-2), which designated times when clients talked about more general aspects of their life circumstances and mode of functioning. These had been thought to be times when material not directly involved in the problematic reaction was brought in. It was assumed that this material probably was not instrumental in the resolution itself but might lead to broader generalization of change. However, closer inspection of these points showed that important higher-order constructs (personal meaning systems) were emerging in these "broadening out" periods.

The first discovery was that some of these points seemed to involve an expression of some personal goal that was relevant at that time. Early in the interview the goal was expressed in a concrete and incidental fashion, such as "I wanted her to understand what I was saying." Later the client recognized this point as involving a very basic personal goal. Once we became aware of these points and had reanalyzed some of the transcripts, it became apparent that the reaction that seemed to the client so exaggerated, distorted, or otherwise problematic was often closely related to this personal goal. For instance, one person's PRP involved becoming incredibly tense during certain seemingly casual phone calls, pacing the floor, getting tangled up in the cord, and being unable to calm down afterwards until he went out and ran a while. It became apparent to him during the interview that he had an intense need to "get through" in some way to the other person; yet for reasons that will be discussed later he was construing the situation as one in which emotionality on his part would be seen as violating social rules or even as being "nuts." The tension and pacing were clearly related to the need to "get through," to be able to communicate his feelings.

The discovery that personal goals were involved in "broadening out" periods fitted in well with the observation that the therapists in several cases had sensed the importance of protecting the client's inner reaction from being invalidated by the client's "reaction to the reaction." For instance, the client just mentioned commented about his PRP, "It's so irrational to get worked up like that. It's just a phone call," and the therapist reflected, "It seems silly to you now, but at the time you just felt ready to burst." If a client is able to explore, while continuing to own his or

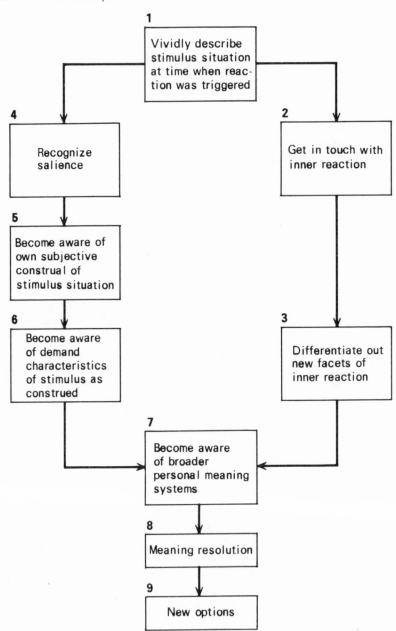

FIGURE 2-3. REFINED PERFORMANCE MODEL.

her inner reaction as organismically real, then the reaction might be seen to be related to some current goal that was being pursued in a distorted or exaggerated form.

The second discovery from this set of interviews was that at other "broadening out" points, as clients explored their own construal of the stimulus situation and their differentiated inner reaction to it, they became aware of broader personal meaning systems (higher-order constructs) that had been previously unexamined. Sometimes these were found to be "shoulds" or other introjected values. In other cases the personal meaning systems were values that were real and owned but much more basic than had been realized. In yet others the personal meaning systems seemed to involve some personal style of relating to one's life situation, some style of which one had been only dimly aware. In the example of the client who became tense during phone calls, his exploration tapped into some assumed "rules" for social interaction and expression. It also tapped into his style of watching for positive feedback in conversations and his awareness that in a phone call he was deprived of some of that feedback. During the process of recognizing and reexamining these higher-order constructs, clients were able to see themselves in a much broader sense as agents in their construal of situations and were able to test their construals in various ways.

The rational analysis, together with its theoretical base, had hypothesized that if clients could get in touch with their subjective, idiosyncratic construal of the stimulus situation in a fine-grained way, their reactions, however problematic-seeming, would be comprehensible. But there was no stated expectation of the source of the schemata (constructs) that led to the faulty construals. Simply, it was assumed that over time individuals may develop inadequate, faulty, or otherwise idiosyncratic schemata relevant to certain classes of situations. The empirical analysis pointed to the importance of getting in touch with the higher-order constructs (personal meaning systems) that were influencing situation-relevant classes of schemata.

Reexamining the transcripts in the light of these findings, it became apparent that successful resolution seems to depend on getting in touch with the nature of one's subjective construals of the stimulus situation and their related higher-order constructs. For some clients the recognition of current personal goals seemed to be the crucial step, for others it was reevaluation of "shoulds" or basic values, and for still others it was the reexamination of personal organizing styles. For most clients some combination of these was involved. The recognition that the reaction, though seen as problematic, does fit the situation as construed constitutes the meaning resolution stage that brings a sense of relief and understanding.

These discoveries changed our concept of resolution and led to another discovery. It became apparent that resolution could be more than the understanding of one's reactions and construals and the relief expressed in the insight "No wonder I felt that way." There was, potentially at least, a further stage in which clients could explicitly examine the possibility of new options for construing and relating to their worlds. In becoming aware of self-as-agent in construals one is able to loosen one's own schemata to make room for new construals. For instance, one client had construed a particular gathering as a situation in which she had complete responsibility for the guests enjoying themselves, and she experienced the whole thing as an enormous burden. Once she became aware that this was her own construal of the "demand characteristics" of the situation, she was able to check her construal against the reevoked memory of the situation and recapture a whole series of little vignettes in which people were having an excellent time without any intervention on her part. Another client mentioned to the research assistant after the interview a plan to try out something new in the outside world that would test the accuracy of his own construal. Of course, some clients may find their own construals to be reasonably accurate, but in getting a fine-grained feel for them, clients are often able to recognize ways in which the construals are unnecessarily limiting the available options. Another outcome may be that the client realizes that the problematic reaction taps into a larger problem, such as a family situation. Resolution in this case is only partial, but at least the client now has clues for approaching the larger problem.

The empirical analysis changed the emerging model and the therapist instructions in two basic ways. In the first place we recognized the importance of clients tapping into their higher-order constructs, recognizing the influence that these had had on their construals of the demand characteristics of different classes of situations, and thus seeing themselves as agents in their own construals. In the second place we recognized that there could be a highly productive stage involving explicit exploration of new options. In most cases the therapist had viewed the interview as finished at the "meaning bridge" stage of Figure 2-2, assuming that generalization of new applications would take place afterwards. Inspection of the few cases in which there had been some further exploration of new options indicated the value of making it an explicit step in the process.

EXAMPLE OF THE UNFOLDING OF
A PROBLEMATIC REACTION

A greatly condensed example of the steps to resolution follows. Large sections of exploration and elaboration have been left out, as well as some secondary themes; such omissions are indicated by the blocks of commentary that separate sections of dialogue. The resolution is not especially dramatic in content, but it proved to have some important implications for the client. She is a perceptive and expressive person for whom vivid reexperiencing was not a problem. In her case the two most important challenges for the therapist were (1) keeping her from staying mainly with her reaction to her own reaction and thus invalidating her own feelings and needs; and (2) refocusing her when each broadening out stage became less relevant.

C1: One of the things that drives me sort of crazy is the kids fooling around when they're eating. My kids and their friends. Particularly when Betty invites a friend for dinner. And they get up and look out the window and come back and eat, and slowly, like an hour to eat. And I get so furious and so controlling and they have to only eat and no silliness and you know very demanding. And really overreacting to little kids against ordinary manners.

T1: Let's make sure that I understand. When the kids are eating and they dawdle and take their time—That just seems to drive you around the bend. And you feel that you're overreacting.

C2: Right.

In the preceding section the client states the problematic reaction and the therapist checks on just what was felt as problematic.

T2: OK. I wonder if we could go back to the situation, the way you visualize it in your mind. So I could get the flavor of that. You say the kids are all sitting around the table, and there's Betty on one side and Larry on the other, and—James is it—across?

C3: Mhm.

T3: So you're watching, maybe standing by the sink in the kitchen?

C4: And I'm watching. Betty is leaning over to Larry, and the place mats are getting moved slightly. And Larry is leaning over there. And then there's some noise outside and he gets up and looks out the window and he comes and sits down and says, "I don't like tomatoes."

T4: And there's something about the way they play and they joke— that really seems to bug you—just something . . .

C5: The way they're dawdling. They don't care. There's absolutely no caring on their faces. And yet I know that the whole eating thing is a lot more than just eating. It's a whole social occasion. And there I am denying it to my kids.

In this section T tries to visualize the particular scene. C quickly brings the scene to life, describing it vividly. T probes for salience, and C responds by first identifying the dawdling and then clearly identifying the lack of caring. This turned out to be an important theme, but at this point she quickly turns on herself with a negative reaction to her own reaction.

T5: So you're telling them, "Cut out all the fun and games. Get down to that task!" Do you have any awareness of what's going on inside you? I imagine you clenching your teeth—

C6: I'm anxious for it to be over. I'm angry. I'm impatient. And then what I mentioned about evaluating myself as a mother.

T6: So then you're not just getting mad at them—

C7: I'm getting mad at myself for being the kind of person I am, the kind of mother.

T7: It's not just the problem of getting upset with them, but you're kind of adding insult to injury by questioning yourself and asking yourself "Maybe there's something wrong with the kind of mother I am." And yet I think what really interests me is what it is about their silliness that seems to upset you so much.

C8: There's a look or a small action that happens. And then they start looking at each other through the corners of their eyes and giggling. And half the meal seems to be made up of giggles.

In the previous section T takes C back to the scene and asks her about her inner reaction. The client identifies it and differentiates it a bit, but then goes back to her reaction to her own reaction. T reflects this and then focuses C back onto what was salient for her. Then, starting at C8, C begins a long exploration, largely omitted here, in which she becomes aware that she is construing the situation as one in which the children are entering into a covert attempt to spite her by getting slower and sillier. She recognizes that this makes her even tenser and angrier and that it is partly her tension that is triggering the added silliness. She had become aware of a part of her own subjective construal, but no real shift takes place until C14.

C9: I feel almost as if they're pulling something on me because they know my needs and despite it all, they're doing this.

T9: At the moment it does feel as if they were doing it to spite you.

C10: I almost don't allow it to feel any way, because at the moment I'm saying "Jeez I'm bitchy." So I don't allow my immediate reaction to come. I'm too busy putting a trip on myself for what I've already done.

T10: And—yet my hunch is that there's something going on that is making you very angry, and that's what we're trying to understand.

C11: Yeah, I think—I don't understand why I get like that. Because sometimes it would be a specific thing that I have to do, and I understand why I'm impatient. But sometimes there isn't anything else I'm supposed to be doing.

T11: Do you have a sense of what that impatience feels like?

C12: (*long silence*) Hmm—It has something to do with feeling the responsibility.

T12: Hmm.

C:13 And it's at that time I'm feeling that my job, my responsibility, is to be there with the kids, and to prepare lunch.

T13: Hmm.

C14: And I separate—I tend to—It's almost like I separate my whole life, or a day or whatever into—little sections. And I can't go on to any section or do anything until one is over. (*pause*) And I can see that in other things too. I used to draw and paint, and I couldn't start a picture because there were going to be other things that interfered with it, so that meant that I couldn't start it at all.

T14: Oh. So by kind of making these little slots for yourself—in a way it—you kind of stop yourself from—

C15: I stop myself from doing anything else. And them being silly and taking a long time—they're stopping my life.

T15: Oh, I see. If they cooperated, then you could be over and finished with that particular section, and you could feel like you did your job well, and then get on to something else.

C16: That's right—(*pause*) And I think the only times I've really enjoyed having lunch with them, is when I've been—when I've been more involved with it and made it . . . part of my life . . . almost . . . as if they were people, rather than seeing it as a job in that slot.

T16: The times you've enjoyed have not been when you've been in the role of the good mother, but when you've just been able to view them as human beings whom you're eating with, just as if they were adults.

C17: That's right. That's when they get into that slot, you know, without that work section. And there's just a *tremendous* difference!

T17: Hmm.

C18: And then I realize that there I am demanding them not to be silly. And I *love* being silly (*laughs*). And I joke with them and we just get right off on it.

T18: Ah—like during those times you're one of them.

C19: Yeah. And there's a tremendous—you know—the whole core is just so different. So much closer and feels so much better.

T19: You don't feel like that nagging mother.

C20: Oh no, no. And the thing is that nagging mother wants so much to be in control of them, for them to hurry up. But when I'm—when I'm part of the whole scene, I *feel* myself being in control.

T20: When you imagine yourself being silly with them and having that good rapport with them, feeling kind of like a *real* sense of control—It's a whole different feeling—

C21: It's just a happier sense, a sense of well-being, of feeling the qualities I like about myself.

In C10 C is beginning to recognize that her reaction to her reaction is a kind of automatic "should," but she doesn't really examine it until later.

T reflects it in a way that keeps her from invalidating her own feelings, and then refocuses her on the PRP. In C11 she makes a key comparison to a situation in which she has the same feelings even though there is nothing urgent to do. T focuses her on the feeling, and after a very long pause she starts exploring, with a very focused vocal quality (as measured on Client Vocal Quality; see description on pp. 53–54). The breakthrough comes in C14, when she recognizes her personal style of dividing her life into little sections. She associates to other situations and realizes that it limits her in all sorts of ways. The meaning resolution stage begins in C15, when she connects her reaction to the children's dawdling with her own construal of the impact of the situation on her life. Then in C16, after a long pause, she begins to contrast her inner reaction with the feeling she has when the children's eating is *not* construed in the work slot. When she sees them as real people and herself as sharing something with them, she not only has fun and feels good about herself as a mother but, ironically, has better control of the situation.

T21: I'm guessing that your life must be quite full, that you've got to structure and organize it this way.

C22: That's right. I've got my studying to do. And the home responsibilities—

T22: And those damn kids are just completely wrecking—

C23: My computer.

T23: And you'd like to say "For heaven's sakes would you just—"

C24: Yeah—"Don't you realize the stress I'm under?" I guess I'm feeling it—but I guess I'm also saying "I have no right to ask them to feel the stress in my life when it's chosen for myself, apart from them." I guess I feel guilty about spending so much time away from them and spending so much time being at the university and writing papers that I didn't want to say "These are my particular needs."

T24: But what comes before that? "Don't these kids know how much stress I have in my life?"

C25: Don't they know how hard I work? Can't they see that they have to cooperate so I can continue doing it?

T25: Mhm.

C26: Can't they see how important it is for me?

C has been talking in detail about the efficiency with which she organizes her time, and in T22 the therapist is trying to focus her on her own reaction. In C24 she brings out her guilt about meeting her own needs and the way in which this guilt is stopping her from sharing her feelings directly with the children. After C26 there was a long segment, omitted here, in which she associates to other family situations. She tells a story about a time when she expressed her feelings of discouragement to her son and he responded in a very understanding way, volunteering to try harder to cooperate. The implication was not made wholly explicit, but it seemed to be a kind of reality testing of her assumption that it would be wrong to tell the children about her own needs, by associating to a situation in which doing so turned out well.

T26: Our time is almost up. And I wanted to ask you where this leaves you.

C27: Well I feel better about it actually. I feel that I *can* go and say— that it is OK for me to say "You know these are all the things I'm doing. This is why I need you to hurry up and not fool around." Because I can see that this is something we can work out together, rather than continuing to feel worse by the minute. Because that's when there's this build-up, you know.

The interview had to be concluded here because of the time limit. C clearly felt better about herself and about the situation. A new option had emerged from her realization that when the children's meals were not construed as belonging to a work section in which she must do nothing but discharge her responsibility as a good mother, she enjoyed their company, and control was no problem. She briefly explores the new option of treating the children as partners rather than viewing them as adversaries, and expresses confidence that they can work it out together.

RELIABILITY AND RELEVANCE
OF OBSERVATIONAL CATEGORIES

The essence of our intensive analysis strategy is a comparison of the emerging performance model with a series of actual client performances. Each cycling from the tentative rational map through a detailed inspection of a successful client performance produces a more interesting and detailed diagram of the steps that the client needs to reach in order to achieve successful resolution. It is here that much of the clinical excitement is generated. And yet it is here that the thoughtful clinician and the empirical researcher often part company. The complexity of even a single tape-recorded therapy hour is so great, and the inferential leaps from client performance to hypothesized inner process so wide, that it is possible to find comfirmation for any one of a dozen theoretical expectations. The thoughtful clinical observer sees patterns that tend to confirm and enrich his or her theory. Some interesting new clinical strategies are developed and shared with supervisees, but the theory remains in the realm of "art." The key process steps that have been identified clinically have not been reliably specified at the fine-grained process-descriptive level needed to establish unequivocally whether and under what circumstances the expected performance patterns do in fact appear. The necessary, though perhaps somewhat tedious, research step is to construct or select observational categories having reliability and construct validity that can serve as criteria for whether or not a certain client process is present at a particular point.

Two levels of observational categories were used in the present investigation, constituting a move from clinical recognition to process description. The two levels involved (1) observational categories generated from clinical recognition of task-relevant processes, and (2) process-descriptive measures in more general use.

TASK-RELEVANT OBSERVATIONAL CATEGORIES

The first level of observation involved the molar codes constructed earlier by the research team as they attempted to describe each actual performance. These were attempts to label at a molar descriptive level the internal processes in which the client appeared to be engaged. Some of these codes refer to essential steps in the resolution of PRP as shown in Figure 2-3. Other codes refer to processes engaged in by clients during the unfolding that are considered to be explorations that may lead to the essential steps. Other codes designate processes that are likely to be irrelevant or to lead to deflections.

Because of the exploratory nature of this study, we used a large number of codes. Inasmuch as some of these codes appeared only a few times in each transcript, the 24 different codes were combined into six clusters for the purpose of checking the reliability of rating. Each cluster was made up of codes that were considered to involve some similar processes, though it was recognized that they were different in some other ways. The 24 task-relevant molar codes, grouped into six clusters, are shown in Table 2-1.

Transcripts of the two most successful interviews studied were given to two raters with instructions to assign one and only one of the molar codes to each client segment. A segment was defined as a client response between two therapist statements. In longer client responses, however, raters were instructed to apply a new molar code whenever the response seemed to shift in midstream and to mark the division point. Tapes were not used in making these ratings. The raters were members of the research team and had participated in the earlier steps of the analysis, but did not have access to the data from the process-descriptive measures.

For Client C there were 64 responses coded, not counting simple confirmation and other fragmentary responses. For 67% of these, the two raters agreed exactly, and for 84% of the responses the codes assigned by

TABLE 2-1. Cluster Groupings of Task-Relevant Molar Codes

Cluster A: Describing
1. Description of stimulus situation
2. Vivid description of stimulus situation
3. Stimulus attribution—descriptions involving inferences about motivation, impact, etc., without any recognition of inference
4. Reaction described in behavioral terms

Cluster B: Recognizing
5. Recognizing salient aspect of stimulus
6. Recognizing new self-relevant information

Cluster C: Focus on internal reaction
7. Identifying internal reaction—involves feelings, physical sensations, etc.
8. Differentiating inner reaction—new facets of feeling qualities emerge

Cluster D: Focus on subjectivity of stimulus construal
9. Subjective construal of stimulus with evidence of awareness of subjectivity
10. Subjective construal of demand characteristics (potential impact) of stimulus, with awareness of subjectivity
11. Comparing ingredients—involves search, using internal referents, for ingredients that trigger the reaction. If there is not clear evidence of internal referents, place in category 17.

Cluster E: Recognition and exploration of relevant higher-order constructs
12. New awareness of basic want or goal relevant to the situation
13. Reexamining shoulds and oughts
14. Reexamining value system
15. New awareness of relevant personal style
16. New options perceived

Cluster F: Cognitive elaboration and unexamined recounting
17. Cognitive elaboration—involves thinking about the PRP in an intellectualized way
18. Reacting to own problematic reaction
19. Recounting miscellaneous information
20. Concrete want mentioned incidentally
21–24. Incidental and unexamined references to shoulds and oughts, values, or personal style

both raters were in the same one of the six clusters. Cohen's κ was .81. For Client J there were 95 responses coded, with 62% exact agreement and 75% agreement on clusters. Cohen's κ was .68.

Process-Descriptive Measures

The two measures selected to represent this second level are both considered to be indicators of the moment-to-moment processing style of the client. The first measure was Client Vocal Quality, which had been designed to assess the client's deployment of attentional energy at any given moment (Rice & Koke, 1981; Rice, Koke, Greenberg, & Wagstaff, 1979; Rice & Wagstaff, 1967). It is a nominal measure involving four mutually exclusive classes based on patterns of vocal features. The four classes are as follows:

1. *Focused.* This pattern seems to reflect a turning inward of attentional energy, which is deployed toward tracking inner experience and trying to symbolize it in words. It is characterized by such vocal features as an irregular accentual pattern, accentuations achieved with loudness and/or drawl rather than pitch rise, irregularity of pace, and the presence of unfilled pauses.
2. *Externalizing.* This pattern seems to involve a deployment of attentional energy outward. It has a premonitored quality that suggests energy being invested in recounting content that is not being newly experienced and symbolized. It is characterized by such vocal features as an extremely regular accentual pattern, accentuations achieved with pitch rather than loudness and/or drawl, and regularity of pace.
3. *Limited.* A withdrawal of energy seems to be involved in this pattern. There is a thin quality to the voice, a distance from what is being said. It is characterized by such vocal features as inadequate push, voice not resting on own platform, and a petering out at the ends of the clauses.
4. *Emotional.* The main distinguishing feature of this pattern is a distortion or disruption of the speech pattern because of emotional overflow.

Although speech content is not filtered out, raters are trained to ignore content, and experienced raters are usually unable to remember content with any clarity. The ratings were made from tapes by someone who knew nothing about the present investigation but had demonstrated satisfactory rater reliability in other studies of vocal quality.

The second process-descriptive measure used was Levels of Client Perceptual Processing, intended for describing therapy process but based on models from cognitive theory (Toukmanian, in press). The measure is a nominal one containing the following seven mutually exlusive classes:

I. *Undifferentiated statements.* Client responses in this class are essentially static and are characterized by a packaged quality. They are undifferentiated and are often used by clients to label their recognition of an event.
II. *Elaboration.* Responses in this class usually contain a series of descriptive statements that often serve to provide a detailed

account of one or more incidents from an observer's standpoint. They give factual information and examples as added information surrounding an event.

III. *Differentiation with external focus.* Client segments in this category are differentiations that reflect an associative type of recognition made primarily from an external frame of reference, using standards, rules, or other people's perspectives to distinguish facets of meaning.

IV. *Differentiation with analytic focus.* Segments in this class reflect an ability to discriminate among available information on the basis of objectifying various elements and making associative references from them through the application of systematic logic.

V. *Differentiation with internal focus.* This class involves differentiations made from an internal frame of reference, using internally generated descriptions to represent the event.

VI. *Reevaluation.* Client segments placed here are characterized by a tentativeness, a reflective process of reappraisal. The client seems to be considering alternative ways of organizing a potentially more accurate perception of the situation.

VII. *Integration.* Segments in this class reflect a synthesis of the differentiated levels of meaning that the client has generated. The client seems to have adopted a new perspective.

Ratings on Levels of Client Perceptual Processing were made from transcripts, not tapes, by an experienced rater who knew nothing about the present study.

Construct Validity of Task-Relevant Observational Categories

Based on our assumptions about the kind of internal process that each of the molar codes represented, we spelled out some hypotheses concerning relationships between the molar codes and ratings on the two process-descriptive measures. The first expectation was that client responses that had been assigned molar codes involving new awareness arrived at by getting in touch with some internal referent would be rated as having predominantly focused vocal quality, while segments having a clearly external cognitive stance would be rated externalizing or limited. The results of this analysis for Clients C and J are shown in Table 2-2. For Client C chi-square was significant beyond the .001 level and the coefficient of contingency was .48. For Client J chi-square was significant beyond the .001 level and the coefficient of contingency was .38. These findings provide some confirmation for the assumption that these codes

TABLE 2-2. Relationship between Molar Codes and Client Vocal Quality

	CLIENT VOCAL QUALITY			
	CLIENT C		CLIENT J	
MOLAR CODES	FOCUSED	EXTERNALIZING OR LIMITED	FOCUSED	EXTERNALIZING OR LIMITED
Internal tracking[a]	18	6	39	20
External stance[b]	5	21	8	27
	$\chi^2 = 15.63, p < .001^c, C = .48$		$\chi^2 = 16.44, p < .001, C = .38$	

[a]Internal tracking codes: 5, 8, 9, 10, 11, 12, 13, 14, 15.
[b]External stance codes: 1, 2, 3, 4, 17, 18, 19, 20, 21, 22, 23, 24.
[c]Inasmuch as the observations for each client are not independent, random variability may be underestimated. Therefore the required probability level was dropped to .001.

do indeed identify moments when clients are engaging in new, internally focused exploration.

Inspection of the ratings suggested further that these moments could be more accurately identified by using Client Vocal Quality ratings to modify the coding based on the transcripts, rather than rating the two aspects separately as was done here. For instance, some of the most difficult coding distinctions were between such categories as Stimulus attribution (code 3), which involves making unrecognized inferences about the stimulus and its impact, and Subjective construal of stimulus (code 9), which requires some evidence of client awareness of the subjectivity of construal. Inspection of the codes assigned and the lower rater agreement on them suggested that these distinctions would be clarified by the vocal ratings.

The second expectation concerned relationships between the molar codes and ratings on Levels of Client Perceptual Processing, and contained five parts as follows:

1. Segments involving new options (code 16) would be rated VII (Integration).
2. Segments involving reexamination of shoulds and own value system (codes 13, 14) would be rated VI (Reevaluation).
3. Codes for operations using an internal referent to differentiate out new facets of awareness (codes 8, 9, 10, 11, 12, 15) would be rated in V (Differentiation with internal focus).
4. Segments involving external cognitive processes would be rated either IV (Differentiation with analytic focus) or III (Differentiation with external focus).

5. Segments with codes having to do with description, recounting, or simple recognition (codes 1, 2, 3, 4, 5, 19) would be rated II or I, which both involve statements made without differentiation.

The results are shown in Table 2-3.

Because of the small numbers of samples involved, the first three groups of molar codes and the first three processing levels had to be combined to permit a statistical test of association. This was not inappropriate since all of the codes required at least the use of the internal referent to arrive at new awarenesses. Thus, hypotheses 1, 2, and 3 could not be tested separately. For Client C chi-square is significant beyond the .001 level, and the coefficient of contingency is .70. For Client J chi-square is significant beyond the .001 level and the coefficient of contingency is .63. Because the first two molar code groups occur infrequently for each client, relationships with perceptual processing levels could not be tested here. Inspection of the figures, however, suggested that with a larger number of items, significant relationships might well be found. For Client C New options (code 16) occurred only once and was rated VII on perceptual processing. For Client J it did not occur. For Client C the reexamination codes 13 and 14 occurred three times, two of which were rated VI. For Client J it occurred eight times, five of which were rated VI.

TABLE 2-3. RELATIONSHIP BETWEEN MOLAR CODES AND LEVELS OF PERCEPTUAL PROCESSING

	LEVELS OF PERCEPTUAL PROCESSING[a]					
	CLIENT C			CLIENT J		
MOLAR CODES[b]	VII, VI, V	IV, III	II, I	VII, VI, V	IV, III	II, I
1, 2, 3	10	5	1	20	7	4
4	0	14	0	0	21	3
5	1	6	22	2	4	10
	$\chi^2 = 57.37, p < .001$[c], $C = .70$			$\chi^2 = 47.7, p < .001$, $C = .63$		

[a]Levels of Perceptual Processing: VII. Integration; VI. Reevaluation; V. Differentiation with internal focus; IV. Differentiation with analytical focus; III. Differentiation with external focus; II. Elaboration; I. Undifferentiated statements.

[b]Molar Codes: (1) New options (code 16); (2) Reexamination of shoulds and values (codes 13, 14); (3) Use of internal referent in differentiating out new facets of awareness (codes 8, 9, 10, 11, 12, 15); (4) External cognitive processes (codes 17, 18, 21, 22, 23, 24); (5) Description, recounting, or simple recognition (codes 1, 2, 3, 4, 5, 8, 19).

[c]Inasmuch as the observations for each client are not independent, the required probability level was dropped to .001.

Although some of the categories in the three rating systems clearly overlap, in the sense of being intended to measure the same thing, the rating systems were developed within quite different frameworks. Furthermore, the raters for the two process-descriptive measures were unaware of the thinking of the research team in developing the molar task-relevant categories. Thus the relationships reported here between the molar codes and the two different measures of momentary processing style provide some confirmation for the identifiability and construct validity of the process steps in the performance model shown in Figure 2-3. It is apparent also from inspection of all the ratings in more detail that using the three different measures together rather than separating them as was done for the purpose of the present analysis would give us a much more complete picture of what was going on at a given point. In fact, this more detailed inspection also suggested some possible revisions of the molar codes and some potentially interesting subdivisions of steps to be included in a later operations model.

CONSTRUCTION OF A CLIENT OPERATIONS MODEL

The goal of the task analysis is to identify and understand the internal operations of the client that are essential for the successful resolution of one class of therapeutic tasks. The eventual aim is to construct a theoretical model of the mechanisms of change, stated in some precise but pantheoretical language, possibly in terms of cognitive–affective information processing. For the present, the decision was made to construct an operations model using a more colloquial language.

The operations are inferred from the client performances as described by the molar codes and the descriptive process systems. The component operations of the model cannot be verified directly, of course, but predictions from the model can be tested in a variety of ways. For instance, once the nature of the basic client operations is well understood, one could make predictions concerning new kinds of therapist interventions that might be effective in stimulating and shaping their emergence. Or one might make predictions about the kinds of individual differences in cognitive–affective processing styles that would affect the ability to carry out these operations.

From the refined performance model in Figure 2-3, together with the interview transcripts rated on the molar codes, Client Vocal Quality, and Levels of Client Perceptual Processing, we began to infer the kinds of client operations underlying the different performance steps. One of the values in attempting to construct such an operations model is that it suggests important but unrecognized intervening steps. We could then go back to the interview transcripts and check whether or not these steps seemed to be taking place. The resulting client operations model is shown in Figure 2-4. The client operations are presented in terms of stages, but in actual performances the exact order followed is not usually as clear-cut.

In the first stage of the unfolding of a problematic reaction the client's task is to reenter the stimulus situation at the time just before the problematic reaction was triggered and to reexperience it vividly, but with an exploratory stance. The therapist interventions are crucial here. As the therapist tries to get a vivid feel for the situation, reflecting back the images created by the client's descriptions, the client is encouraged to reconstruct the stimulus situation, often describing aspects that had not previously been symbolized. As the reconstructed stimulus situation comes alive, the client begins to reexperience the situation. It is this reentering of the scene at a fairly high level of arousal, but with the focus on exploration, that positions the client for the differentiation stage.

In this next stage the client's task is to differentiate out new facets of his or her own inner reaction on the one hand and new facets of his or her perception of the stimulus situation on the other. The therapist's interventions help to keep the client focused inward in order to make the necessary identifications and differentiations while also maintaining a high level of immediacy. The focus of both client and therapist may switch back and forth between the reaction and the situation, but the focus is placed on one side at a time. On the reaction side the client first focuses attention on the inner reaction and then identifies the rearoused inner reaction. The client next attempts to give a differentiated description of the inner reaction that matches the internal referent and finally recognizes the precisely unique quality of the inner reaction.

At some point the client and therapist switch their focus to the stimulus situation with a high level of sensory awareness. The client scans the situation for salience, recognizing aspects that had stood out. The therapist's reflections should help the client to deliberately adopt a personal, subjective stance while elaborating his or her own idiosyncratic, subjective construals of the situation. Finally, while maintaining a subjective stance, the client differentiates out the nature of his or her own construal of the demand characteristics (potential impact) of the situation. The unique quality of the inner reaction and the awareness of one's own construal of the demand characteristics of the situation together form its experiential quality.

The differentiation stage is usually followed by a broadening out into other aspects of the client's life. This is not initiated by the therapist, but seems to involve the client's making exploratory associations to his or her own inner reaction and/or construals of the stimulus situation. The client's task here seems to be a kind of focused association that is neither free association nor cognitive analysis, but a sliding, with an exploratory and observing stance, to other life situations that have the same experiential

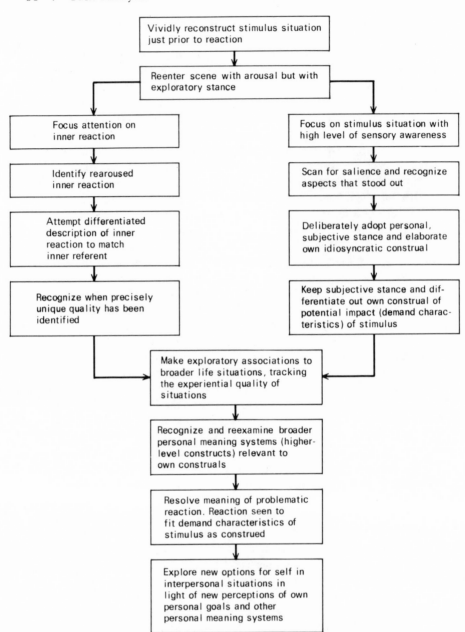

FIGURE 2-4. CLIENT OPERATIONS MODEL.

quality. The therapist's function is to facilitate this broader exploration, but to refocus the client vividly on the original situation whenever the explorations begin to lose relevance.

This broadening out into other life situations seems to enable clients to recognize and begin to reexamine some of their relevant higher-order constructs. These may be personal goals, basic values, "shoulds" and other introjected values, personal organizing styles, or, as in most cases, some combination of these. Inasmuch as the client is conducting a focused search and is thus open to new meanings, the implications of these higher-order constructs are usually recognized immediately. It is this recognition and reexamination of previously unexamined constructs that are influencing one's construals that seems to lead into the meaning resolution stage.

The client reprocesses the original situation and understands that the reaction that seemed so problematic fits the demand characteristics of the stimulus situation as construed. This brings with it a sense of relief in understanding a previously incomprehensible reaction and a kind of self-acceptance.

The new awareness, together with freedom from the self-blame that often characterizes the reaction to the reaction, generally leads to a further loosening and reorganization of constructs and an increased attentional capacity. In the light of their own personal goals and other personal meaning systems clients can explore new options for themselves that go beyond the particular situation. These may involve a loosening of "shoulds" and other introjected values or a reaffirmation of one's own values enhanced by greater understanding of how those values affect one's options. Although one's construals may be found to be fairly accurate, awareness of them reveals whether there are ways in which they limit one's options unnecessarily, and thus compromises become possible. A client may reality-test his or her construals by "returning" to the stimulus situation in the interview or making plans to do it outside. In some cases the client may thereby recognize that he or she has tapped into a much larger problem area. For these clients the relief is only partial, but they now have a clearer focus for beginning to work on the problem.

THE THERAPIST AS TASK FACILITATOR

One of the goals of the present research program was to gain a greater understanding of the ways in which therapists could facilitate the client in the unfolding and resolution of PRPs and related tasks. Once we had identified the client processes involved in the essential steps of task resolution, we could then use the occurrence of those processes as the criterion by which to evaluate the impact of different kinds of therapist interventions at particular points in the unfolding process. Rather than making any questionable assumption that certain kinds of therapist responses are by nature facilitative, it became possible to study the kinds of therapist interventions that actually seemed to facilitate the client's achieving each essential step. In this approach one first makes a systematic and detailed study of what *does* happen and then, by a series of successive approximations, one learns more and more about how to make it happen more effectively. Although the therapists involved had felt that at many points in the process they were "flying blind," they were experienced client-centered therapists who were following implicit guidelines of which they were only partially aware and did in fact make many highly facilitative responses.

Some illustrative findings should clarify this clinical–inductive process. In scrutinizing the transcript of Client J's interview we noted that at times when he was on some sidetrack involving repetitive statements or cognitive elaborations in an externalizing or limited vocal quality, the therapist refocused him with a vivid fragment of the stimulus situation, leaving an "open edge" that pushed for client awareness of salient features of the stimulus. The client not only tended to respond with awareness of salience or even awareness of perceived demand characteristics of the stimulus situation, but more interestingly, his vocal quality usually moved from being primarily externalizing or limited to being primarily focused. This clearly suggested that the client was not just following the directional lead of the therapist but was engaged in a real exploration, a turning inward of attentional energy.

The following interchange from Client B provides an example.

C: I can't remember much more about it. We were just driving along in the rush hour and he kept talking to me.

T: And he was telling jokes and leaping up and down, and—I'm not sure—and something about his leaning over you—kind of leaning half way into the front seat?

C: Not really. But I was aware of his head there, just by mine, and then the shocked look on his face.

In order to check this observation more precisely we went over the two transcripts and marked each point at which the therapist had made this kind of response at a time when the client was not productively engaged. We then looked at the Client Vocal Quality ratings of the client segments immediately preceding and immediately following these points. For Client J there were six such points, and in four of the six the proportion of focused voice increased after the therapist statement. In the other two the level of focused voice remained the same. For Client C there were five such therapist responses, and in four of them the proportion of focused voice increased, and in one remained the same. In no case did the proportion of focused voice drop after the intervention.

This kind of therapist intervention, at times when the client seems to be losing touch with the experiential search, is a sufficiently common occurrence in the evocative unfolding process to permit testing its effect by means of a formal sequential analysis, using a greater number of interviews. One could then compare the probability of an increase in focused voice following such therapist responses (the conditional probability) with the base rate of occurrence (unconditional probability) of such shifts in client vocal quality (Garner, 1962; Gottman & Markman, 1978).

FUTURE RESEARCH

Further verification steps are clearly necessary in the intensive analysis of this event. In the first place a new sample of interviews needs to be collected, made up of clients in ongoing therapy, for whom standard outcome measures as well as session-by-session productivity measures are available. The therapists will be trained by means of the improved therapist manual previously discussed. The generality of the process findings for actual client performances will be tested on the new sample. The performance model shown in Figure 2-3 will be further differentiated and altered by comparisons with the intensively analyzed new sample, including some comparisons between successful and unsuccessful resolutions, and this in turn will lead to an improved client operations model. It would be desirable at this stage to obtain information from the clients' perspective concerning the essential steps toward resolution, by means of an adaptation of interpersonal process recall (Elliott, Chapter 8). Finally, of course, it will be necessary to relate the presence of the essential processes to other criteria for successful resolution and then to relate degree of success in the resolution of problematic reactions to measures of the outcome of therapy.

THEORETICAL YIELD

On the basis of the third and much revised performance model and the operations model we have begun to consider a theoretical model of the underlying mechanisms of change for the present class of change episodes, as well as for other classes having some similar characteristics. The essential characteristics of the process seem to be reexperiencing and reprocessing, bringing to bear on the reevoked experience an exploratory stance and a processing capacity that for various reasons were not available on the original occasion. This model makes use of Zajonc's (1980) recent argument for the relative independence of the cognitive and affective processing systems. The assumption is made that these two systems are involved in different sequences in the original experience and in the reprocessing of it. Although such tentative theorizing is not within the scope of this chapter, we will briefly sketch out some of the directions in which the present line of research might expand client-centered theory.

One immediate implication for client-centered theory lies in the importance attached to the exploring of one's idiosyncratic, subjective construals of the situations one encounters. Roger's (1957, 1959) theory statements clearly imply a perceptual–conceptual base for personality and behavior change: The assumption is that if we can perceive self and the world differently, then we will react and behave differently. Yet in the preoccupation with "responding to feelings" in most client-centered writings little encouragement is given for clients to explore and examine their own idiosyncratic ways of construing their worlds. The present model would place more emphasis on understanding the interactions of affective and cognitive processing operations involved in the therapeutic exploration of the client's interactions with and construals of the environment.

The resolution of a PRP clearly bears some resemblance to the tasks addressed in cognitive therapy (Beck, 1976; Goldfried, 1979; Meichenbaum, 1977) and in Kelly's (1969) approach. The preceding discussion may even appear to suggest that client-centered theory should be extended by incorporating the techniques of cognitive therapy; yet the processes in which the client engages and the prescribed therapist interventions in evocative unfolding are quite different. The first basic difference concerns the probable primacy in time of affective reactions as compared to cognitive processes (Zajonc, 1980). The assumption that people can get in touch with their own highly differentiated affective processes and that this new awareness will prove to be essential in effectively guiding one's own life is basic to client-centered theory and to the kinds of exploration considered to be productive.

The second, related, basic difference is the importance given to identifying and unfolding the motivational element in the affective reaction rather than focusing on its inappropriateness. In most cognitive therapies the "inappropriate affect" is assumed to follow distorted cognitions or maladaptive self-statements resulting from them. That is, the inappropriate affect is merely an unfortunate by-product of the cognition. In the present formulation the affective reaction is seen as being influenced by cognitions at certain stages, but also as related to some genuine personal goal which it is important to understand. In the unfolding of PRPs, therapists attempt to keep the clients from focusing on the reaction to their reaction and thus invalidating their own affective reaction before it can be explored and its different facets can be differentiated out.

The most basic difference, perhaps, is the importance given to clients' discovering for themselves in a live, irrefutable fashion their own agency in their idiosyncratic construals and recognizing the possible new options available. In the present approach the crucial first step is to have clients develop a vivid feel of a single stimulus situation, together with a sense of what was salient for them. This approach is the opposite of seeking patterns and comparing and contrasting the clients' reaction in different situations. The assumption is that the vivid but focused reexperiencing of a stimulus situation and its evoked inner reaction in their idiosyncratic detail can lead to discovery and reexamination of one's own construals and personal meaning systems, including goals.

Furthermore, this approach is assumed to be powerful in inducing change for several reasons: (1) The constructs are reexamined while being reexperienced emotionally, not just recognized as patterns; (2) the idiosyncratic nature of what is discovered leads to more revealing personal awareness than could be predicted in advance on logical grounds; and (3) new options grow naturally out of the exploration.

These comparisons are not intended to demonstrate that one therapeutic approach is more "correct" than another, but to illustrate a point suggested earlier: Conducting rational–empirical task analyses of a number of different classes of events from a variety of different orientations might enable us to arrive at a kind of informed eclecticism that would combine some of the crucial insights of each orientation.

ACKNOWLEDGMENTS

The authors wish to acknowledge the valuable contributions of the other members of the research team, Gillian Kerr, Katherine McDermott, Nancy Schmidt, Michael Church, Kenneth Enns, and Greg McVeigh. Productive discussions were also held with Dr. David Rennie and Dr. Barbara Peterson.

REFERENCES

Barrett-Lennard, G. T. Dimensions of therapist response as causal factors in therapeutic change. *Psychological Monographs*, 1962, *76* (43, Whole No. 562).
Beck, A. T. *Cognitive therapy and the emotional disorders*. New York: International Universities Press, 1976.
Butler, J. M., & Rice, L. N. Adience, self-actualization, and drive theory. In J. M. Wepman & R. W. Heine (Eds.), *Concepts of personality*. Chicago: Aldine, 1963.
Garner, W. R. *Uncertainty and structure as psychological concepts*. New York: Wiley, 1962.
Gendlin, E. T. A theory of personality change. In P. Worchel & D. Byrne (Eds.), *Personality change*. New York: Wiley, 1964.
Gendlin, E. T. *Focusing*. New York: Bantam, 1981.
Goldfried, M. R. Anxiety reduction through cognitive–behavioral intervention. In P. C. Kendall & S. D. Hollon (Eds.), *Behavioral interventions: Theory, research, and practice*. New York: Academic Press, 1979.
Gottman, J. M., & Markman, H. J. Experimental designs in psychotherapy research. In S. L. Garfield & A. L. Bergin (Eds.), *Handbook of psychotherapy and behavior change*. New York: Wiley, 1978.

Husserl, E. *Experience and judgment.* (L. Landgrebe, Ed.; J. Churchill & K. Ameriks, Trans.). Evanston, Ill.: Northwestern University Press, 1973. (Originally published, 1939.)

Kelly, G. A. *Clinical psychology and personality: The selected papers of George Kelly.* New York: Wiley, 1969.

Krantz, D., & Tversky, A. Conjoint measurement analysis of composition rules in psychology. *Psychological Review,* 1971, *78,* 151–169.

Meichenbaum, D. A. *Cognitive-behavior modification: An integrative approach.* New York: Plenum Press, 1977.

Pascual-Leone, J. Metasubjective problems of constructive cognition: Forms of knowing and their psychological mechanisms. *Canadian Psychological Review,* 1976, *17,* 110–125.

Rice, L. N. The evocative function of the therapist. In D. A. Wexler & L. N. Rice (Eds.), *Innovations in client-centered therapy.* New York: Wiley, 1974.

Rice, L. N., & Koke, C. J. Vocal style and the process of psychotherapy. In J. K. Darby (Ed.), *Speech evaluation in psychiatry.* New York: Grune & Stratton, 1981.

Rice, L. N., Koke, C. J., Greenberg, L. S., & Wagstaff, A. *Manual for client vocal quality.* Toronto: York University Counselling and Development Center, 1979.

Rice, L. N., & Wagstaff, A. K. Client voice quality and expressive style as indexes of productive psychotherapy. *Journal of Consulting Psychology,* 1967, *31,* 557–563.

Rogers, C. R. The necessary and sufficient conditions of therapeutic personality change. *Journal of Consulting Psychology,* 1957, *21,* 95–103.

Rogers, C. R. A theory of therapy, personality and interpersonal relationships, as developed in the client-centered framework. In S. Koch (Ed.), *Psychology: A study of a science* (Vol. 3: *Formulations of the person and the social context*). New York: McGraw-Hill, 1959.

Toukmanian, S. G. A measure of client perceptual processing. In L. S. Greenberg & W. M. Pinsof (Eds.), *The psychotherapeutic process: A research handbook.* New York: Guilford Press, in press.

Wexler, D. A. A cognitive theory of experiencing, self-actualization, and therapeutic process. In D. A. Wexler & L. N. Rice (Eds.), *Innovations in client-centered therapy.* New York: Wiley, 1974.

Zajonc, R. B. Feeling and thinking: Preferences need no inferences. *American Psychologist,* 1980, *35,* 151–175.

3
A Task Analysis of
Intrapersonal Conflict Resolution

LESLIE S. GREENBERG
University of British Columbia

The event analyzed in this chapter was chosen from the practice of Gestalt therapy. One of the key methodological innovations of the Gestalt approach was the introduction of the "graded experiment" to promote the actual "living through" of particular psychological experiences, in order to help people discover how they interfere with themselves. As Perls, Hefferline, and Goodman (1951) note, engaging in experimental tasks in order to discover "what interferes with the successful completion of the task becomes the center of the [Gestalt] work." Task analysis, on the other hand, is a method designed to explore the moment-by-moment performance of clients engaged in resolving tasks, in order to identify the components of successful performances. It is therefore a research method that is highly congruent with the therapeutic approach in Gestalt therapy.

SELECTION AND DESCRIPTION OF THE TASK

The selection of a therapeutic event for study is governed by the investigator's intuitions about what processes are important in therapeutic change. The event is chosen in the belief that understanding the processes involved in the event will illuminate the workings of psychotherapeutic change. Both explicit and implicit theory guide selection of the event. It is important for the investigator to spell out as explicitly as possible the theoretical assumptions guiding the selection in order to explicate the theoretical framework that will influence the study of the event. The investigator's tacit knowledge (Polanyi, 1966) or cognitive map of how solutions are achieved in particular tasks is part of the data of this approach and therefore needs to be explicated as clearly as possible at the start.

In the present study the underlying general theory of human functioning comes from Gestalt therapy. In this approach a healthy organism is regarded as operating by satisfying a hierarchy of values that determines its most urgent current need. Needs are seen as emerging at the organism–environment boundary and as organizing the perceptual field into figure–

background formations that determine behavior. In addition, people are conceived of as systems, composed of parts, in which integration of diverse aspects of the system leads to the greater utilization of system potential. The different aspects of the personality are seen as either working in harmony or being in conflict. Describing the role of conflict in the personality, Perls *et al.* (1951) state, "Situations in which you encounter blocks in carrying out tasks which you have set for yourself are conflict situations—and furthermore, the conflict is between one part of your personality and another." A dialogue between Topdog and Underdog is seen as central to the experience of conflict. Topdog is the authoritarian, bullying part of the personality which has introjected societal "shoulds." Underdog is the more manipulative, excusing part of the personality which engages in a dialogue with Topdog and evades the shoulds with "Yes, but. . . ." As long as these dialogues are left unattended to, they involve the person in useless struggle, self-cancellation, and self-control.

In working with these dialogues, the therapist does not formulate an idea of an underlying conflict which becomes reified as the client's "issue," but rather works with a client's presently experienced split. If clients bring their conflicts fully into awareness and the opposing parts into lively contact, reconciliation is seen as occurring by an integration of opposites. The goal of Gestalt work is awareness and integration of the partial aspects of the self, and the goal of integration is upheld as far superior to control over one aspect by the other.

This theoretical framework guided the selection of client splits as the focus of study. As a therapist I had noticed, guided by the theory of the significance of splits in human functioning, that people in therapy often described momentary states in which aspects of themselves were experienced as being in opposition. They would make statements such as "One part of me wants to do this but another part of me doesn't want to," "On the one hand I feel this but on the other hand I feel that," or "I want to do this but I can't." Such statements of splits were observed to occur often both within, and across, clients. Gestalt therapists whom I had observed almost always intervened at these points, in an attempt to get at the opposing parts. When clients explored these splits and experienced deeply some aspects of their experience, they often appeared to be no longer stuck, confused, and conflicted. Resolving important splits seemed to open people to a new way of viewing themselves in their situations and to offer them new approaches to their problems. In addition, therapeutic change did appear to take place when splits were resolved, but how this change took place was not very clear. On inspection both theory and therapists alike said two things: (1) that present experiencing and awareness was important and (2) that integration was the way in which splits were resolved. More than this on the process of resolution was not readily available in the literature or in the oral tradition in Gestalt therapy. An understanding of how change took place in these experiences of conflict seemed to hold promise of helping explain change in psychotherapy for a class of events of considerable significance to therapeutic practice.

DEFINITION OF A CLIENT MARKER

The events to be studied began with a client marker, a statement that indicated the client was experiencing a conflict. In order to clarify the features of a split and develop a formal definition of its structure, a number of samples of conflict markers were selected for study. Using a method of distinctive feature analysis adapted from linguistics (Greenberg, 1975), raters constructed rules that described the distinguishing features of splits. This was done by a process using naive raters who described, at as low a level of inference as possible, the features that differentiated a sample of statements labeled Type A (splits) from a sample labeled as Type not A (nonsplits). Without prior knowledge of what was being looked for, the raters then constructed rules that described splits. Three types of splits, called conflict splits, subject–object splits, and attribution splits, were defined by this method (Greenberg, 1979).

Performances related to the resolution of one of these types of splits, conflict splits, are the focus of the studies described in this chapter. A conflict split is essentially a direct statement of internal conflict defined by four distinct features (Greenberg, 1979): (1) a statement of tendency or partial aspect of self (e.g., "I want to get closer," "I have all these feelings," "I want security"); (2) a statement of a second tendency or partial aspect of the self (e.g., "I seem to pull away," "I'm afraid to let my feelings out," "I want freedom"); (3) an indication of intrapersonal contradiction indicating the two parts are in opposition (e.g., yet, if, but); and (4) an indication that the person is involved in a present experience of struggle, striving, or coercion indicated verbally by "I can't." "I'm afraid," "I don't know whether to" and nonverbally by voice and gesture. Examples would be a client working on intimacy who says, "I want to get closer to people, yet I can't; I just seem to pull away," someone working on control who asserts, "I have all these feelings inside; I'm afraid. If I let them out I don't know what would happen," or someone experiencing a decisional conflict who says, "I don't know whether to stay in this relationship or leave. I want the security but I also want more freedom."

It was found that conflict splits reported in therapy as having been experienced in the past and lacking indicators of a present struggle could be worked with, but they had first to be brought to life and experienced as conflicts in the present. In addition, it is important to note that a statement of a split does not represent a statement of a reified conflict in which the content remains static throughout the therapy. Often an initial split will evolve into a more and more refined or differentiated split, until some core conflict is experienced. The initial stated split does not remain as a static focus of therapeutic work. Rather, the content of the conflict often changes; it is the experience of being in conflict, torn between opposing sides, that remains the same. In fact, one of the major goals for both client and therapist when working on splits is to correctly sense the opposed forces in the personality that are operating in the conflict.

DEFINITION OF RESOLUTION

In the beginning of a task analysis it is important to study *successful resolutions* in order to isolate the components crucial to resolution. Some idea of successful resolution was therefore needed in order to select resolution events for study. Gestalt therapy theory suggested that resolution of a conflict split occurred through a process involving the two parts listening to each other and thereby achieving integration. Perls has stated that it is "by listening [that] we can bring about a reconciliation." (Perls, 1969, p. 19). He maintained that only when the two sides "come to their senses (in this case listening to each other) does the door to integration and unification open" (Perls, 1969, p. 5). He went on to affirm the following:

> [The] basic philosophy of Gestalt therapy is that of nature—differentiation and integration. Differentiation by itself leads to polarities. As dualities these polarities will easily fight and paralyze one another. By integrating opposite traits we make the person whole again. For instance, weakness and bullying integrate as silent firmness. (Perls, 1970b, p. 7)

It appeared to the investigator that, Perls's descriptions of resolution notwithstanding, there were no clear formulations of resolution that would facilitate a reliable identification of "correct" solutions to the affective problem of being in conflict. Instead it seemed that a solution, vague and indeterminate at the start, emerged for the client as a sense of completion, a sense of a new gestalt having been formed. The client appeared to achieve solutions by fitting evolving pieces of a puzzle into a new configuration, and at the point at which there was no longer a sense of confusion, perplexity, or struggle, "resolution" could be said to have occurred. Resolution could therefore be best identified by a client's sense of completion, the feeling that something had shifted and that the problem had ceased to exist. It was decided therefore to use client reports of resolution as the primary criterion by which to identify successful performances. In addition to client reports, a therapist report confirming resolution was obtained. Finally, in order to obtain an observer's point of view on client process, ratings of Stage 6 on the Experiencing Scale (Klein,

Mathieu, Kiesler, & Gendlin, 1969), which indicates a synthesis of readily accessible and more fully realized feelings to resolve issues or produce personally meaningful structures, were used to confirm resolution. Events in which these three perspectives converged would provide a sample of clear resolutions.

DESCRIPTION OF THE TASK ENVIRONMENT

The notion of a task environment, borrowed from the cognitive psychology domain, provided a solution for the vexing problem of how to study client performance when the client is always interacting with the therapist. We had observed that therapists carefully trained in specific interventions could often provide a fairly standard task environment; this was particularly true for the same therapist across clients. Given that therapists could be selected and trained to work with splits according to the same theoretical beliefs and the same theories of practice, it appeared useful as a heuristic device to assume that the task environment could be regarded as relatively constant and that the client performance could be studied on this standardized environment as a phenomenon in its own right. Although therapists' moment-by-moment behaviors varied across situations, the basic structure or press of the clients' task environment could be regarded as similar. Further, it was felt that even if some therapists did provide different environments, the focus of the investigations would still be on identifying components of client performance that were related to resolution, and variations across task environments that influenced resolution would not detract from the validity of the components of client resolution performance.

An effective environment for working on the affective task of split resolution appeared to be Perls's (1969) empty chair work, defined for working with splits as Gestalt two-chair work (Greenberg, 1979). The therapist uses two-chair work in order to separate the two parts of the split and then create contact between them. Even though much of the Gestalt approach relies on the creative intuition of the therapist, there exist some basic principles around the two-chair technique that can be abstracted and used as guides toward the resolution or integration of the opposing aspects of clients' splits (Greenberg, 1975). The five basic principles of two-chair work are (1) separation and the creation of contact, (2) the responsibility of the client, (3) the attending function, (4) the heightening function, and (5) the expressive function. A description of these principles follows.

The primary and most basic task for the client is to *separate and create contact* between the partial aspects of the self. Only when the client is able to establish a dialogue between both sides of himself or herself will the client experience the difference and the validity of each pole. Almost invariably, when contact is restored between these poles, the individual discovers that these disowned parts can come to terms with each other.

The next aspect of the task environment to be held constant was that of encouraging the client to assume *responsibility* for the different aspects of the conflict rather than viewing them as experiences imposed from the outside. The client may avoid responsibility by blocking awareness or by ignoring feelings or experience—here the therapist must intervene. The client is encouraged to "own" his or her experience by, for example, using "I" when referring to inner feelings. The client is encouraged to contact and express in an authentic fashion the characteristics of each role. He or she is asked to identify with aspects of present experiencing, such as the tension in the neck, the tightness in the chest, the tears, or the wavering voice.

The *attending* function of the task environment entails promoting an increased awareness in clients of different aspects of their experience. The therapist can direct the client's focal beam of attention inside by requesting that he or she pay attention to internal experience or direct a client's attention to overt phenomena by inquiring about what is going on with a wiggling foot, tapping fingers, or an interesting quality in the voice.

The *heightening* principle calls for the therapist to increase the impact of an experience by increasing the client's level of arousal. This is attained by suggesting that the client exaggerate some movement, repeat some statement, or act out the style of one of his or her partial aspects of self. The therapist also heightens and creates higher levels of arousal by making explicit messages that had remained implicit in the interaction between the parts.

The principle of *expressing* promotes doing, rather than talking about. The impact of actually doing something is far greater than just talking about it. Clients are asked to become aware of what they are doing to themselves and to enact this process in specific ways. The therapist stimulates this by requesting that clients embody what they are talking about by, for example, becoming a judge or actually withdrawing into a little ball. In these enactments clients are encouraged to reveal the particular content of the inner dialogue instead of remaining with generalities.

These principles serve as a type of therapist manual and provide a definition of the task environment. Although the moment-by-moment therapist behaviors vary in working with splits on different occasions, it is the overall intent and function of the therapist operation that must remain constant across situations. This specification of the task environment allowed the study of client performance in a relatively standardized intervention environment. Measures of client-perceived therapist empathy (Barrett-Lennard, 1962) were also taken to ensure that the task atmosphere perceived by the client was also standardized as an empathic environment.

Greenberg and coworkers (Greenberg & Clarke, 1979; Greenberg & Dompierre, 1981; Greenberg & Rice, 1981) showed that when these five basic principles were utilized in the two-chair operation there was a resulting greater increase in depth of experiencing and greater attainment of conflict resolution than when empathic reflections were used at splits. This provided evidence that the event was potent and was worthy of intensive study.

DESCRIPTION OF CLIENT PERFORMANCE:
RATIONAL AND EMPIRICAL ANALYSES

For any human problem one can ask oneself, "How could I solve this problem?" This type of questioning forms the basis of the rational task analysis. Starting with this kind of question, and guided by one's clinical knowledge and a general theory, one engages in a "thought experiment" (Husserl, 1939/1973) in order to explicate the essence of a resolution performance and thereby map out the idealized client performance by rational means. This idealized performance is what Husserl referred to as an "intuition of essences"; it is the investigator's best creative integration of everything he or she knows about the essential elements of resolution performances. This idealized performance will probably contain errors and certainly omissions, but it will serve as a framework for organizing the vast amount of data to be obtained from a study of actual resolution performances and will be modified and refined as the research progresses. An important aspect of this method is that one loops around through the rational description of idealized performances and the empirical description of actual performances in a number of cycles in order to develop a model of resolution performance. At any stage of the research program the idealized description is a model of hypothesized performance to be confirmed or disconfirmed by the study of the next case.

The empirical description of client performance in the intensive analysis that follows was not formulated by uninformed observers operating without guidelines as to what they wished to observe. The naturalistic therapy observer in fact is usually guided by some explicit or implicit notions as to what to look for; these represent his or her best intuitions at that time. Sometimes these guidelines may be in the form of carefully constructed categories of possible behaviors; sometimes the framework guiding observation may be, as in the first cycle of analysis, global and implicit notions of what constitutes good performances in therapy. The important point is that the observers do have some ideas of possible performance and these guide their investigations. When actual performances are described in an objective manner, by process scales, they take on meaning in the context of the concepts of possible performances. This practice of comparing actual performances in specific situations to possible performances is an important aspect of empirical analyses.

The procedure used below of reflecting actual, concrete performances off possible idealized performances is an attempt to put some of the investigator's research energy directly into the creative activity that underlies much research but is often neglected or relegated to the "private" realm. Research methodologies that explicitly draw out this private realm (Polanyi, 1966) in order to tap it as a source of discovery will be important in turning the art of psychotherapy into a science.

The First Cycle: Constructing the Model

Rational Analysis

The first idealized performance model of split resolution identified by rational means some possible resolution strategies and some possible error strategies. These were arrived at by reviewing the literature and by explicating clinicians' notions of resolution. The possible ways of resolving conflict in Gestalt two-chair work appeared to be (1) a resolution by some form of integration; (2) a resolution by a release of previously unexpressed feelings, in Gestalt terms, an explosion (Perls, 1969); or (3) a resolution by a change of perspective which made the conflict no longer appear relevant. In addition, the following error strategies were identified as indicating that the performances were not really on task, that is, that the client was not attempting to resolve the conflict. These were (1) talking about the conflict or (2) avoiding the conflict by minimizing it or not wanting to discuss it in personal terms.

Empirical Analysis and Model Construction

The first empirical description was developed by rating the dialogues in the two chairs for three events from each of three clients on depth of experiencing, using the Experiencing Scale (Klein et al., 1969), and on Client Vocal Quality (Rice, Koke, Greenberg, & Wagstaff, 1979). These variables were chosen because they could accurately identify the experiential processes regarded as important in a phenomenologically oriented therapy.

The nine events were separated from the sessions. Each began with a client statement of a split, contained a two-chair dialogue performance in an environment consistent with the principles of two-chair work, and ended with the termination of the two-chair work (including summary discussion) or the end of the session, whichever came first. Raters achieved a 100% agreement on identification of splits. Intensive analysis of the ratings of all the 2-minute segments that made up each of these nine events began to reveal some interesting patterns in the data, which were tabulated and graphed in various ways. The first observation from the graphs was that the experiencing levels of the two chairs seemed to be somewhat different, particularly in the earlier part of the event. A graph of the experiencing levels of an event is shown in Figure 3-1 to demonstrate the pattern discovered in each group. In this figure it can be seen that the two chairs initially proceed at different levels of experiencing until at a certain point, called the merging point, the experiencing levels become similar. At this point the levels of both chairs increase to higher levels. Thus, the dialogue can be seen as possessing two phases, the preresolution and resolution phases, pivoting on the merging point. This pattern repeated itself in each event.

The details of the analysis of the experiencing data presented elsewhere (Greenberg, 1975, 1980) demonstrated that the mean level of experiencing of the two chairs in the preresolution phase was significantly different. In addition, the preresolution and resolution phase scores for each chair were significantly different. The mean experiencing levels for each client are shown in Table 3-1.

The data revealed the following patterns:

1. The chair initially higher in experiencing, called the experiencing chair, proceeded initially at or around Stage 4 on the Experiencing Scale, indicating an expression of feeling.
2. The chair initially lower in experiencing, called the other chair, started at experiencing levels below Stage 4, and increased in depth at the merging point to levels comparable to the experiencing chair.
3. After the merging point resolution was attained by both chairs, increasing in depth of experiencing to Stages 5 and 6. Attainment of the merging point by the other chair appeared to be a sufficient condition of resolution and could be regarded as signaling entry of the resolution phase in the dialogue.

Comparing the detailed observations of the experiencing data across clients with the idealized performance description led to the construction of the first model, which suggested that the two chairs could be regarded as initially functioning as independent subsystems characterized by different levels of experiencing. Furthermore, at a certain point in the performance, a merging of these two subsystems appeared to take place by an increase in the level of the experiencing of the lower one. The two systems thereafter proceeded to task resolution at levels of experiencing which were indistinguishable from each other, but which were on the average higher than before the merging point.

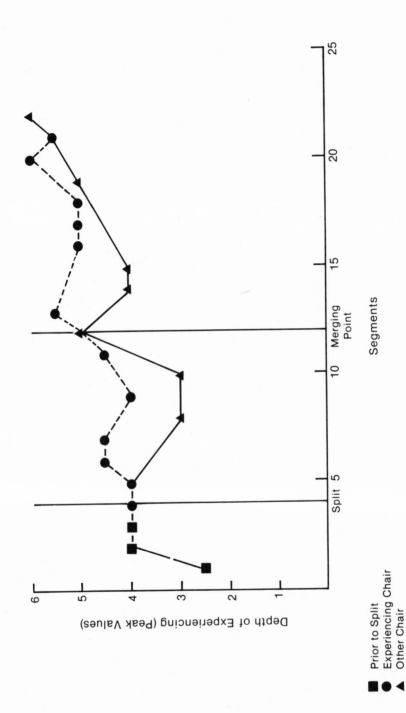

FIGURE 3-1. EXPERIENCING LEVELS OF THE TWO CHAIRS IN A GESTALT DIALOGUE.

TABLE 3-1. MEAN EXPERIENCING IN THE PRERESOLUTION AND RESOLU-
TION PHASES

CLIENT	PRERESOLUTION	RESOLUTION	MANN-WHITNEY U
	OTHER CHAIR		
GOF	3.2	4.5	0^a
GAT	3.5	4.5	
KAT	3.7	4.6	
	EXPERIENCING CHAIR		
GOF	4.2	5.2	0^a
GAT	4.5	4.9	
KAT	4.2	5.1	

[a]Significant at the .05 level

Given this model, the next step was to see if a measure of an independent dimension, Client Vocal Quality, in any way corroborated these findings. If voice was different in the two chairs, this would strengthen the model's depiction of the two chairs as independent systems. Changes in voice after the merging point would similarly strengthen the model's conception that there was some change phenomenon occurring in the resolution phase.

Analyses showed that the other chair used significantly more of a combination of an energetic, outer-directed voice (externalizing: X) and an energyless, restricted voice (limited: L), whereas the experiencing chair used more of a combination of a high energy, inner-directed voice and an expressive voice (focused: F, and emotional: E). From the analysis of voice data it was concluded that the other chair was less involved and made poorer contact with itself than the experiencing chair (Greenberg, 1980). However, the *proportion* of good contact voice (focused and emotional) in the other chair increased significantly in the resolution phase; in addition, this *change* of voice appeared to begin consistently, around the merging point. Change to focused voice in the other chair therefore appeared to be a necessary condition for resolution and emerged as an important therapeutic cue. When this voice change in the other chair was accompanied by an increase in experiencing to the level of the experiencing chair, the dialogue always entered the resolution phase.

The findings of this study seemed closest to the concept of "a reconciliation of two parts by integration," although the voice data and inspection of the transcripts suggested a more distinctive mechanism of resolution in the resolution phase: The other chair appeared to soften its attitude towards the experiencer. Integration did occur in the sense of two chairs becoming similar in depth of experiencing. Inspection of the transcripts revealed in some instances some form of listening or negotiation between the sides. However, the voice data showed a change in the other chair from the predominant use of a "lecturing at" voice, in which preformed meanings were expressed, to a greater use of a voice characterized as "searching internally" for new information. This was corroborated in the Experiencing Scale by the shift in the other chair from externally oriented descriptions and reactions to a style of participating in which it was more subjectively involved and described its own feelings and concerns. Inspection of the transcript showed that the shifts in the other chair accompanied a change in attitude from critical to more accepting. This softening in the attitude of the critic seemed to be a necessary and sufficient condition for integration.

Comparison of the first idealized notions of performance with the first empirical analysis provided evidence showing that one of the original models, integration, was far more descriptive of resolution performances than the other two, that is, explosion or change in perspective. Resolution performances could be characterized as involving two subsystems, the experiencing chair and the other chair, which merged on experiencing prior to resolution. Finally, a change in voice in the other chair was found to occur at the merging point and was an important signal of resolution.

A few excerpts from a dialogue in which a client is working on a split between feeling vulnerable and wanting herself to be strong follow. The chair delivering each statement is indicated.

PRERESOLUTION PHASE

Other: I am ashamed that you should say things like that—Come on Sue, *smarten up*.

T: Change. Tell her what you feel.

Exper: I feel sad because I'm alone.

T: Is that hard for you to say?

Exper: Yes, my voice went right up.

T: Change.

Other: Don't get into your sadness. You're coping well. Keep coping.

Exper: I'm sick of coping. I'm sick of trying to prove . . .

* * *

Exper: I'm afraid life is going to pass by me. I feel very weak.

T: What's it like for you inside?

Exper: I'm soft. I'm alone and soft. I'm tender and passive.

T: Be your softness.

Exper: I am my softness and I'm alone . . . I am my softness and I'm afraid.

T: Mhh.

Exper: I'm my softness and I'm vulnerable (*cries*) . . .

T: What do you say to your toughness?

Exper: Help me not to be as afraid—not to be pushed around.

T: What do you experience?

Exper: This is a kind of trance and I'm kind of sad.

T: Tell her about this.

Exper: Um—I'm sad. God I don't dare get to be myself . . . (*sniff*)

T: What do you want?

Exper: I want to be given a chance to be myself.

RESOLUTION PHASE

T: Tell her.

Exper: I want to be given space so I can be, without being so sad just to be me. Give me some time—just give me some time.

T: Change. What do you say?

Other: (*gestures with her arms*)

T: What's this? [referring to the gesture]

Other: What shall I do?

T: Mhm.

Other: Why do I do that? I was just wondering. . . . I'm aware she's tired. (*changes body position*)

T: Now what happens here? [referring to body position]

Other: I was conscious that I put my feet here [on the chair in front of her]. I want to get my shoes off and put them on the chair.

T: What do you feel as you do this?

Other: Um—sort of um—closeness.

T: Tell her this.

Other: I feel a closeness. It is the first time she's asked.

T: How does that feel?

Other: Um—that makes me feel softer and a little happier.

T: How do you feel toward her?

Other: Not really trusting yet but pleased. I feel you deserve a place like you've earned it. I don't know how you are yet—ah it's different to the whining. I want you to have a place.

T: Mhm.

Other: (*laughs*)

T: What's happening?

Other: Seems like you're growing up.

T: What do you feel?

Other: I'm feeling like—uh, I feel like my mother. I feel (*laughs*) proud—like I don't have many judgments.

T: Anything you want from her?

Other: I have some good points—don't discard me.

T: Tell her some of your good points.

Other: My good points are that I do have desirable strengths. I can help you through tight spots where you could bleed unnecessarily.

T: What's happening?

Other: I feel close again. I feel as if I'm talking to a child but in a caring way.

T: Change. What are you experiencing?

Exper: Um—a sting of sadness I guess but some sense of being protected. I feel cared for. I really sense the way my legs were. I sense there is a semicircle.

T: Mhm—sort of cradled.

Exper: Like I have the word delicate in my mind—fragile, but not in a negative way. Yeah, I feel delicate.

T: I like your delicateness.

Exper: Yeah, me too. . . .

Resolution performances frequently contain some of the same components as the preceding dialogue—one side criticizing the other side, which often reacts with compliance, but then goes on to oppose. In successful dialogues the experiencer then expresses its feelings and wants and the critic softens its attitude.

THE SECOND CYCLE: REVISING THE MODEL

Rational Analysis

Informed by the first empirical analysis and on the basis of informal observation of a few new resolutions, a new rational analysis was engaged in to break down the process of resolution into more minute components. Figure 3-2 presents an eight-step model developed by Johnson (1980), in which each identified step was like a task that had to be completed before the next step could be reached. Each step therefore represented a level of performance competence necessary for problem resolution. Possible tangential performances in which other issues might come up were also indicated. This diagram represented an idealized performance model of split resolution and contained the idealized notion of resolution by integration, as well as the idea of softening discovered in the first empirical analysis.

This second rational analysis addressed itself to the more detailed steps involved in the resolution of splits. Possible process indications of each step of the idealized performance path were specified as part of the rational analysis in terms of the following five process indicators:

1. The Experiencing Scale
2. Quality of voice

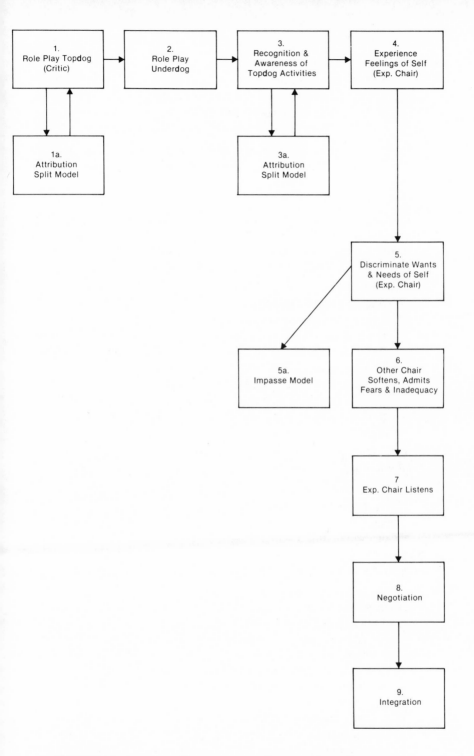

FIGURE 3-2. IDEALIZED DESCRIPTION OF CONFLICT SPLIT RESOLUTION.

3. Language content
4. Behavior and gesture
5. Client comments made during the interview or during interpersonal process recall (IPR) sessions

A brief description of each step in the diagram and the process indicators of the step that we expected to find are detailed as follows.

Step 1: Role-Play Topdog (Critic)
The client plays the part of a bully or critic and attempts to intimidate or overwhelm the opposite party either by citing moral, social, or ethical obligations or by demonstrating superior verbal force.

Indicators:
1. Experiencing Scale—Stages 2–3
2. Quality of voice—externalizing
3. Language—abundant use of "you," "if," "should," "ought," "must"
4. Behavior—upright, rigid posture; intimidating hand gestures (e.g., pointed finger, raised hand); cold, glaring looks
5. Client comments (made during interviews or IPR session)—allusions to authority figures (e.g., parents, priest, teachers); words or phrases indicating coercion (e.g., "I was laying a real heavy. . . .")

Step 1a: Tangential Performance Where the Shift Evolves into an Attribution Split.

Step 2: Role-Play Underdog
The client takes on the role of a weakling who appears to succumb to the power of the Topdog. He or she acts meek and passive and attempts to counter the Topdog by whining, making excuses (i.e., "Yes, but . . .") and being crafty and cunning.

Indicators:
1. Experiencing Scale—Stage 3
2. Quality of voice—limited or emotional
3. Language—abundant use if "I," "can't," "don't know," "yes, but," "maybe," etc.; apologetic, submissive, whinning; indirect
4. Behavior—closed, hunched, crouching posture; limited eye contact; bowed head
5. Client comments—allusions to reaction to criticism, feeling helpless, powerless, etc.; allusions to feeling small and weak (e.g., little girl, young child)

Step 3: Recognition and Awareness of Topdog Activities
The client realizes that the attitudes and behavior ascribed to the Topdog role are not entirely external, but that they represent one aspect of himself or herself. The client becomes aware of and acknowledges how he or she actually goes about intimidating and pressuring himself or herself.

Indicators:
1. Experiencing Scale—Stages 2–3 (peak of Stage 3)
2. Quality of voice—externalizing; some focused
3. Language—abundant use of "you," "it," "should," etc.; some use of "I" at recognition point
4. Behavior—upright, rigid posture; intimidating hand gestures; cold, glaring looks
5. Client comments—verbal statements indicating awareness and recognition (e.g., "This is what I'm always doing!"); comments symbolizing activities (uses similes, e.g., "like a school teacher")

Step 3a: Tangential Performance Where the Shift Evolves into an Attribution split.

Step 4: Experience Feelings of Self (Experiencing Chair)
Faced with the recognition and reowning of actions by the Topdog, or other chair, the experiencing chair sheds the role of Underdog and begins to explore and express feelings true to the self. Typically, these feelings will initially reflect vulnerable emotions such as inadequacy, loneliness, sadness, and fear, although more aggressive expressions may also appear.

Indicators:
1. Experiencing Scale—Stage 4
2. Quality of voice—focused; possibly emotional
3. Language—"I" statements; present tense statements; affective statements (e.g., "I feel . . .")
4. Behavior—possibilities include sighs, fatigue, slouched body, looking down, tears, or trembling
5. Client comments—statements concerning feeling, particularly related to the "newness" (i.e., not stereotyped feelings of "ain't it awful"); indications of recognizing idiosyncratic feelings ("I realized that's what I felt")

Step 5: Discriminate Wants and Needs of Self (Experiencing Chair)
In the Experiencing Chair, the client proceeds to separate his or her feelings into specific statements of and demands for what he or she intrinsically wants and needs. The process is one of clarification, differentiation, and assertion.

Indicators:
1. Experiencing Scale—Stage 4, possibly 5
2. Quality of voice—focused, possibly emotional
3. Language—"I want" and "I need" statements; demands placed on other chair; increasing specificity and idiosyncratic meanings
4. Behavior—possibilities include looking up and more assertive features and hand gestures (i.e., open palms and sitting straighter and more solidly)
5. Client comments—statements concerning awareness of wants and needs; statements indicating increasing clarity of wants and needs

Step 5a: Terminal Tangential Performance. The Impasse.

Step 6: Other Chair Softens, Admits Fear and Inadequacy
In the other chair, the client relaxes the rigid, "tough" pose and proceeds to expose, initially in a tentative fashion, feelings of compassion, concern, weakness, trepidation, or incompetence.

Indicators:
1. Experiencing Scale—Stage 4, possibly 5
2. Quality of voice—focused
3. Language—"I" statements by other chair; present tense statements; affective statements (i.e., "I feel")
4. Behavior—relaxed, nonrigid posture, possibly leaning forward
5. Client comments—statements relating to feelings of compassion or of fear, weakness, inadequacy, nervousness, etc.; statements indicating "newness" or surprise quality of feelings

Step 7: Experiencing Chair Listens
In response to the other chair, the client in the experiencing chair adopts an empathic, understanding manner, which indicates that it is listening to the other chair and giving full consideration to the remarks made.

Indicators:
1. Experiencing Scale—Stage 5
2. Quality of voice—focused
3. Language—empathic statements (i.e., "I understand")
4. Behavior—good eye contact with other chair; leaning forward in chair
5. Client comments—statements concerning recognition and understanding of feelings expressed by other chair (i.e., "I didn't know you felt that way"); frequent statements of surprise concerning feelings of other chair

Step 8: Negotiation
Both the experiencing chair and the other chair put forth the terms and conditions related to their feelings and wishes that they would like met. They then proceed to bargain with each other.

Indicators:
1. Experiencing Scale—Stage 5
2. Quality of voice—focused
3. Language—"I" statements from both chairs; tentative, qualified statements; structures of the nature of "If you will . . . , then I will . . ."; hypotheses examined (i.e., "What if . . . ?")
4. Behavior—relaxed, assertive posture
5. Client comments—allusions to process of bargaining or trade-offs; comments concerning feelings of equality and equal power distribution

Step 9: Integration
The two chairs reach a satisfactory agreement that resolves the conflict and creates integration by incorporating aspects of both sides.

Indicators:
1. Experiencing Scale—Stage 6
2. Quality of voice—focused
3. Language—statements of agreement by both chairs (i.e., "That sounds good to me")
4. Behavior—possibilities include calm, relaxed, serene posture, or excitement and vivaciousness related to resolution (i.e., spirited activity)
5. Client comments—statements concerning resolution (i.e., "I feel finished"); statements indicating attainment of integration (i.e., "I can do both!"); expressions of relief over resolution of conflict

Empirical Analysis

Having specified the idealized performances possibilities and their indicators, two successful performances and one unsuccessful performance were chosen for study in order to compare actual and possible performance steps and to determine whether the successful performances indeed differed in similar ways from an unsuccessful performance. One of the methodological concerns at this stage was how to segment the transcripts. Once a transcript of the event, beginning with a split and ending in a resolution, was obtained, it was segmented by dividing it into steps comparable to the model. It was decided that it would be appropriate at this discovery-oriented stage to have the investigator and one judge, guided by the idealized description and the process indicators, break the transcript into transitional steps to determine whether the idealized performance description was at all representative of an actual performance. This was not a test but a postdictive description of what actually occurred. The judges first segmented the transcripts into the two tracks of experiencing and other chair. Then each of the chairs was segmented into the steps of the rational model according to the judgment of the judges, who read the transcripts and identified when the client entered and left a step. They also made judgments of tangential performances which were not on task, according to the model. A descriptive client performance diagram was then constructed depicting each of the on-task segments as rated by the judges. This brought the investigators close to the data, and guided by the idealized model and the process indicators, they were able to track the two successful and one unsuccessful dialogue(s) quite closely. A condensed sample of a few segments from an actual performance diagram is shown in Figure 3-3.

In this figure each box represents one of the steps or components of competence which was proposed in the idealized model and occurred in the actual performance. A short quotation from a client statement is given in each box to provide a flavor of the performance by that chair. Experiencing level and quality of voice ratings are indicated, and the presence of IPR statements that confirm the attainment of the stage is indicated by a "+" sign. Client statements from the session or IPR statements that confirm the stage are also shown in summary form under the comments heading.

In the first box shown, the individual is in Step 3, in a state of "recognition and awareness of Topdog activities." An injunction to the self to "be spontaneous" is issued at Stage 3 on the Experiencing Scale in an external voice, and the words "you should" are used in the interaction. On the IPR the person gave no response to this segment. In the second segment the person is in the same state, but the voice is focused and on the IPR the person says, "That hit it on the head. I know I keep people at a distance." In the next two segments the experiencer expresses feelings and then wants and needs, and, as shown in the last box, the other chair softens.

Although an actual performance is complex, with many repetitions, circular transactions, and some tangential performances and subtask issues that have to be resolved, it was possible to track the essential resolution performance. It was found that the actual resolution performances, with some refinements to be discussed later, closely matched the idealized performance description. In addition, the nonresolution performance showed, as expected, that the dialogue traversed similar steps but did not get as far along the path as did the resolution performances. This close inspection of some actual data, although not a verification, did add confidence to what was previously rational conjecture and produced a more refined description of resolution performances.

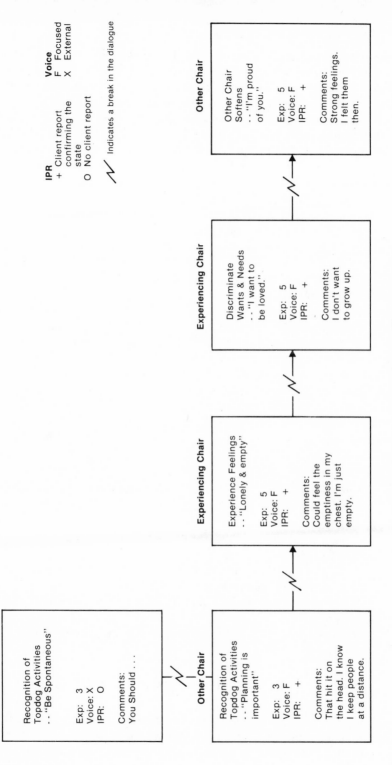

FIGURE 3-3. SAMPLE OF AN ACTUAL PERFORMANCE.

87

From the empirical analyses we made two discoveries about process in the other chair and clarified the process of facilitating the experiencing of feelings in the experiencing chair. We found that in the other chair, between the period in which individuals were harshly critical of themselves and the time at which they softened their attitude toward themselves, little islands of focused voice appeared with content that was still external and critical. This previously unidentified process in the other chair came to be called a statement of "standards and values." In working on a split concerning her anger toward her mother, which evolved into a conflict between being secure and taking risks, a client (in the nonresolution performance) speaking from the other chair approaches the statement of a standard, but it is in an externalizing, lecturing voice:

T: What would be too far?
C: Too far would be going further. I mean a little bit is enough.
T: A little bit . . .
C: Moderation, yeah—moderation in all things.
T: Tell her this.
C: Yeah, moderation, moderation is the key to being successful, moderation is the key to happiness.

The experiencer after some work replies:

C: I'm aware that I will forever miss out on something for not going any further (*sobs*). I want both. I want the safety and I want the other side, too.

After further dialogue the other chair experiences the personal meaning of the statement of standards made earlier.

C: It's not good for you to forget yourself.
T: Tell her why.
C: Cuz then you're not in control.
T: Tell her this, "If you're not in control, then. . . ."
C: If you're not in control then you want to be in control—I mean . . .
T: And then . . .
C: And something bad will happen—just something that you're not controlling.

This last sentence is said in a focused voice, with a great sense of personal meaning.

The discovery of this phenomenon of experiencing the personal meaning of an expectation in the other chair was facilitated by the fact that although the unresolved event given in the excerpt did not achieve integration, there was, according to therapist and client, a significant shift in the person's perception and experience of herself in that session. As we looked at this tape and the resolvers' tapes, and freely varied in our imagination the dialogues we had observed, we realized that an important shift or "component of competence" was the ability of the other chair to express its personal meaning or standards of values not in a harsh derogatory fashion, but more as a statement of an ideal. It appeared that it was the contact between clients' personally aspired-to values and standards and their organismically experienced wants that provided the fertile soil of resolution. The outstanding characteristic of the expression of values and standards was that the other chair, although not yet softened in attitude and still stating expectations, was doing so in a focused voice, as though it were freshly experiencing or newly discovering what its hopes or values were for the self. Statements such as "If you don't work you'll never be able to do all the things you want" or "If you let out your vulnerabilities you'll get hurt again. That will be too much for you," said in a focused voice, occurred frequently in our maps of dialogues. Although stated as an expectation, these utterances were spoken from within and appeared to be experienced not as totally coercive acts, but more as statements of ideals or guidance statements. This experience of the critic not as a punitive lecturer but rather as a realistic center of ideals appeared to be a necessary step to resolution.

Out of the confrontation between clients' newly discovered standards and values and their wants in the context of present feelings arose either the "stuckness" of the impasse or the shift into a new relationship between their sides. This shift resulted in the softening of the other chair and the experiencer either contacting new feelings in a fuller, more integrated fashion or adopting a listening stance and attempting to understand the softened perspective of the other chair. The dialogue then evolved into a negotiation between two equal partners, which resulted in some form of agreement or integration.

We discovered, in addition, two characteristic styles of softening. One style was nurturing while the other style involved going inside to express fears of loss of autonomy or inadequacies that appeared to be driving the shoulds. The observations provided interesting clinical pointers as to what to look for in a softening and how to recognize both these types of softening. An example of a nurturing softening follows:

C: You are coming out of the corner at times and . . . and so . . . I, well, would only like to say keep trying, and, uh, and . . . and . . . give it, you know . . . have some . . . have some compassion for whatever is happening there. And also see a bit . . . that it isn't all grey, that it's becoming also a bit rosy at the edges . . . ah.

T: Tell her that. . . . I don't see you as all grey [as she had previously seen herself].

C: I—I see you not just as all grey and—I see . . . I see a lot of . . . light spots in there, and a lot of softness around the edges . . . um . . .

T: Can you tell her about some of that? What's the softness that you see here?

C: Ah . . . um . . . the—listening and the . . . and the . . . joyfulness when . . . you've gotten over that . . . you know, when you've left the grey one behind a little bit . . . a real good feeling, sense of worth . . . that comes when . . . when I . . . ah, when you . . . when you have actually done a few steps and . . . it's really great to see that . . . um . . . and you have a lot of courage, you know . . . you have a . . . a lot of . . . strength there . . . um . . . (long pause)

T: What's happening?

C: I feel a lot of compassion for that p . . . (cries)

A softening by an expression of fear is shown in the following excerpt:

C: (to therapist) Over there I see the person that just waits to be and, uh, maybe not be famous, or maybe make a contribution totally different than what I, sitting over here see that person . . . and it's kind of scary.

T: Tell her about that. It's scary for me. Tell her about your fear.

C: (pause) See, I don't know where you're going to take me (laughs) and that's scary for me, because it's a whole area I don't have very much experience with. I can tell you how to think and I can tell you—how to do things, and what you should be doing, but when it comes to feelings . . . and yet I sense you being very strong in your feelings, you know, but they probably rule you many ways that I rule you and you haven't made such bad judgments, if it, if it's been judgment based on your feelings in the past, so maybe I, maybe I should trust you but it's . . . I'm very tempted to. . . .

In addition to these two new understandings of styles in the other chair, we saw that to obtain the component called "experience of feelings" a lot of therapeutic work was often done which took the person on an extended path of exploration. The therapist consistently worked to deepen feelings in the experiencer until some new feeling state emerged and did not encourage the progression of the dialogue until this component state called feelings had been attained.

Model Construction

Comparison of the second intensive empirical analysis of three performances, consisting of two resolutions and one nonresolution, with the idealized performance diagram led to the crystallization of a model of split resolution shown in Figure 3-4, which depicts the essential com-

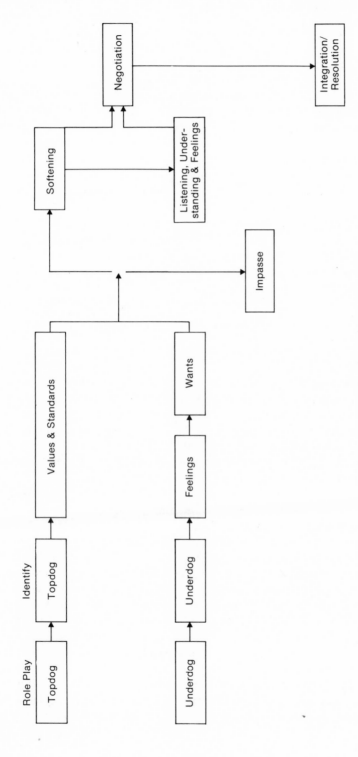

FIGURE 3-4. REVISED PERFORMANCE MODEL.

ponents of competence in a resolution performance. First the person usually role-plays the two sides of the conflict more as an act than a real experience, but this rapidly changes as the person begins to identify with the role. From the one side the person blames, criticizes, and commands, and from the other makes excuses, avoids, or complies. Thereafter the other chair differentiates its blaming into a statement of standards and values while the experiencing chair engages in an expression of previously disowned feelings. The experiencing chair eventually becomes assertive of its wants and needs. The confrontation between wants and needs on the one hand and values and standards on the other results either in an impasse in which no further steps are attained or in the softening of the other chair. This leads to listening and understanding by either or both sides or possibly an experience of new feelings by the experiencer, which is often followed by a stating of terms by each side, that is, a negotiation and a final agreement between the sides or an integration of perspectives in which the conflict is resolved.

THE THIRD CYCLE: REFINING THE MODEL

Empirical Analysis

The intensive analyses indicated that the addition of a content scale would greatly enhance the description of the dialogue. Benjamin's (1974, 1981) Structural Analysis of Social Behavior (SASB) system, which measures the degree of interdependence and affiliation in interpersonal interaction, was tried on a dialogue to see if it could help characterize the interaction between the chairs. It seemed most promising and was therefore added to our battery of process measures.

The SASB was developed from Leary's (1957) system of interpersonal behavior and is composed of three two-dimensional grids. The first grid measures behaviors that focus outward on others: for example, behavior 118, "Encourage separate identity." In the Gestalt two-chair dialogue this grid was employed to measure the statements of either the other chair or the experiencing chair when those statements were focused away from themselves and on the opposite chair. Statements issued from either chair that were focused inwards toward the sender of the statement were measured on the second grid. This grid measures behaviors that focus on "self," for example, 218, "Own identity, standards," the corresponding behavior to 118. The third grid measures intrapsychic behaviors and was not used in this probject.

All these grids are two dimensional and composed of four quadrants. The horizontal axis is characterized by affiliation and the vertical axis by interdependence. The first number in the three-digit behavioral code describing each category pinpoints grid 1, 2, or 3; the second number specifies the quadrant on that grid 1, 2, 3, or 4; the third number identifies the specific chart point in that quadrant (1 to 8).

In the empirical analysis of the second cycle we had lacked a reliable system for measuring the language content of the chairs or the interpersonal style of communication between the chairs, so we had looked at language, behavior, and gesture in a free-form manner. The introduction of SASB allowed a more rigorous measure of language content and categorized these utterances along interdependence and affiliation dimensions. The reliabilities achieved on this instrument were high, with a Cohen's κ of .9. Using the *revised* model now as a rational framework to guide our observations of the statement-by-statement interactions of some new actual performances, we looked for patterns on voice, experiencing, SASB, and IPR that would reflect the different steps along the path to resolution.

The transcripts of the dialogues were unitized according to client statement, and each statement was rated on SASB. According to the rules for SASB ratings, a statement can be broken into key phrases or elements. A key phrase is defined as a codable, understandable, and complete thought statement that is often, but not always, a sentence. The key phrase conveys in a few words the essence of an interaction. A single client statement predominantly contained one key phrase and therefore obtained one rating. Each performance was diagrammed in terms of key phrase units, and voice category and experiencing level were indicated on the performance diagram (McDonald, 1982). As an example of this level of description, a dialogue sequence from a resolution performance is diagrammed in Figure 3-5. Each node in the client performance diagram shown in Figure 3-5 represents a different SASB behavior. As the client adopted new SASB behaviors in each chair, new nodes were generated toward the right of the page. As the client returned to a previously expressed SASB behavior in the particular chair, a node was drawn below the node of the same category and a vertical line added to connect them. Thus, the diagram is linearly ordered by time of generation of behaviors, with time running to the right and down, as in Newell and Simon's (1972) problem behavior graph, discussed in Chapter 4.

We see that in the first row of the diagram the sequence starts with the other chair engaging in behavior 137, "Intrude, block, or restrict," in an externalizing voice at Stage 2 on the Experiencing Scale. The other chair continues in a criticism pattern with behavior 135, "Accuse, blame," in an emotional voice, Stage 3 experiencing, and a standard value pattern then emerges in with behavior 148, "Specify what's best," in a focused voice, Stage 3 experiencing. The experiencer responds with 238, "Whine, defend, and justify," in an emotional voice at Stage 4 experiencing, followed by two statements of 214, "Clearly express," in an Externalizing

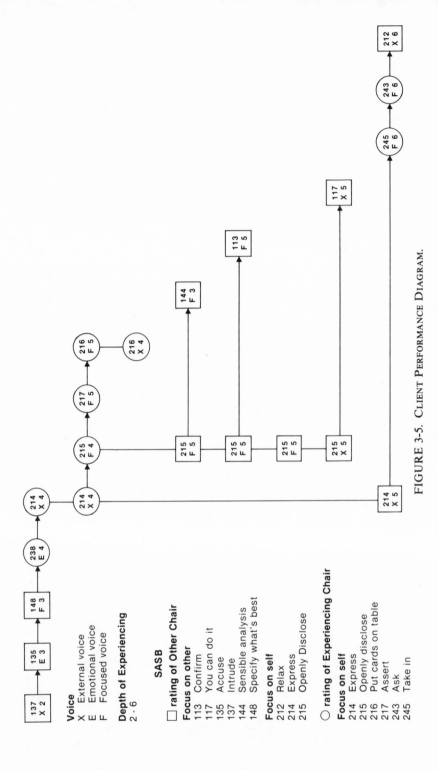

FIGURE 3-5. CLIENT PERFORMANCE DIAGRAM.

Voice
X External voice
E Emotional voice
F Focused voice

Depth of Experiencing
2 - 6

SASB
☐ rating of Other Chair
Focus on other
113 Confirm
117 You can do it
135 Accuse
137 Intrude
144 Sensible analysis
148 Specify what's best

Focus on self
212 Relax
214 Express
215 Openly Disclose

○ rating of Experiencing Chair
Focus on self
214 Express
215 Openly disclose
216 Put cards on table
217 Assert
243 Ask
245 Take in

94

voice at Stage 4 experiencing. This is followed by a cluster of four statements in which the experiencer openly discloses and reveals (215), asserts on own 217, and puts cards on table (216), twice. In this sequence there is a shift to focused voice, and experiencing increases to Stage 5. This cluster is a good example of felt wants. It is followed by a softening pattern in the other chair with behavior 215, "Openly disclose and reveal" in a focused voice and at Stage 5 experiencing, followed by a "Sensible analysis" (144), another three "Openly disclose and reveal" (215) statements with a "Confirm as okay as is" (113) between the first two, in voice and experiencing levels as shown in Figure 3-5. The other chair ends the sequence with a statement of "You can do it fine" (117) and a "Clearly express" (214). The experiencer "Takes in and learns from" (245) and then "Asks, trusts, and counts on" (243). The other chair responds by "Releasing, flowing, and enjoying" (212). This begins the resolution of the problem with Stage 6 experiencing levels and the voices shown.

A transcript of the actual dialogue diagrammed in Figure 3-5, plus the therapist interventions, follows. This transcript constitutes the last 28 statements of a resolution dialogue. The chair delivering each statement is indicated in the left column and a brief commentary of what is occurring according to the models developed is indicated in the right column.

TRANSCRIPT	COMMENTARY
Other: You should have been able to . . . you should have been able to get through to him . . . when nobody else could, you could! You could have somehow . . . gotten him to see what he was doing . . . somehow . . . somehow communicated to him in a way that you could, you could see he was going down a path of. . . .	*The other chair selects a particular attribute of the client's behavior in the past situation and delivers a specific critical statement.*
T: Tell her how she failed . . . you failed to get through to him.	
Other: Yeah, you failed . . . you failed to get . . . to get through to him (*voice breaking*). You who, who knew him, who loved him, you . . . (*crying*) failed him. . . .	*The client becomes aware of her critical feelings as her own, and her criticism is differentiated from "You should have been able to . . ." into "You who knew him, failed him."*
T: Say this again.	
Other: You failed him. You didn't cause his breakdown—he did. But you failed somewhere up the road (*sniff*) . . . by not . . . not being able to just show him what was happening . . . but then . . . it was, it was. . . .	*The standard or value emerges when she says in a Focused voice, "But you failed somewhere up the road by not being able to just show him what was happening." It was this that was of great personal significance to the client.*
T: Change. Change.	
Exper: But I was buried in what was happening (*voice breaking*) (*crying/sigh*) . . . and I was just about . . . having a breakdown myself. I had more than I could cope	*The experiencer focuses inward on her aroused reaction, expresses and differentiates her feelings.*

TRANSCRIPT	COMMENTARY

with. (*sniff*) (*sigh*) And somehow all we seemed to have left was just a physical relationship (*sniff*) (*sigh*) . . . And even there . . . we'd be together, and I'd just explode in tears. I felt out of control. I felt like I was the one who was having the breakdown. And he was just angry.

T: How do you feel when you say that?

Exper: (*sigh*) I feel angry towards him . . .

The experiencer applies a new concept to organize what she is referring to and anger emerges as a new experience.

T: Right, right.

Exper: . . . for not being there for me.

T: Tell him this. I'm angry.

Exper: I'm angry . . . I'm angry with *you* for not being sensitive to me (*sigh*) . . . for not caring . . . for . . . for thinking that I should just be there for you. That I didn't really matter.

T: You failed me.

Exper: (*softly*) You really were the one who failed me (*pause*) . . . And I was too stupid (*sniff*) . . . and too in love with you . . .

Experiencer develops the implications of the new view and the accompanying experience.

T: Right.

Exper: . . . to realize that . . . and too stupid to understand when we came back that . . . that really . . . the ending point was when you went back to your wife. But somehow I was hanging on . . . I was trying to be . . . committed and work things through. And there had to be a way through —and there wasn't. . . .

T: What do you want from that other part that says you failed him down the road?

Exper: I want her to understand . . . I tried everything I could . . . I think she knows that . . . I'm not perfect. I can't be there for everybody.

Experiencer expresses a want to the other chair.

T: Say this again.

Exper: I'm not perfect. And I can't be there for everybody . . .

Experiencer affirms her newfound sense of direction.

T: I couldn't.

Exper: . . . I couldn't be there for J. I was hardly there for me.

T: Um hmm. Try: You ask too much of me.

Exper: You want too much . . .

T: What happens?

Other: I sort of feel softer, melting inside. I really do . . . expect too much.

The other chair focuses inward and softens her critical perspective.

T: Um hmm. Tell her this. I expect . . . I do expect too much.

TRANSCRIPT

COMMENTARY

Other: I do expect too much of you.

T: How do you feel as you . . . ?

Other: I guess I'm aware of another piece, sort of . . . thinking about how I take other people's "shoulds" and expectations and sort of hit her, especially with the commitment thing . . . when I really know that if anything, she hangs on too long even when it looks like from the outside that you're not committed. I guess I'm so concerned with appearances that I mess things up.

The other chair reevaluates her values about "failing him up the road." She reexamines her framework and begins to generalize to other situations.

T: Ummm. I'm not clear, so let's clarify things. It's kind of like . . . "I should you, in order to save face or to look good. I make you hang on in order to satisfy other people's expectations."

Other: Instead of just . . . letting her . . . trusting her . . . and like, like trusting the wisdom of my own experience. Like I knew . . . that's one of the healthiest things I've done in my life was to get out of that relationship.

T: I see, so you're more sort of saying that I realize I do have really high expectations, but it's almost like I know I do it sometimes just to . . .

Other: Just to look good.

T: Just to look good.

Other: For other people.

T: Right. And that's what I don't really want to do.

Other: Yeah.

T: I want to be able to trust you.

Other: Instead of look good for other people I want to be there for myself.

T: Right. Say this to yourself. I want to be there.

Other: I want to be here for you.

Boundaries between the selves begin to dissolve.

T: Right.

Other: And I do trust you. I mean that. I'm just kind of slow. It's sort of more than trust . . . that I respect you really. Sometimes I'm amazed at the wisdom of experience inside that's really (*inaudible*) . . . and yet I get distracted so easily and start— being overly concerned with what other people are thinking.

T: What are you experiencing right now?

Other: I'm flipping to my head and thinking that this is sort of a typical conflict in all kinds of ways for me. Um . . . my struggle to risk-take . . . I struggle in so many ways

Generalizes her new point of view.

TRANSCRIPT

to just trust myself and be myself . . . and not conform to other people in order to be liked and to fit in.

T: Look . . . so will you change and be yourself and speak to your image manager here. You know, you're saying this is a conflict that's ah . . . So you're yourself.

Other: Okay.

T: What do you want from her? She's saying: I do want to trust you. What do you say to her?

Exper: I, I feel more hopeful . . . I'm finally beginning to see . . . um . . . how . . . you go out . . . how you take on other people's expectations . . . how your focus is outside, and away from me.

T: And you want . . .

Exper: And I, I want . . . I need you to trust me. I need you to . . . I need you in order to clearly know what I want . . . and to give me the strength to . . . the courage to simply be me. And I have got all the resources I need . . . except sometimes you. . . .

T: Mm hmm. Mm hmm. Change. What do you say?

Other: Um, I just sort of feel lighter.

COMMENTARY

Negotiation and integration.

Model Construction

The client performance diagrams of resolution dialogues became an important observational base for discovering patterns which occurred across client-resolution performances. These descriptive diagrams became part of a postdictive discovery-oriented procedure which gave us insight into the more characteristic patterns of cues associated with the statement-by-statement occurrences in the dialogue.

From the statement-by-statement analyses of nine resolution dialogues, McDonald (1982) showed that some additional performance components along the path to resolution could be clearly discriminated. A refined model of conflict resolution containing additional steps in each chair is shown in Figure 3-6. In this refined model we see that after entering the dialogue by role playing, the critic begins to identify its harsh critical evaluations of the experiencer, which in turn expresses its affective reactions to the harsh criticism. The harsh critic moves from global general statements to much more concrete and specific criticisms in which particular changes are demanded or specific characteristics of the person or specific situational behaviors are negatively evaluated. In response to these criticisms, the experiencer begins to react in a more differenti-

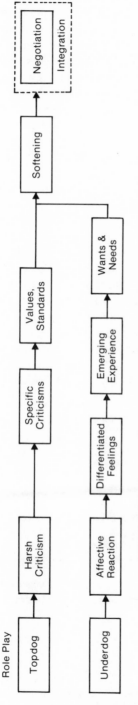

FIGURE 3-6. REFINED PERFORMANCE MODEL OF CONFLICT RESOLUTION.

99

ated fashion until a new aspect of its experience is expressed. A sense of direction then emerges for the experiencer, which is asserted as a want or need to the critic. The critic, having become more specific, moves to a statement of standards and values, and it is at this point in the resolution dialogue—when there is an assertion of a want or need in the face of a standard and value—that the critic softens. This is followed by a negotiation or an integration, or both, between the two parts. These steps are refined in the commentary on the preceding transcript.

The more detailed components-of-competence model allowed us to look at client performance at a level at which we could begin to specify client mechanisms of change involved in resolving splits. The degree of specificity obtained by describing statement-by-statement client process helped in the provision of a framework for investigating what clients were doing *internally* in order to change from one moment to the next. A new type of model which described the possible internal mental operations involved in generating the observable performances was therefore constructed. The language used to specify the operations is at this stage a descriptive rather than a technical one, and it attempts to describe the cognitive strategy the client has to adopt each step of the way to resolution. A preliminary operations model is shown in Table 3-2.

This client operations model shows the internal client operations in each chair that we believe are associated with the measured client processes. The operations numbered 1 to 9 in each chair are placed in the sequence of their occurrence in that chair. At two points in each chair (Steps 4

TABLE 3-2. CLIENT OPERATIONS MODEL

OTHER CHAIR INTERNAL OPERATIONS	EXPERIENCER INTERNAL OPERATIONS
1. Deliberately acts like a critic.	1. Deliberately acts like a responder.
2. Identifies the most alive sense of criticism and speaks from it.	2. Formulates reaction
3. Increases arousal to intensify criticism.	3. Protects self by (a) justifying, (b) withdrawing, or (c) attacking.
4a. Selects particular attributes to criticize.	4a. Focuses inward on aroused reaction.
4b. Realizes that the locus of criticism is internal.	4b. Matches words to feelings.
5. Elaborates the criticism.	5. Differentiates out new facets of feelings.
6. Recognizes a core standard or value.	6. Constructs new concept for organizing experience.
7a. Reexamines and reevaluates.	7a. Explicates implications of new experiencing.
7b. Focuses inward on feelings aroused by new perspectives.	7b. Affirms new direction.
8. Dissolves differences.	8. Dissolves differences.
9. Integration of aspects from both perspectives.	

and 7) the operations indicated by "a" and "b" appear to operate in a circular feedback-loop fashion, building on each other, with neither necessarily coming first, but the pair occupying a particular place in the overall sequence. Each of the operations shown in the table serves to cognitively position the client to engage in the next operation along the path to resolution. At different points not only the preceding client state but also the interaction between the chairs seems to serve the function of positioning the client appropriately to proceed to the next step along the resolution path. In addition, therapist interventions applied at the right moment help to position clients for a particular operation, and clearly this combination of the correct therapist intervention at the correct time would be most effective for facilitating change.

In this model we see that clients, induced by therapist intervention, start off the dialogue by deliberately *acting like* Topdog and Underdog, that is, like a critic and responder. This proceeds until, because of the increased arousal brought about by deliberate expression in the role play, the clients become spontaneous in their expression by *speaking from the most lively sense of criticism* which they can now feel. They now react more spontaneously to these criticisms. *Intensification of the criticisms* by exaggerating and repeating them leads to a building of the hostility, brings the warfare out into the open, and induces the experiencer to react to the attack by *selecting* protective strategies from its repertoire, such as justifying, withdrawing, or attacking.

The critic at this point becomes less abstract and more specific by *selecting for criticism particular attributes or actions* from recent situations in the person's life. By criticizing themselves in a detailed and specific fashion, individuals come to experience themselves as their own harsh critics and *realize* that they are the locus of the criticism—their own attackers or punishers. The particularity of the criticisms induces the experiencer both to *focus inward* on its aroused reactions to the detailed criticisms and to *match words* to these reactions. This begins an exploratory process in the experiencer. The critic meanwhile explores and elaborates its criticisms until it *recognizes a core meaning or scheme* (standard or value) underlying the many things it is saying. The experiencer, already in an inner exploratory stance, and stimulated by the elaborated, but less harsh criticisms, *differentiates its feelings* into more and more idiosyncratic and varied facets until such time as a new *construction (scheme) is formed* which most adequately represents the new experiential information available.

At this stage each chair enters a loop which leads to resolution. The other chair, in response to increased assertion from the experiencer, turns around on its own core values in order to *reexamine and reevaluate* them and also *focuses inward* to the feelings aroused in it by the new information coming both from its own explorations and those of the experiencer. The processes of reexamining and softening feed each other and result in a final reevaluation. The experiencer, having created a new perspective, begins to *explicate new meanings* from this perspective, assert them to the other chair, and *affirm this new direction* from an inner sense of confidence. These combined internal operations seem to lead to a dissolving of the differences between the two parts, which now begin to be seen and experienced not as having a separating boundary but rather as being much closer and more unified in outlook.

The refined performance model and the operations model move us closer to what is actually occurring in the moment-by-moment performance in a two-chair dialogue. Certain general cognitive information-processing strategies, such as selection of particular information, intensification, realization of responsibility, focusing of attention, recognizing core meanings (schemes), differentiating affect-laden experience, constructing new meanings (schemes), and reexamining and reevaluating, emerge as being highly important in this change process. In addition to the importance of illuminating the client operations that move the person from one state to the next, this more momentary description of client process allows us to begin studying which therapist interventions will best facilitate movement at particular points. These models act as a type of road map of the path to resolution. If a client engaged in resolving a split strays from the path of resolution and is not engaging in the appropriate internal operations at a particular point, the therapist can guide the client back onto a resolution path by facilitating the required mental operations. In addition, with this map of resolution performance, further research questions can be asked about which interventions return the client to the resolution path or facilitate particular client mental operations.

As we have shown, task analysis has provided models of resolution. Validation of these models is required in order to move these models beyond description of a few memorable cases and into the realm of generalizability.

VERIFICATION OF THE MODEL

Verification studies were undertaken at different stages of this research program. Even before inspecting the process data and searching for patterns in successful resolutions, verification studies were undertaken to demonstrate the differential effectiveness of the therapist interventions which facilitated the client processes to be studied. These initial verification studies involved the use of differential intervention designs, in which the efficacy of two-chair dialogue was compared with that of empathic reflection (Greenberg & Clarke, 1979; Greenberg & Dompierre, 1981; Greenberg & Higgins, 1980; Greenberg & Rice, 1981). These studies showed that two-chair dialogue was more effective than the use of empathic reflection in facilitating the resolution of specific conflicts as measured by in-session depth of experiencing and postsession client report and goal attainment. In the task analytic approach it is essential, before investing too much in the intensive analysis and model building phase, to establish that the processes to be studied intensively contain some of the active ingredients of therapy and are worthy of the effort of intensive analysis. The differential intervention studies accomplished this and encouraged continuing study of the process of two-chair dialogue.

In addition to the differential efficacy studies involving two-chair dialogues and empathic reflection, Clarke (1981) has recently shown that two-chair dialogue was more effective than the rational problem-solving approach proposed by D'Zurilla and Goldfried (1971) in facilitating the resolution of decisional conflict in a two-session program of counseling. These findings provided further evidence that something worthy of intensive study occurs when conflicts are worked on using two-chair dialogue procedure.

Once the intensive analysis of patterns and model construction was begun, it was essential to check that the models generated from the rational and empirical investigations extended beyond the few cases from which they were derived. The creative–inductive phase of the research program, although essential in generating clinically meaningful patterns and fine-grained hypotheses, needs to be followed by a rigorous verification phase to support or disconfirm the models constructed in the first phase. A number of verification studies of aspects of the model of split resolution were therefore undertaken. The logic of the verification steps will now be spelled out briefly and then followed by a description of the studies conducted.

Having developed a model of resolution from the investigation of a number of selected cases, the first step was to be able to generalize the model to further cases. This could be tested by whether or not the model generated by intensive analysis could discriminate between a new sample of resolution and nonresolution performances. If the model succesfully discriminated between resolvers and nonresolvers, a certain degree of validity would be added to the model. It would show that those events, which both clients and therapists reported as conflict resolution events, did contain the component processes predicted by the model. A stronger test of the validity of the model, however, would be to show that component processes of resolution were *predictive* of treatment outcomes. This type of design (relating process to outcome), comparing the outcomes of cases in which hypothesized mechanisms of change do occur with the outcomes of cases in which the mechanisms do not occur, is one of the better ways of establishing the relevance of specific therapeutic processes to change. Short of an experimental design in which the mechanisms of change hypothesized by the model are experimentally induced and manipulated, a difficult task in psychotherapy field research, a design relating process to outcome would be the strongest field test of the model. It was decided therefore to first test for the generalizability of the model and if this was successful to perform a study to relate process to outcome.

GENERALIZING

A three-stage sequence of intrapsychic conflict resolution was apparent in the earlier, revised model of conflict resolution (see Figure 3-4). This sequence, consisting of an *opposition phase* followed by a *merging phase* and ending with an *integration phase*, was proposed for testing on a larger population. Fourteen successful conflict resolution performances were selected on the basis of client, therapist, and rater report and were compared with fourteen unsuccessful performances, in order to test the proposed three-stage model of conflict resolution. The resolution events were selected for this study on the basis of three criteria: (1) a report by clients of at least a level 5 on a 7-point Conflict Resolution Box Scale (Greenberg & Dompierre, 1981) and a reduction over the session of at least 5 points on the Target Complaints Discomfort Box Scale; (2) a report by the therapist of at least a level 5 on the Conflict Resolution Box Scale (Battle, Imber, Hoehn-Saric, Stone, Nash, & Frank, 1966); and (3) a judgment by raters of a Stage 6 on the Experiencing Scale (Klein *et al.*, 1969) in the final 4 minutes of the dialogue, indicating that a problem had been resolved.

The overall prediction for this study was that clients who resolved conflicts would progress through three sequential stages as they worked toward resolution of a personal conflict. The occurrences of the three stages of opposition, merging, and integration were to be demonstrated by the use of process instruments that measured the degree of affiliation and independence between the two chairs in a Gestalt two-chair procedure, the vocal quality of each chair, and the depth of experiencing in each chair.

Two sets of hypotheses generated from the model were tested. The first set distinguished between resolvers and nonresolvers. The model's most salient claim was that resolution and nonresolution groups could be distinguished by the difference in the degree to which the internal critic softened its attitude. This was tested by examining whether the critic in the group which resolved became more affiliative in the quality of its interactions than the critic in the nonresolver group, as measured by SASB; whether, at a related point in the dialogue, the critic in the resolving group began using more "good contact" voice quality in place of a "lecturing at" vocal quality; and whether the critic at this point began to experience its own feelings more deeply. If these observable processes occurred differentially in the two groups it would suggest that the model was indeed identifying a process that could discriminate resolvers and nonresolvers.

In addition to these between-group hypotheses, the model suggested the existence of a certain sequence and pattern of performance within resolution performances. It was therefore hypothesized that in the resolution group (1) the two chairs would start off at different levels of experiencing, but would merge and become indistinguishable on this variable as the dialogue progressed, and that (2) the experiencer would progress from a more hostile stance at the beginning of the dialogue to a more affiliative and independent stance at the end of the dialogue, as measured by SASB.

Identifying the Components

The SASB coding system (Benjamin, 1974, 1981) was used to measure the degree of interdependence and the degree of affiliation in the dialogue. Each client statement in the dialogue was identified as belonging to one of 36 categories of a circumplex model with dimensions of affiliation and interdependence. Two surfaces of the model, "focus on self" and "focus on other," were used in this study. This instrument was discussed more fully on pp. 92–93.

The events under study, which all begin with a split and contain a two-chair dialogue, were broken into phases in the following fashion: The final, integration phase was defined as that portion of the gestalt event that began with a Stage 6 score on the Experiencing Scale. There were therefore, by definition, no integration phases for the nonresolvers. This was consistent with the intent of the study—to determine whether certain performance patterns which led up to and were associated with the attainment of conflict resolution could be distinguished. The merging phase was defined as occurring when the other chair began to affiliate with the experiencing chair, as defined by the SASB scores. Merging occurred when the other chair responded with more than two consecutive responses from the affiliative quadrants (1 and/or 4); this point was, thereafter, referred to as the merging point. The merging phase ended when the integration phase began. This definition of the merging phase made its occurrence in each group contingent upon the degree of affiliation shown by the other chair. The opposition phase was defined as the portion of the gestalt event that preceded the merging point.

As the three-phase sequence on the criterion variables did not occur in the nonresolution group events, it was necessary, in order to compare the two groups, to phase the nonresolution events in the following manner. The mean proportion of statements corresponding to each phase in the resolution group was calculated and these proportions were transposed onto the nonresolution group events. The resulting proportions were opposition phase, .6; merging, .3; and resolution, .1. Each nonresolution event was then segmented into three phases according to these proportions. This allowed a comparison to be made between the variables of interest in the resolution group and a control sample of dialogue, to test if the predicted pattern characteristics occurred significantly more than the chance occurrence of these in similar events.

At this point all the data were charted on graphs according to chair, phase, and rating on the three scales; summary statistics were then calculated for each phase. Mean level of experiencing was calculated for each chair for each phase. For voice, proportions of good contact voice (focused and emotional) in each chair were calculated for each phase. On SASB, proportions of affiliative and autonomous behavior were similarly calculated. The use of proportions compensated for the differing total lengths of performances and phases and the varying number of clients' statements for each chair or phrase.

Results

Analyses of the data, reported in detail elsewhere (Greenberg, 1983), showed that the two groups differed on the variables measured. The proposed sequential phase model of intrapsychic conflict resolution and the more detailed hypotheses concerning the performance of each chair were confirmed. The mean or median scores on the three variables for each phase are shown in Table 3-3.

Tests of the between-group differences showed that the two groups started off in the opposition phase, indistinguishable in terms of the interaction between the chairs, on the depth of experiencing, quality of voice, and degree of affiliation. As the dialogue progressed, the resolution group became significantly more affiliative in the other chair than did the nonresolution group, as measured by Fisher's exact test ($p < .001$); this process of becoming more accepting of the experiencer clearly distinguished the two groups. This increase in affiliation, which marked the beginning of the merging phase, was accompanied by significantly higher depths of experiencing ($t = 5.3$, $p < .001$), and significantly more use of "good contact" voice ($U = 10, p < .001$, Mann-Whitney) in the other chair in the resolution group. The other chair in the resolution group was also shown to change from an externalizing to a focused or emotional voice at the beginning of the merging phase (three statements before or after the merging point) significantly more often than the other chair in the nonresolution group, ($p < .001$, Fisher's exact test). These indices reveal that a "softening" of the attitude of the harsh internal critic took place in the resolution group.

In addition, it was found that the experiencing chairs in the two groups, having begun the dialogue at similar levels on experiencing, became significantly different ($t = 12.1$, $p < .001$) as the dialogue pro-

TABLE 3-3. Means and Standard Deviations of Depth of Experiencing and Modes and Ranges of Voice Quality and Structural Analysis of Social Behavior

GROUPS		MEASURES								
		DEPTH OF EXPERIENCING		VOICE QUALITY		STRUCTURAL ANALYSIS OF SOCIAL BEHAVIOR				
		MODAL EXPERIENCING		GOOD CONTACT (F + E)		AFFILIATIVE (Q1 + Q4)		AUTONOMOUS (Q1)		
		Mean	SD	Median	Range	Median	Range	Median	Range
Resolution									
Opposition	Ch 1	2.5	.26	.31	.07–.45	.17	0–.35	.1	0–.27
	Ch 2	3.0	.2	.475	.21–.63	.67	.29–.86	.59	.15–.86
Merging	Ch 1	4.1	.37	.71	.3–1.0	.92	.7–1.0	.61	.38–1.0
	Ch 2	3.9	.47	.665	.38–1.0	.98	.52–1.0	.67	.29–.9
Integration	Ch 1	5.7	.55	.625	.4–1.0	1.0	.75–1.0	.71	.4–1.0
	Ch 2	5.7	.33	.95	.15–1.0	1.0	.87–1.0	1.0	.48–1.0
Nonresolution									
Opposition	Ch 1	2.5	.24	.175	.0–.85	.2	0–.27	.16	0–.27
	Ch 2	2.9	.26	.37	.1–.78	.66	.4–1.0	.57	.33–1.0
Merging	Ch 1	2.6	.26	.1	0–.7	.15	0–.35	.12	0–.33
	Ch 2	3.0	.44	.41	0–.84	.65	.45–.9	.65	.45–.9
Integration	Ch 1	2.5	.45	.17	0–.67	.05	0–.1	0	0–0
	Ch 2	2.9	.51	.32	0–1.0	.71	.30–1.0	.58	0–1.00

Note. Ch 1 = other chair, Ch 2 = experiencing chair; F + E = focused plus emotional voice; Q1 = Quadrant 1—independent and affiliative; Q4 = Quadrant 4—dependent and affiliative.

gressed. This was expected because the resolution group was chosen on the basis of high experiencing scores at the end of the dialogue, but it was not known when this increase had occurred. Analysis of the data revealed that the shift to deeper experiencing in the experiencing chair in the resolution group occurred in the merging phase. This shift to a more internal sense of the feelings of the previously rejected part was shown not only by the deepening of experiencing, but also by the use of more good contact voice. The proportion of good contact voice (focused plus emotional) in the experiencing chair was significantly higher in the resolvers in the merging phase ($U = 35.5$, $p = .01$) indicating that in conjunction with the change in stance of the critic, the experiencer explored more deeply. These results showed, therefore, that the two groups differed significantly on observable process indices.

Shifting attention to the pattern over time between the chairs in the resolution group alone, it was found that the chairs indeed started at different levels of experiencing and as predicted became indistinguishable in the merging phases. This resulted from an increase in depth of experiencing by other chair, which moved from fairly low level, externally oriented statements to more inner, focused statements. In addition, as predicted by the model the experiencer changed from being somewhat hostile in the opposition phase to being more affiliative in the integration phase. Inspection of the data showed that in the opposition phase the critic, as required by the demands of the task environment, was predominantly controlling with a "focus on the other," using SASB behaviors such as 135, "Accuse, blame," 136, "Put down, act superior," and 138, "Enforce conformity." The experiencer, although somewhat affiliative in this phase, often reacted in a yielding manner, with behaviors with a "focus on self" which were complementary to those used by the other chair, such as 235, "Whine, defend, justify," 236, "Sulk, act put upon," and 238, "Follow rules; proper."

Analyzing the change in behavior over time in the resolution group, using Wilcoxon tests to compare phases, it was found that in the merging phase the critic changed significantly ($p < .01$) to more tender behaviors with a "focus on the other," such as 147, "Benevolently monitor, remind" and 142, "Provide for nurture," or to revealing behaviors with the "focus on self," such as 215, "Openly disclose and reveal." In the integration phase the experiencer was significantly ($p < .01$) more affiliative than it was in the opposition phase. It was predominantly in quadrant I, the affiliative and independent quadrant, with a "focus on self," using such behaviors as 213, "Enthusiastic showing," 215, "Openly disclose and reveal," and 218 "Own identity, standards." The critic in the integration phase of the resolution group also used a significant ($p < .05$) predominance of behaviors from the affiliative, independent quadrant with a "focus on the other," such as 113, "Confirm as okay as is," 115, "Friendly; listen," and 118, "Encourage separate identity."

What we have, therefore, is a picture of a dialogue in which the parts begin in opposition, and those that resolve do so by a process of experiencing previously unaccepted feelings more deeply, thereby bringing about an affiliative relationship between the critic and the experiencer. This greater acceptance of the experiencer of the self by the critic is followed by a more affiliative and autonomous stance by both aspects in the conflict and a type of negotiation between two equal parties that leads to Stage 6 on the Experiencing Scale, that is, "a synthesis of . . . more fully realized feelings and experiences to produce personally meaningful structures or to resolve issues" (Klein et al., 1969, p. 61).

A point of great clinical interest, the change of voice of the other chair at the merging point, was confirmed. It appears as though the "turning inwards" by the other chair, indicated by focused voice, is a critical aspect of the process of softening. No longer is there the "lecturing at" quality of the critic, but rather a true looking inside for what is to be said. This change of voice in the other chair seems to be an important indicator that something new is happening, and almost always accompanies the affiliative content. Change to a focused voice by the other chair is a good clinical cue that the client may be ready to integrate the two sides. Voice is a subtle, moment-by-moment indicator of change which is not easily subjected to conscious control or external influence and is therefore a good cue of the "true" process of softening in the other chair.

It thus appears from these results that aspects of the performance model can be used to distinguish resolution and nonresolution performances. This finding serves as supportive evidence for the validity of the model. Softening in attitude by a previously harsh critic clearly distinguishes resolvers from nonresolvers. In addition, the model of two systems initially in opposition, which integrate by a process in which one side experiences itself more deeply and the other side becomes more affiliative, appears to be an accurate description of resolution performances.

RELATING PROCESS TO OUTCOME

In order to further validate components of the performance model, a study relating process to outcome was undertaken. Four components of the revised model of conflict resolution (see Figure 3-4) were judged to be essential to the attainment of resolution. These essential components were criticism in the other chair (identifying with Topdog), feelings and wants in the experiencer, and softening of the critic. For the purposes of measuring these components, feelings and wants were combined into a performance element called felt wants, thus yielding three essential components of resolution—criticism, felt wants, and softening.

It was the purpose of this validation study to relate to decision-making outcomes the in-session process of intrapsychic conflict resolution in the solution of decisional conflict. Decisional conflicts (Janis & Mann, 1977) were chosen for study in the belief that they provided a specific behavioral index of outcome, and because it was felt that they could be dealt with in a brief therapy. The process was related to outcome by comparing treatment outcome effects of in-session resolvers and non-resolvers. Resolvers were defined as those clients who manifested all three of the essential components—criticism, felt wants, and softening—in the sessions. It was hypothesized that the occurrence of the three resolution components in two-chair dialogue sessions would correlate with improved outcome. Outcome effects were measured on four separate occasions: immediately after the resolution session, that is, the session in which the final resolution component, softening, was expressed; a week after this resolution session; at the termination of the treatment; and at a 1-month follow-up.

Resolution session outcomes were measured on a Conflict Reduction Box Scale (Greenberg & Dompierre, 1981), Target Complaints Discomfort Box Scale (Battle *et al.*, 1966) and mood change (Epstein, 1979). The prolonged effects of the resolution session were measured on mood change over the week after the resolution session. Treatment outcomes were taken at termination and at 1-month follow-up on the Scale of Indecision (Osipow, Carney, & Barak, 1976), State Anxiety (Spielberger, Gorsuch, & Lushene, 1970), Target Complaints (Battle *et al.*, 1966), and Goal Attainment (Kiresuk & Sherman, 1968), and on two instruments constructed for this study to measure attitude and behavior change.

The clients in this study were 31 urban adults who voluntarily sought counseling in response to an advertisement offering to help them resolve a decisional conflict that they were experiencing. At an introductory interview subjects were screened for evidence of severe disturbance. Acceptance criteria were based on Malan's (1976) criteria for brief analytic therapy and ensured that the client was able to engage in a relationship and was not highly suicidal, depressed, or anxious. Only persons who were relatively well functioning and were experiencing a decisional conflict were accepted for treatment.

Identification of Resolvers

Process instruments were used in this study to identify resolvers and nonresolvers. Resolvers were defined as those people who attained the performance components of criticism, felt wants, and softening during a session. These three components will now be described in more detail.

Criticism

Criticism was viewed as that type of behavior most often associated with Perls *et al.*'s (1951) Topdog: controlling, bullying, lecturing, or threatening remarks issued from an omnipotent and/or moralistic stance assumed by one aspect of the personality (other chair). For example, the harsh internal critic delivered such general statements as "You are a failure as a father," "You've got no backbone," "You'll never make it," and "You should do better for yourself." These statements were delivered with an outward focus, a focus on the other—as if they were an attack in a "lecturing at" voice quality. This performance component was measured according to the following criteria.

1. At least two client statements in the other chair had to be rated in either quadrants 2 (Invoke Hostile Autonomy) or 3 (Hostile Power) of the other chair grid on SASB.
2. At least two client statements had to be rated as being in externalizing voice on Client Vocal Quality.

Feelings and Wants

For the purposes of this study, feelings were thought to be intuitive appraisals (Arnold, 1960) which persons rely upon to provide meaning. Gendlin (1969) refers to feelings as bodily felt sense from which meaning emerges, while Zajonc (1980) stresses the precognitive nature of feelings, which provide an impression or sense of what we encounter even before the conscious phases of cognition begin to arise. The presence of significant expression of feeling was to be indicated on the 7-point Experiencing Scale as Stage 4 or higher. "Description of feelings and personal experiences." (Klein *et al.*, 1969, p. 64.) The client, at this level, is no longer concerned exclusively with external or remotely experienced feelings; instead the client draws directly from his or her experiencing to describe feelings and personal reactions. Gendlin's process of "experiential focusing" begins here as the client begins to attend to and grasp the direct inner referent of his or her experiencing and make it the core of his or her communications (Gendlin, 1969; Gendlin, Beebe, Cassens, Klein, & Oberlander, 1968). The focused and emotional categories on the Client Vocal Quality system were used as additional measures of expression of feeling. Focused voice involved the turning inwards of attention as individuals focus on their own experience and struggle to symbolize and communicate the process. Emotional voice is characterized by an overflow of emotion into the speech pattern.

Wants were regarded in this study as statements of desires or needs by the experiencer. To resolve an issue a client must first know what he or she wants. The want is an orienter—a compass on the journey to resolution. Wants mobilize and channel a person's intentions by providing a sense of direction for newly discovered feelings. Wants were regarded as occurring when the experiencer asked for or asserted some desire based on a sense of an inner felt sense of direction. Feelings and wants were regarded as occurring when a want appeared in the context of feelings. This combined component was measured according to the following criteria.

1. At least one client statement in the experiencing chair on SASB had to be rated in the categories 243, "Ask, trust, count on," 217, "Assert on own," or 216, "Put cards on table."
2. At least one of the client statements listed in #1 had to have reached Stage 4 on the Experiencing Scale. A secondary judgment was made on whether there was only one or more than one statement at Stage 4. One statement at Stage 4 satisfied the criterion, and more than one provided a stronger statement of experiencing.
3. At least one client statement coincident with the SASB statement had to be in focused voice.
4. The client must have met the semantic criterion of expressing a desire directly to the other chair, for example, "I want . . . ," "I need . . . ," "I'd like . . . ," or some other equivalent of want.

Softening
The concept of "softening" was the third of the essential resolution components. The term refers to a change in the other chair to an expression of compassion, caring, or understanding, or an expression of underlying feelings, such as inadequacy or fear. Phenomenologically, it appeared as if the harsh internal critic had melted—expectations were suspended and there was a softening in attitude toward the experiencing chair. Softening occurs by a deepening in experiencing of the other chair, accompanied by a shift from a poor contact, externalizing lecturing voice to a good contact, focused or emotional voice and a change to a more accepting attitude. The following criteria were used by the raters for classifying this component.

1. At least two consecutive client's statements from the other chair had to be rated as affiliative on SASB, that is, rated in quadrants 1 or 4. (A client statement was defined as everything occurring between two therapist statements.)
2. At least one client statement in focused voice had to be coincident with the above affiliative SASB rating (i.e., one of the two consecutive SASB statements must have been in focused voice).
3. At least one statement in the other chair must have reached Stage 4 or above on the Experiencing Scale. Stage 4 was used rather than Stage 5, as in previous studies, because smaller units (i.e., one statement) were being measured.

The clients were seen once a week for 6 weeks or until they resolved their conflict, whichever came first. When, in the therapist's judgment, the client had manifested a resolution performance, that is, when the three resolution elements (an expression of criticism, an expression of felt wants, and a softening) had taken place, the session in which softening occurred was defined as the therapist-judged resolution session (later to be evaluated by process raters as a possible resolution session). If a client failed to manifest the resolution elements, the fifth session was declared the resolution control session. At these resolution sessions, both those who, according to their therapists, had manifested the resolution elements and those who had not were reminded that the next session was the termination session. They reported in 1 week for the session and then again 1 month afterwards for a follow-up interview.

In order to be classified as an actual resolver, clients had to manifest the three components of criticism, felt wants, and softening as rated by the two raters on the specified criteria. Nonresolvers were individuals who showed two or less of these components. By listening to tapes of the sessions of 31 clients and using therapist and client report to guide the search for components, a judge isolated 158 8-minute tape segments of possible resolution components. A rigorous procedure, described in (Greenberg & Webster, 1982) which involved listening to all the session material of the clients in which not all of the components were found, ensured that all possible resolution components were identified. These 158 segments were then submitted to the two raters for rating as containing criticism, felt wants, softening, or none of these.

Each rater independently rated two-thirds (105) of the total number of statements in order to provide an interrater reliability check. The one-third overlap upon which the rater's reliability was checked was composed of 53 8-minute segments. These overlapping segments were designed to contain all the therapist-indicated softenings.

To determine the extent of agreement between the raters, Cohen's κ (Cohen, 1960), a procedure that yields a coefficient of agreement for nominal scales, was used. The coefficient of agreement of these data was $\kappa = .925$, indicating very high agreement between raters on the identification of the resolution components. This suggested that the rating criteria were clear, independent, and mutually exclusive with respect to the defining of resolvers and nonresolvers. The raters were found to be more stringent than the therapists, eliminating two therapist-judged resolvers.

Results

The analyses of the session and treatment data, which are reported in detail elsewhere (Greenberg & Webster, 1982), revealed that in-session resolvers attained outcomes consistently superior to those of the non-resolvers. Analysis of variance revealed that, although there was no difference between groups on initial measures, the resolvers were significantly less undecided at termination and follow-up and significantly less anxious (A-state) at follow-up than nonresolvers. Using nonparametric tests for the data which did not satisfy the assumption for analysis of variance, the resolvers were found to be significantly more improved on their target complaints at termination and follow-up and on a report of behavior change at follow-up. The resolvers also revealed (1) a significantly greater sense of self-acceptance, greater integration, and greater feelings of power after the resolution sessions; (2) significantly greater self-acceptance, integration, and feelings of power during the week following the resolution session; and (3) significantly greater goal attainment and attitude change 1 week after the resolution session and at follow-up. The means and standard deviations of the postresolution session and follow-up data are given in Table 3-4 as an indication of the results obtained.

In light of these findings, it appears that the ability of resolvers to resolve an intrapsychic conflict in the session according to the specified process criteria was suggestive of differential outcome. In other words, the in-session process of criticizing the self from one side of the conflict, expressing a desire embedded in a feeling context from the opposite side, and then experiencing a softening in the attitude of the critic toward the self appears to be related in this sample to positive outcome in Gestalt two-chair work. A trend, although based on a small number of clients and not significant, was also evident in the data for those clients who attained both the criticism and feelings and wants states. These clients improved more on most of the outcome measures than the people who never attained the feelings and wants state, but did not improve as much as those who achieved a softening in attitude.

It remains possible that some variable other than the in-session performance of the resolution components could explain the relationship between group membership and outcome. It is possible, for example, that the conflict resolution performances described took place only in particular types of clients or that some aspect of the relationship was decidedly different in the two groups. The relationship environment was in fact controlled in this study to ensure that all clients perceived the therapist as empathic (Barrett-Lennard, 1962) and the two-chair dialogue as relevant to their goals (Horvath, 1981). This ensured that all clients, resolvers and nonresolvers, were in a good working alliance with their therapists, and differences between them could not therefore be attributed to nonresolvers being uninvolved in the therapeutic process. However, even if a third variable was found which accounted for a greater degree of the variance than the process indicators, the performance pattern in the two chairs, because of its multidimensional and highly specified nature, could not be a chance correlation and would still possess a high degree of explanatory power regarding the mechanisms of change in the process of conflict resolution.

TABLE 3-4. MEANS AND STANDARD DEVIATIONS FOR RESOLVERS AND NONRESOLVERS ON POSTRESOLUTION SESSION AND 1-MONTH FOLLOW-UP SCORES

OCCASION	MEASURE	RESOLVERS		NONRESOLVERS	
		MEAN	SD	MEAN	SD
Post session	Conflict resolution	6.46	.66	4.94	1.73
	Target complaints discomfort[a]	11.92	1.11	10.05	3.08
	Pleased with self	7.61	.77	6.55	1.38
	Integrated	7.85	.69	6.44	1.38
	Powerful	7.46	.97	6.53	1.25
Follow-up	Indecision	24.38	5.09	33.83	7.25
	State anxiety	24.08	5.94	39.78	11.22
	Target complaints discomfort[a]	4.85	.38	3.94	.94
	Behavioral reports	5.61	.51	2.78	1.22
	Goal attainment	60.77	6.40	49.44	7.25
	Attitude	9.38	.77	7.17	1.38

[a]Higher score indicates less discomfort.

In relation to the session change measures the resolvers experienced a significantly greater sense of conflict resolution over the resolution session than did the nonresolvers over the fifth session. This finding suggests that the softening manifested by the resolvers in their resolution session is a key component of resolution. That is, when the critic experienced a change in attitude toward the organism and its experience, a reduction of the sense of internal conflict resulted. In addition, over the resolution session, the act of softening was related to the report by the resolvers of significantly greater relief of discomfort associated with the target complaint. This was most likely attributable to relief of the underlying sense of struggle and hence improvement in the related discomfort.

Finally, over the resolution session, the resolution of the intrapsychic conflict appeared to relate to the resolvers experiencing significantly greater self-acceptance, integration, and feeling of power than did the nonresolvers over their fifth session. It appears that the resolvers' increase in feelings of self-acceptance was directly related to the critical aspect changing its attitude and becoming more accepting of the organism. The increase in integration was a result of the merging of the disparate, disorganized, partial aspects of the personality that were formerly in opposition to each other; and the increase in feelings of power was a result of experiencing more self-direction, having resolved the conflict. The act of resolving an intrapsychic conflict in the session was powerful enough to maintain these changes in mood stages over 1 week.

The resolution process was, in addition, related to significantly greater goal attainment for the resolvers at both 1 week and 1 month following the resolution session. This is an interesting finding which showed that intrapsychic conflict resolution appeared to promote the attainment of a specific goal. Nonresolvers, who also set a goal at the end of their fifth session as to what behavior they would like to change, did not attain their goal as well as the resolvers who had resolved a conflict.

Finally, the ability of the resolvers to resolve their intrapsychic conflict appeared to be related to significantly more conflict-related attitude change for them as compared with nonresolvers, at both 1-week and 1-month follow-up measures. Engaging in a conflict resolution performance resulted in an attitude change: When the critic's attitude softened, an old cognition or introjected value was restructured into a new one, with greater worth placed on the organism's experience.

These results relating process to outcome provided further support for the validity of the conflict resolution performance model and showed that in the context of a good helping alliance characterized by client perceptions of the therapist as empathic and the therapeutic task as relevant, conflict resolution performances follow a particular path. This path is characterized by an initial expression by one part of the personality of criticism toward, and lack of acceptance of, another part, followed by a deepening of experiencing and assertion of wants and desires in the previously unaccepted part. The final essential component of this performance is a softening in the attitude of the critic, which results in an acceptance of the client's deeper experiencing and a resolution of the conflict, often by negotiation between the two parts. The verification studies to this point provided support for the hypothesized relation between core aspects of the model and outcome. The model, however, had continued to evolve and possessed a number of details that required further study.

VALIDATION OF DETAILS OF THE MODEL

A third verification study was therefore undertaken by McDonald (1982) to generalize some of the more detailed aspects of the model of conflict resolution beyond the cases from which they were derived. Increasing knowledge of the structure of two-chair dialogues from the intensive analyses had convinced us that, although a softening in attitude appeared to be the critical component of competence without which resolution did not occur, the two *preceding* components were essential for the occurrence of the softening in attitude. It appeared that the "dual" process of deeply experiencing felt wants in the experiencing chair and contacting and clearly expressing differentiated values and standards in the other chair were the soil from which softening emerged. It was the purpose of McDonald's (1982) study to see if these preceding components discriminated between groups of reported resolvers and nonresolvers. More specifically, this study tested (1) whether a resolution group contained more softening client performance patterns than a nonresolution group (a replication and extension of the first verification study) and (2) whether the two groups differed significantly on the frequency of occurrence of the values and standards performance patterns in the other chair and felt wants patterns in the experiencing chair. In addition, we were interested in finding out from the IPR review of the resolution dialogues which points in the dialogues clients perceived as the most significant change point.

Eighteen two-chair dialogues, nine resolution and nine nonresolution performances, were studied. Four therapists were represented in this sample of 18 clients. The resolution performances for this study were chosen from a population involved in counseling at a university counseling facility on the following criteria: Both client and therapist had to indicate a postsession score of 5 or above on the 7-point Conflict Resolution Box Scale, and clients had to report a shift of 5 or more points between the pre- and postsession scores on the Target Complaint Discomfort Box Scale. Nine sessions of dialogue which did not show these gains were selected as a control sample.

Identifying the Components

Using an Interpersonal Process Recall (IPR) method, the client reviewed the session with an investigator and made a 9-point rating of the most significant change points in the dialogue (Elliott, Chapter 8). The "most significant change point" was selected as that moment in the client's experience rated on the 9-point scale to be of the most significance to the resolution of his or her conflict. For the nonresolution performances, a "control change point" was selected by taking the mean time of the most significant moments across resolution performances. This was found to be 47 minutes into the interview.

A search for specific process patterns was then performed around the identified change point across each of the 18 performances. The unit of analysis for identifying the components preceding softening was 20 dialogue statements preceding the indicated "most significant change point." This unit was chosen on the basis of our clinical observations that the statement of values and standards generally closely preceded softening and that feeling and particularly wants usually occurred in response to standards and values.

Each of the 20 statements was rated on experiencing, vocal quality, and SASB to determine the presence of the client performance patterns under study. A new factored form of SASB had been developed by the originator of the system (Benjamin, 1981), by clustering neighboring groups of items of the original circumplex categories into factors. The new factors of SASB were used at this stage of our research program, as they described interactions between the chairs more succinctly. For this more detailed study of the components of the model softening was defined more tightly than in previous studies as (1) other chair statements which were rated as attaining Stage 5 on the Experiencing Scale, displaying focused voice, and belonging in any of the following four factors of SASB (Benjamin, 1981): "Helping and protecting," "Nurturing and comforting," "Affirming and understanding," or "Disclosing and expressing." Standards and values were defined as other chair statements, Stage 4 or below on the Experiencing Scale, focused voice, and a factor on the newly constructed SASB called "Watching and managing," which ranged from category 137, "Intrude, block, restrict," to category 147, "Benevolently monitor, remind." Felt wants were defined as statements in the experiencing chair with level 4 or above on the Experiencing Scale, focused voice, and either category 217, "Assert on own," or category 143, "Ask, trust, count on," on SASB. Procedures and results are reported in detail elsewhere (McDonald, 1982) and findings are summarized here.

Results

Resolvers and nonresolvers were compared on frequency of occurrence of the softening, values and standards, and felt wants patterns. The two groups were found to be significantly different on the occurrence of the softening pattern ($p < .001$). In fact, all clients in the resolution group showed the softening pattern, but none of the individuals in the control group did. Using Fisher's exact test throughout, the two groups were found in addition to be significantly different ($p < .05$) on the presence of the values and standards pattern, with eight out of nine resolvers and three of the nonresolvers manifesting the pattern. The groups were also significantly different on the felt wants pattern ($p < .001$), with eight resolvers and no nonresolvers showing this pattern in the 20 statements rated. The groups were also significantly different on attainment of the combined patterns prior to softening ($p < .01$), with seven resolvers and no nonresolvers showing the combined pattern of values and standards and felt wants. In addition, all nine resolvers indicated that the most significant moment was during softening: Five clients indicated the moment co-occurred with the presence of the softening pattern, three indicated the moment occurred one statement prior to the occurrence of the softening pattern, and one client indicated the moment occurred three statements after the softening pattern.

This study added further support for the significance of softening in attitude in resolving splits, but more importantly showed that the values and standards and felt wants patterns occurred with high frequency in the 20 statements before the softening pattern. In the one case where the values and standards pattern did not occur in the 20 statements preceding the change point, it was found earlier in the session. In the case where felt wants were not found, the person was engaged in a split that evolved into a dialogue with a dead parent, and there was an expression equivalent to a felt want, with the client saying, "You should have been there for me." This was rated as a 230, "Desperate protest," on SASB and as an emotional voice and Stage 3 experiencing. Although it did not meet the criteria of our definition of felt want, it appeared to serve some of the same function in being an assertion of a desire expressed with feeling. These findings suggest that the combination of values and standards and felt-wants patterns, although not a sufficient conditon for softening, did appear to be a highly important prerequisite for the occurrence of softening.

The study validated, for the first time, the presence of the values and standards pattern as an identifiable entity important in the resolution process. This suggests that the process of resolution of conflict in two-chair dialogue involves deeper experiencing of some previously rejected desires of the self, and contact between these desires and the person's newly articulated ideals. When both of these aspects are experienced in the moment, the feeling part, which had previously pulled back from being criticized as bad or unworthy, no longer feels invalidated and is more able to claim legitimacy for itself as a vital part of the person. Values and standards in turn are affirmed as a strong independent center of valuing that guides the person. With the attainment of the experience of the legitimacy of each part in the opposition, contact between these two separate but now more equal subsystems becomes possible. A shift then occurs with values and standards going through a reevaluation process and adopting a more affiliative stance toward the feeling part, that is, softening, and accepting or validating it in some way. The feeling part then either becomes more understanding of the person's aspirations or feels less need to be defensively separated, and a dissolution of boundaries seems to occur. This process allows either a negotiation between the sides or an integration of the two views to form a new perspective which resolves the conflict.

SUMMARY AND CONCLUSIONS

When we look back on this research program and ask what has been learned, we find the answer spans two domains. Our research team has learned more both about method and about promoting therapeutic change. Our knowledge of how to do intensive description of complex change episodes has been vastly expanded, and in addition we know more about facilitating intrapsychic conflict resolution.

This research program has taught us the value of tracking client process intensively using a rational framework to guide this tracking.

Repeated observations of actual performances in specific situations forced us to think about what occurred for the clients step-by-step and moment-by-moment as they worked their way along the path to resolution. The benefits of making rigorous, fine-grained observations of actual therapeutic performances were great, and vastly improved our ability to discern order and pattern where previously there appeared to be only complexity or chaos. On many occasions this work, particularly at the stage of preparing material for rating, seemed tedious and overwhelming; we were often pulled by the lure of studying more clients less intensively, by premature verification attempts and by the attractiveness to journal editors of studies with large *n*'s and outcome studies. However, whenever we turned to intensive observation our eyes were again opened, new aspects of the phenomena became visible, and our research program became revitalized. Further intensive observation and specification of the details of client split resolution performance is still possible and will still yield greater understanding of both client change and the information processing involved in this change.

At the level of practice and theory of practice our ideas about the process of struggle between opposing tendencies in humans were illuminated. Many of the process components we observed, such as the critic, the experiencer, even the softening in attitude of the harsh critic, have been observed before in clinical practice and noted in theoretical writings. It was the detailed explication and measurement of these phenomena in a rigorous fashion that gave them a validity they previously lacked. Rigorous observation revealed recurrent patterns on measurable variables that grounded the phenomena, such as the softening in attitude of the critic, in consensually reliable terms. It was in this sense, by showing that posited global phenomena did in fact occur and manifested themselves in observable performances that could be tracked, that we learned something new about the process of conflict resolution. We learned that a process of experiencing previously disavowed feelings and shifting in attitude from self-criticism to self-acceptance did indeed take place in resolving conflicts expressed in therapy and that by being clear on the components of resolution we became much more skilled in its facilitation.

It became clear that in working with in-session conflict it was profitable to follow two aspects or tracks of client process in order to promote resolution: one a more cognitive, rational track and the other a more affective, experiential track. Movement on both of these tracks was required in order to resolve intrapsychic conflicts. In the more cognitive, rational domain the person needed to clarify guiding ideals and beliefs and to reinspect and reevaluate these in the light of newly emerged desires. On the affective, experiential track the person needed to construct an experientially grounded new perspective which encompassed newly emerged appraisals and attendant feelings, in order to develop a sense of direction, desire, or personal ambition. Some suitable form of interchange, such as "listening," between the desires and the values and standards then led to a dissolving of differences between the parts and a restructuring and resolution of the problem.

This process of working with clients by going back and forth between the more rational, sometimes obsessive, processes and the more affectively laden, warded-off content can be found in many therapeutic contexts. Facilitation of this process does not require that a therapist use Gestalt two-chair work. Two-chair work as defined here helps to make the processes of resolution particularly apparent, but it is clear that skilled clinicians of many different orientations can make use of our findings without having to use Gestalt methods.

ACKNOWLEDGMENTS

I would like to thank all my students who have helped me with the arduous work of intensive analysis. I would like especially to thank Kathy Clarke, Nancy Johnson, Linda McDonald, and Mike Webster for their significant contributions and the many raters who spent untold hours rating the material. The research reported in this chapter was supported in part by Social Science and Humanities Research Council of Canada grant 410-80-0210.

REFERENCES

Arnold, B. *Emotion and personality* (Vol. 1: *Psychological aspects*). New York: Columbia University Press, 1960.

Barrett-Lennard, G. T. Dimensions of therapist response as causal factors in therapeutic change. *Psychological Monographs*, 1962, *76*(43, Whole No. 562).

Battle, C. C., Imber, S. D., Hoehn-Saric, R., Stone, A. R., Nash, E. H., & Frank, J. D. Target complaints as criteria of improvement. *American Journal of Psychotherapy*, 1966, *20*, 184–192.

Benjamin, L. S. Structural analysis of social behavior. *Psychological Review*, 1974, *81*, 392–425.

Benjamin, L. S. *Manual for coding social interactions in terms of structural analysis of social behavior* (SASB). Madison: University of Wisconsin Press, 1981.

Clarke, K. *The effects of the Gestalt two-chair experiment and cognitive problem solving on decision making.* Unpublished doctoral dissertation, Loyola University, 1981.

Cohen, J. A system of agreement for nominal scales. *Journal of Educational and Psychological Measurement*, 1960, *20*, 37–46.

D'Zurilla, T., & Goldfried, M. Problem solving and behavior modification. Journal of Abnormal Psychology, 1971, *78*, 107–126.

Epstein, S. The stability of behavior: On predicting most of the people much of the time. *Journal of Personality and Social Psychology*, 1979, *37*, 1097–1126.

Gendlin, E. T. Focusing. *Psychotherapy*, 1969, *6*, 4–15.

Gendlin, E. T., Beebe, J., Cassens, J., Klein, M., & Oberlander, M. Focusing ability in psychotherapy, personality, and creativity. In J. M. Shlein (Ed.), *Research in psychotherapy* (Vol. 3). Washington, D.C.: American Psychological Association, 1968.

Greenberg, L. S. A task analytic approach to the study of psychotherapeutic events (Dissertation, York University, 1975). *Dissertation Abstracts International,* 1977, *37,* 4647B. (Available from National Library of Canada, Ottawa K1A OBA; Order no. 26, 630)

Greenberg, L. S. Resolving splits: The two-chair technique. *Psychotherapy: Theory, Research and Practice,* 1979, *16,* 310–318.

Greenberg, L. S. An intensive analysis of recurring events from the practice of Gestalt therapy. *Psychotherapy: Theory, Research and Practice,* 1980, *17,* 143–152.

Greenberg, L. S. Toward a task analysis of conflict resolution in Gestalt therapy. *Psychotherapy: Theory, Research and Practice,* 1983, *20,* 190–201.

Greenberg, L. S., & Clarke, D. The differential effects of the two-chair experiment and empathic reflections at a conflict marker. *Journal of Counseling Psychology,* 1979, *26,* 1–8.

Greenberg, L. S., & Dompierre, L. Differential effects of Gestalt two-chair dialogue and empathic reflection at a split in counseling. *Journal of Counseling Psychology,* 1981, *28,* 288–294.

Greenberg, L. S., & Higgins, H. The differential effects of two-chair dialogue and focusing on conflict resolution. *Journal of Counseling Psychology,* 1980, *27,* 221–225.

Greenberg, L. S., & Rice, L. The specific effects of Gestalt intervention. *Psychotherapy: Theory, Research and Practice,* 1981, *18,* 31–37.

Greenberg, L. S., & Webster, M. Resolving decisonal conflict by means of two-chair dialogue: Relating process to outcome. *Journal of Counseling Psychology,* 1982, *29,* 468–477.

Horvath, A. *An exploratory study of the working alliance: Its measurement and relationship to therapy outcome.* Unpublished doctoral dissertation, University of British Columbia, 1981.

Husserl, E. *Experience and judgment* (L. Landgrebe, Ed.; J. Churchill & K. Ameriks, Trans.). Evanston, Ill.: Northwestern University Press, 1973. (Originally published, 1939).

Janis, I., & Mann, L. *Decision making: A psychological analysis of conflict choice and commitment.* New York: Free Press, 1977.

Johnson, N. *Model building and intensive analysis of Gestalt events.* Unpublished master's thesis, University of British Columbia, 1980.

Kiresuk, T. J., & Sherman, R. E. Goal attainment scaling: General method for evaluating comprehensive community mental health programs. *Community Mental Health Journal,* 1968, *4,* 443–453.

Klein, M., Mathieu, P., Kiesler, D., & Gendlin, E. T. *The experiencing scale.* Madison: Wisconsin Psychiatric Institute, 1969.

Leary, T. *Interpersonal diagnosis of personality.* New York: Ronald Press, 1957.

Malan, D. H. *Toward the validation of dynamic psychotherapy: A replication.* New York: Plenum Press, 1976.

McDonald, L. *Essential process components of conflict split resolution.* Unpublished master's thesis, University of British Columbia, 1982.

Newell, A., & Simon, H. *Human problem solving.* New York: Prentice-Hall, 1972.

Osipow, S. H., Carney, C. G., & Barak, A. A scale of educational vocational undecidedness: A typological approach. *Journal of Vocational Behavior,* 1976, *9,* 233–243.

Perls, F. *Gestalt therapy verbatim.* New York: Bantam Books, 1969.

Perls, F. Four Lectures. In J. Fagan & I. Shepherd (Eds.), *Gestalt therapy now.* Palo Alto, Calif.: Science & Behavior Books, 1970.

Perls, F., Hefferline, R., & Goodman, P. *Gestalt therapy.* New York: Delta, 1951.

Polanyi, M. *Tacit dimension.* New York: Basic Books, 1966.

Rice, L., Koke, C., Greenberg, L. S., & Wagstaff, A. *Manual for client voice quality.* Toronto: York University Counselling and Development Centre, 1979.

Spielberger, C. D., Gorsuch, R. L., & Lushene, R. E. *Manual for the state-trait anxiety inventory.* Palto Alto, Calif.: Consulting Psychologists' Press, 1970.

Zajonc, R. B. Feeling and thinking: Preferences need no inferences. *American Psychologist,* 1980, *35,* 151-175.

4

Task Analysis:
The General Approach

LESLIE S. GREENBERG
University of British Columbia

RATIONALE FOR TASK ANALYSIS

In 1865 Claude Bernard, writing *An Introduction to the Study of Experimental Medicine,* made an impassioned plea for medical science to move beyond the use of averages and statistics, which he argued kept 19th-century medicine as a conjectural science. He urged medicine to move toward becoming a determinate science which regulates its phenomena according to general laws. Psychological clinicians of the present age are in much the same position as the medical physicians of a century ago. The 19th-century physician of Bernard's era believed that medicine could not be anything but conjectural and indeterminate and that physicians were artists who had to make up for the indeterminate of particular cases by what was called "medical tact." The parallel between the state of medicine in the 19th century and the present state of psychotherapy is striking. Psychotherapy practitioners today still believe more in the "intuitive art" of psychotherapy than in the possibilities of a determinate science of psychotherapy.

Psychotherapy research is at present a science of statistical inference in which the true relations of phenomena disappear in the average and result in findings that apply only to population means. Findings in which the cause of the facts observed is not clearly determined can only lead to a science of the indeterminate and to practitioners who believe that one cannot move beyond an "art" based on conjecture and intuition. Statistics that taught physicians of the previous century little about the nature of the phenomena and yielded results that were true in general but false in particular can do little more for psychological clinicians. What must be done in psychotherapy (as in physiological medicine of a century ago) is to study clinical phenomena more intensively in order to accurately define the conditions of their occurrence. As soon as the circumstances that produce a particular phenomenon are sufficiently well known, researchers can stop global treatment evaluations. When the cause of the phenomenon is defined accurately enough, the effects can be produced without exception (Sidman, 1960).

It may appear that studies which yield determinate knowledge in medicine are easier to perform because the phenomena to be observed are more concrete. The complexity of psychological subject matter should not, however, deter us from adopting an intensive investigative approach in hunting for revealing phenomena. Bacon (1890) pointed out that scientific investigation is like "hunting" and that the facts that the investigator observes are like the wild game the hunter discovers in the forest. Claude Bernard (1865/1957) provides some excellent examples of this "hunt." In investigating how blood leaving the kidney eliminated injected substances, he "chanced to observe that the blood in the renal vein was crimson, while the blood in the neighbouring vein was dark like ordinary venous blood" (p. 155). This observation led to the further one that secretion from different glands altered blood color. Thus, intensive observation became the starting point for an idea that guided investigations of the chemical cause of the change in the color of glandular blood during secretion. In another situation, while investigating the cause of carbon monoxide poisoning Bernard observed that the blood of a poisoned dog was "scarlet in all the vessels, in the veins as well as the arteries, in the right heart as well as in the left" (p. 159). This observation, with the help of further experiments, led to the discovery that carbon monoxide permanently replaced the oxygen in the blood by combining with the substance of the blood molecule. These examples illustrate the importance of an intensive investigative approach. The interpretation of the observations was verified through further hypothesis testing and was translated into a theory that deductively accounted for all the known facts. This method of investigative analysis entailing observation (the hunt for facts), followed by interpretation, testing, and model or theory building, is what is required in psychotherapy research.

If we must investigate our subject matter, become hunters in order to discover phenomena of interest, for what phenomena should we hunt? We have no simple observational referents such as color of blood; what, therefore, are we, as psychotherapy researchers, to observe? Fiske (1977) points out that while therapy interaction has been studied at many levels, our ultimate concern in these studies should be with the observation of actions of people and their immediate effects in the interaction. The more global levels of analysis of client and therapist factors affecting outcome (e.g., demographic information, personality, biographic variables, views about therapy, etc.) have not produced useful findings. In any event, it is only in the specific acts of the participants that these variables take effect. A more productive level of analysis, therefore, would be to study the participants' immediate responses to particular acts or statements of the other. What is required in a study of client change is the observation of what clients actually do in therapy: Client performance is as available a referent to psychotherapy researchers as the color of blood is to medical researchers.

The problem that psychotherapy researchers have to overcome in studying client performance is a measurement problem. In the hard sciences, what is usually measured is some change in quantity, often of a single dependent variable. In studying complex human performance we do not need to know about change in quantity as much as about change in form. A change in the manner or style of what is being done or said is often far more important than a change in quantity. The different arrangements or orders of the numerous component elements of a performance convey more meaning about the nature of the performance than a tally of those elements. But how does the investigator determine that the form of the performance has changed? This problem of measurement has until recently kept investigators from studying complex human performance.

John von Neumann (1961), the pioneer of game theory, pointed out that in the past science has dealt with concepts related to material substance, such as "force," "energy," and "motion." However, he predicted that in the future science would be more concerned with problems of form and make use of concepts such as "system," "information processing," "organization" (Burks, 1970). When one shifts, as von Neumann suggests, from the domain of energy to the domain of information, measurement becomes an issue of recognizing *difference* rather than of measuring *dimensional quantity* (Bateson, 1972). Measuring change in performance is therefore a task of recognizing differences in form, from one instance to the next. Measurement becomes a type of pattern analysis. Using dimensionless coding systems to recognize differences in patterns, change in complex phenomena can be "seen," much as the difference in blood color can be seen by the medical investigator.

STUDYING COMPLEX HUMAN PERFORMANCE

There is an increasing convergence in a number of areas in the social sciences toward the study of structure and form of human performances in order to reveal their meaning (Chomsky, 1968; Piaget, 1954). One such area in psychology of particular interest is the study of the symbolic processing that occurs in complex human performance. The majority of these studies use verbal protocols and audio and visual recordings of subjects' performances on tasks in order to understand human information processing (Byrne, 1977; Farnham Diggory, 1972; Gagné, 1968; Lindsay & Norman, 1972; Newell & Simon, 1972; Pascual-Leone, 1976a, 1976b; Piaget, 1954; Reber & Lewis, 1977; Resnick, 1976; Simon, 1979;

Winograd, 1972). It has proven possible in these task analyses to describe and track complex human performance in particular situations in terms of characteristic steps or sequences in the performances. These studies suggest that task analysis can be used to productively describe and measure complex human performance and change.

Task analysis, similarly, can be applied to a study of client in-therapy performance, to increase our understanding of how change takes place in therapy. Some description of moment-by-moment in-therapy performance has already been accomplished in psychotherapy research through the use of process measures. As has been pointed out in the previous chapters, however, these have been applied without sufficient attention to context and could be more powerful tools of investigative analysis if used to study the process associated with the characteristic steps of complex performances.

In addition, many a well-intentioned process researcher has immersed himself or herself "in the process" without the aid of a disciplined investigative strategy and has been overwhelmed by the data. What is needed is an organizing method to guide the intensive analysis of process. Task analysis has developed a set of procedures for describing and analyzing the vast amount of human behavior generated in complex problem-solving tasks (Gagné, 1968; Newell & Simon, 1972; Pascual-Leone, 1976a, 1976b; Resnick, 1976). Task analysis was primarily developed in the information-processing area to aid in the construction of models capable of simulating the performance of a single individual in a particular task situation. It is beginning to be recognized as an approach that can help illuminate how psychotherapy works (Gottman & Markman, 1978; Greenberg, 1975). Task analysis is essentially an approach in which the components of competence of successful performances are specified in order to understand problem-solving. When combined with the measurement sophistication developed in psychotherapy process research, task analysis holds promise as an investigative approach to help in the discovery of mechanisms of client change.

The following section will provide a brief overview of the origins of task analysis. This will be followed by a discussion of the use of task analysis in cognitive problem solving. The remainder of the chapter will focus on the adaptation of task analytic procedures to the study of client change in psychotherapy.

TASK ANALYSIS

The term "task analysis" originated in the 1940s in the area of industrial or work psychology from the analysis of the competencies that a task, such as the operation of a lifting vehicle, required (Miller, 1955). These initial task analyses were often more behavioral than psychological. Task analysis is characterized by the study of subjects' actual task performances. Whenever performances are analyzed into components, a task analysis of some kind is involved.

Recently, in the information-processing field, Newell and Simon (1972) used a task analytic method in developing their theory of human problem solving. They constructed information-processing systems that modeled the behaviors of single subjects in single-task situations by making detailed observational records of single individuals engaged in solving reasoning problems. The experimenters noted the approach tried and the blind alley encountered, then the backing up and search for a new approach. From these records they inferred the way the problem was construed, the hypotheses tried, the ways in which task instructions influenced solution, and, finally, the mental processes required to generate this performance.

In addition, educational psychologists have been placing an increasing emphasis on task analysis as a way of constructing learning hierarchies (Gagné, 1974), establishing instructional objectives (Klahr, 1976), and diagnosing performance disorders (Ysseldyke & Salvia, 1974). In instructional theory and design, task analysis is playing a central role in the study of the psychological processes involved in solving intellectual tasks (Gregg, 1976; Resnick, 1976) in order to locate elements of the task that are instructable. In the cognitive–developmental area a number of researchers (Baylor & Lemoyne, 1975; Case, 1974, 1975; Pascual-Leone, 1976a, 1976b) have been studying and modeling how children progress from one stage of cognitive development to another and how conservation and other cognitive competencies are attained.

These modern task analyses all take root in one of three traditions, the associationist/behaviorist tradition, the Gestalt tradition, and the cognitive information-processing tradition. The approaches to task analysis that grew out of these traditions differ in their goals and theoretical positions. Only relevant versions will be described here. One of the simplest current task analytic procedures, called *component* or *constituent* analysis, has grown out of the behaviorist tradition. A typical behaviorist analysis used by Gagné (1968) to break down the performance on a learning task into its hierarchical constituents or components, by describing the skills used in the task, is an example of this approach. Such an analysis is strictly behavioral, with no emphasis on cognitive mediating events or client error strategies.

Competence or *structural* analyses grew out of the Gestalt tradition and are more complex, emphasizing internal events and overall strategies of the subject. Competence models are built by theorists such as Chomsky (1968) and Piaget (1954), who construct, based upon observations of the task and the subject's performances, as well as an intuitive theory of the psychological system, a structural system that explains the performances. These systems can only be used in explaining correct performances and do not account for errors.

Process–structural or information-processing analyses provide a much finer process description of the steps required to generate the performance and utilize error strategy analysis to inform model building (Pascual-Leone, 1976a, 1976b). They differ from the purely structural Gestalt and Piagetian (1970) approaches by attempting to describe the actual flow of performance and organize it into temporally ordered sequences of actions. A process–structural approach works backwards from performance to the starting situation, repeatedly unfolding the steps required to generate smaller and smaller temporal performances until the grain of the process description corresponds to the level used by the subject during task performance. These information-processing analyses of tasks are based on certain assumptions about how the human mind stores, accesses and operates upon information.

The latter approaches to task analysis are clearly distinguished from behavioral approaches by their explicit attempts to describe internal processing. Process–structural, information-processing analysis incorporates both an analysis of performance and an analysis of the information-processing competencies required to produce the performance. It is this type of task analysis that holds the most promise for use in psychotherapy research. In order to specify mechanisms of client change, the moment-by-moment unfolding of client performances must be described in detail in order to delineate the components of successful performance. A model of the underlying information-processing operations and competencies that produce this performance can then be developed.

TASK ANALYSIS IN THE STUDY OF COGNITIVE PROBLEM SOLVING

To perform a task analysis and to be able to predict task performance we need, according to Newell and Simon (1972), to know three things:

1. The problem solver's goals or task, that is, statement of the problem.
2. The structure of the task environment, that is, nature of task, instructions, and aids.
3. The invariant characteristics of the problem solver's processing mechanism, for example, duration of short-term memory.

From this information, Newell and Simon suggest, one can predict with great accuracy what methods are available to the subject, and from the method one can predict what the subject will do.

By its very nature, a task analysis can only be carried out on one performance by a single individual at any one time. Consequently, it is a form of single-case research with replication. A number of cases, all involving the same problem and its resolution, are studied, but each analysis is conducted individually. The performance of one subject in the specific situation is observed and a descriptive model of that person's performance is developed. The pattern or sequence that leads to resolution is determined, and then other cases are analyzed in order to discover whether or not similar performance patterns occur. In this research what is being studied is not the individual per se but the event of resolution of a particular problem. The "population" of the study consists of problems that are resolved by the same strategy; thus, it consists not of individuals but of units of behavior.

The study of problem solving has generated a number of concepts useful to the task analysis of therapeutic events. These include "states," "tangents," "graphing," "protocol analysis," and "model building."

STATES

The first concept that is helpful in analyzing problem-solving performances is the idea of states of knowledge. In the study of cognitive problem solving, "All the information the subject knows about the problem at any moment is called his state of knowledge. Each time he applies some operation to some new fact, he changes his state of knowledge. A description of his problem-solving behavior, then, should trace out this progression in the subject's 'states of knowledge'" (Lindsay & Norman, 1972, p. 505). In terms of the therapy situation, states of knowledge are synonymous with the client's awareness and present conceptualization of the problem and can be thought of as "experiential states" or states of mind (Horowitz, 1979). These are transitory states which one achieves during the process of working on a problem and which may be left and reentered repeatedly in any single problem-solving attempt and across attempts. The state represents where the client is at the moment in relation to the task and situation.

Embodied in this concept of a state is the assumption that each new state represents a step in the process of problem solving. Thus, each state is an accumulation of information and understanding of the elements that form part of the overall process of problem solving. For instance, in an arithmetic problem, a final state of knowledge might consist of knowing the product of two times two. The path to this state may involve a number of computational steps, each of which represents a state along the path to the final state. Some of the states along the way might make use of the subject's knowledge of numbers, the concept of multiplication, and the "times table."

TANGENTS

The concept of a tangent is useful in following complex problem solving. It is often difficult and confusing to track the process followed by a person working on a particular problem because the person will go off on tangents which are either unrelated to the task or aimed at achieving subgoals necessary to help attain the major goal. These diversions from the main goal can be elucidated by tracking the client states as tangents, in anticipation of the person returning to work on the main task. For example, tracking the process of the product of two times two is direct and straightforward. If, however, rather than being the process of resolution of the problem, these steps had to be accomplished as a subgoal within the context of solving some more complex problem, then the sequence would appear as a tangent to the primary process. The process might thus be diagrammed as follows:

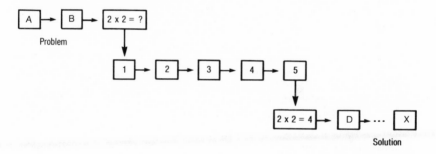

In the affective problem-solving situation of therapy, many of the states required for resolution must be created, constructed, or developed during the problem-solving process, thus entailing numerous tangents to achieve subgoals. There are, as yet, no clearly defined elements and aids such as multiplication tables for perceptions, feelings, and experiences. If there were, therapy would possibly consist of recalling and combining the right elements and performing the different operations required to reach the "correct" answer. As it is though, clients, in addition to recalling past awarenesses to create present states of knowledge, must also create new states as they progress.

The states in the therapy situation may be conceptualized as "experiential states" rather than "states of knowledge," in order to capture both the cognitive and affective aspects of an emotional state. The process of working on tasks in therapy thus involves the exploration and creation of new experiential states. Aspects of the self that were previously unclear are brought out in the open and examined; new methods of acting or interacting are sampled and perfected. In other words, the client tries experimental avenues in order to arrive at new awarenesses which, when incorporated into the problem-solving process, can be symbolized as new states and then tracked as part of the resolution process.

In a therapy situation an example of the tangential creation of a new state might begin when a client says, "I feel trapped." (This state could be characterized by ratings on stylistic and content variables.) The client could then, with the help of the therapist, explore and experiment with how this feeling is created. As the client accepts personal responsibility for the feeling and becomes fully aware of what he or she does to produce it, a new experiential state, that of an increased sense of control, is created. This new state might be indicated by the client saying, "I realize I'm feeling trapped because I'm not wanting to face the alternatives." This state also could be characterized on stylistic and content variables, to confirm the existence of a new state. The new state is then used in tackling the main problem on which the client is working, for example, the resolution of a conflict between a desire for and a fear of intimacy. It is in this way that engaging in tangential processes can add to a person's awareness and create new states useful in affective problem solving.

GRAPHING

A third concept presented in the literature on problem solving which is valuable to intensive psychotherapy research is that of *graphing* the problem-solving performances of individuals. In a problem-solving performance each person progresses, through some operation, from one state to another. By tracing these steps and creating a visual representation of the process, investigators are able to identify more clearly approaches or strategies used in attempts to solve a problem. Lindsay and Norman (1972) describe this graphing as follows:

> The problem-behaviour graph is one method of dissecting the stages of problem-solving, decomposing the process into a series of small steps. It graphically illustrates the mixture of successes and failures that go on in a problem-solving task. (p. 509)

The procedure of graphing provides a clear-cut means of analyzing the structure of problem-solving behavior. Common elements or patterns can be identified and categorized, and strategies, or plans of attack, can be recognized. It is important to note that it is the exploratory nonexpert performance of people struggling with problems that is to be studied, not necessarily the behavior of experts. Only the former reveal for observation their problem-solving behavior; behavior based on considerable expertise in a particular area involves rapid and covert, complex processes not available to introspection or observation.

By using a graph to illustrate the overt problem-solving process, the strategies of novice problem solvers can be quickly and readily identified. This type of graph would reduce the "clutter" resulting from the specifics of the content that occurs in therapy by diagramming these as tangential pathways. What remains is a clear, concise performance diagram with a recognizable resolution strategy. As Simon (1979) points out, even in a relatively simple problem domain a number of alternative, basically different strategies have proved efficacious for finding solutions. He points out that in studying specific cognitive problems "something has been learned about the range of strategies available and the circumstances under which they are likely to be adopted and most of the strategies that have been identified have been successfully modeled" (p. 365). The graph of problem-solving behavior thus provides a method of discovering different resolution strategies and of illustrating the actual process of a specific resolution using a particular strategy.

PROTOCOL ANALYSIS

The first step in the investigation of any phenomenon is observation of the performance associated with it. One way of getting at some of the internal mental operations in which problem solvers are engaged is to have them describe aloud what they are doing as they attempt to solve a problem. This results in a verbatim transcript of their verbalized processes, referred to as a verbal protocol in the problem-solving literature. These protocols bear a striking resemblance to therapy transcripts. Although there are difficulties in interpreting protocols, they provide extremely useful information about the process involved in problem solving.

Newell and Simon (1972) have been concerned with making protocol analysis into a useful tool for the study of problem solving. They introduced a series of steps in their data analysis procedure, steps which function to isolate relevant variables for measurement and to make evident the important regularities in the protocol. The first step divides the protocol into phrases. Each phrase represents a single act of task-oriented behavior. This is the problem of segmenting or unitizing, familiar to psychotherapy process researchers (cf. Kiesler, 1973). Having segmented the performance, a "problem space" is constructed to help researchers understand the problem solver's performance. The problem space is the problem solver's internal representation of the problem situation and the method of tackling the problem. The initial situation, the desired situation, that is, the resolution, and the problem-solving strategy are all represented in this space. Specification of the problem space is an attempt to understand how the problem solver is tackling the problem. The problem-solving behavior is then studied empirically to see how the problem solver gets from the initial to the desired situation.

This construction of the problem space is followed by plotting of a problem behavior graph (PBG). Proceeding through the protocol phrase by phrase, a plot of each phrase is made on the graph. The key constraint is that all changes in states (as defined for the problem space) that are detectable in the protocol must be shown on the graph. The PBG segments the protocols into a population of occasions for action. The PBG is suggested by Newell (1977) as a method for tracking the search for resolution in order to reconstruct its history. An example of a PBG is shown in Figure 4-1.

In using a PBG, the problem solver is viewed as always being located at some node in the graph and having available exactly the information contained in the state of knowledge characterizing that node. This graphing of actual problem-solving performances and the subject's states furnishes highly specific and complex descriptive information about the problem-solving behavior. The data upon which it is based, however, have been "plugged in" to the structure of the graph and thus categorized, organized and analyzed. Without the diagram one would be swamped by the overwhelming amount of information.

The construction of a PBG represents the groundwork for the final step of model building. The structure of the graph provides a framework that can be used to express diagrammatically the sequences of the performances. The PBG serves in this research as the link between the models and the data obtained through the task analysis. The graph can be used as a diagram of both the possible performance the investigator might expect to find (i.e., a model) and the actual problem-solving performances found. Graphing therefore provides the means of comparing, in detail, what is found with what one expects to find and thereby provides an opportunity for confirming or refuting expectations and assumptions about performances. It is this comparison of actual performances with hypothesized performances that leads eventually to the testing of the validity of the models.

MODEL BUILDING

Model building is concerned with the description and explanation of a system of events in the real world. The term "model" is an alternate name for a theory that carries the implication of a somewhat shorter life span than that of the sought-after eventual theory. The model builder is

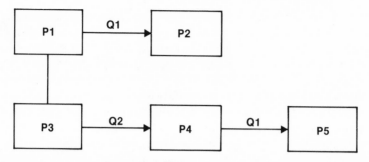

FIGURE 4-1. PROBLEM BEHAVIOR GRAPH (PBG). *Rules for PBG.* (a) A state of knowledge is represented by a node (the labeled boxes in the figure). The application of an operator to a state of knowledge is represented by a horizontal arrow to the right; the result is the node at the head of the arrow (Q1 to position P1 gives position P2). (b) A return to the same state of knowledge as node X is represented by another node below X and connected to it by a vertical line (P3 results after abandonment of P2; it constitutes the same state of knowledge as P1). (c) Time runs to the right and down; thus the graph is linearly ordered by time of generation (from P1 to P5).

confronted by the problem of conceptualizing a real system in terms of intellectually manageable variables and relationships that will validly represent the real system and be effective in yielding insight and understanding into its workings. The model builder must consider the problem of translating his or her conceptions of the system into a rigorous symbolic language such as mathematics or logic. In addition, if a test of the model is required, the problems of measurement and analysis of empirical data must be considered to enable a test to be made.

It is important to realize that different valid models can be developed for the same set of real events. Engineers have developed different models for many processes ranging from petroleum refinement to optimal resource allocation policies. The structural and operational characteristics of a model are determined to a high degree by the purpose it is to serve. Some models are more useful than others for a particular purpose. Although a system of events can be conceptualized in different ways, not all are equally effective in accounting for all observations or for explaining new phenomena. Copernicus's view of the solar system as centered around the sun was more useful than the previous view of the universe. Kepler produced a more accurate model, Newton a still more powerful explanatory model, and Einstein and modern astrophysics an even more powerful model of the behavior of matter in the universe. A model must therefore be evaluated as more or less useful for a particular purpose.

Morris (1967), in writing on the art of modeling, suggests two basic principles to guide the approach to model building. The first is that the process of model development may be usefully viewed as a process of *enrichment* or *elaboration*. In building a model one starts with very simple models quite distinct from reality and attempts to move in evolutionary fashion toward more elaborate models which more nearly reflect the complexity of the actual situation.

The second principle is that this process of elaboration or enrichment involves at least two sorts of *looping* or *alternation* procedures. The first is the alternation between modification of the model and confrontation by the data: As each version of the model is tested, a new version is produced which leads in turn to a subsequent test. The second type of alternation is between exploration of the deductive power of the model and the assumptions that characterize it: If a version of the model permits the attainment of the investigator's deductive objectives, the investigator will be satisfied with the assumptions underlying the model. If it has no deductive power the assumptions will be reinspected.

The importance of the first of these looping procedures is to make clear that the research need not be conceived as a grand one-shot test of a single model. In addition it shows that the investigator need not absolutely decide whether to develop the model first or "get the data" first. The second of these alternations, the selection and modification of basic assumptions, is to a large extent what characterizes model building and is the process by which the underlying structure of the phenomena is revealed. The essential task of the model builder is to discover a set of assumptions that are both descriptive of the problem and deductively useful.

Model building therefore proceeds by means of an iterative process. The investigator alternates between a sensitive and selective observation of real situations and a conceptual structuring process which reveals patterns or brings some order to the available data. The key to this process is the specification and consideration of a concrete instance of the phenomenon which allows a working back and forth between the phenomenon and the model.

Two types of models, which will be called performance models and information-processing models, are useful in understanding problem solving. The performance model describes the actual component behaviors involved in a successful performance. It acts as a descriptive guide of what to look for in these performances. The second type of model depicts the psychological system that could have generated the performance. This information-processing model attempts to simulate the operations of the mind by using different information-processing operators, such as "if–then" production rules (Bower, 1978; Newell & Simon, 1972), to explain how particular performances might have been generated.

One type of information-processing model that could be constructed would be a computer simulation of the client's cognitive processes. A simulation of this sort tests initially for the consistency and completeness of the theoretical ideas embodied in the model but it also provides a means of discovering where the model may fail by observing its behavior under a variety of simulated conditions. A simulation can also provide a means of empirically discovering task demands placed on the information-processing systems by revealing where the system is unable to respond to the demand (Pylyshyn, 1978).

Another type of information-processing model that can be constructed is a descriptive simulation in which the performance is symbolically modeled without the researcher actually writing a computer program. This symbolic modeling, possibly more feasible in psychotherapy research, has less power to test the model across situations than a computer model but is still a refined theoretical demonstration of the adequacy of the assumptions and operations on which the model is based.

Model building is one of the important aims of task analysis. The phenomenon to be ultimately modeled in a study of problem solving is the psychological system that could generate a specific problem-solving performance in a particular task. The data base is the subject's protocol, that is, the transcript of what the subject said and did, plus any other non-verbal performance records that are made, such as eye movements, voice quality, etc. Once measurements of the performance have been made, the model builder constructs a performance model by looking for structure and relationship between the measured variables. This performance model serves as a base for constructing an information-processing model which would generate the performance.

What we have gained, therefore, from the cognitive problem-solving area are some ideas on how to study complex performances with model construction as the final goal. Using protocols of a subject's problem-solving performances, the investigator attempts to understand the problem solver's representation of the problem and its possible solution. The changes in states in actual problem-solving performances are plotted on the problem behavior graph, including tangents as well as advances toward the resolution. This detailed descriptive model of performances provides the data base for the construction of a model of the mental operations that could have generated the observed performance. With this background on the task analysis of cognitive problem solving, it is now possible to turn our attention to the application of these ideas to a task analysis of therapeutic events.

TASK ANALYSIS OF THERAPEUTIC EVENTS

The approach to be discussed here assumes that within the complex stream of performance exhibited by the client and therapist during therapy there are discriminable recurring *events* which possess a high probability of affecting change (Rice & Greenberg, 1974). An "event" consists of an interactional sequence between client and therapist. It is a performance sequence that has a beginning, an end, and a particular structure that gives it meaning as an island of behavior distinguishable from the surrounding behaviors in the ongoing psychotherapeutic process. To the client the event has the quality of a whole and its completion is experienced as a closure of some interaction with the therapist. For the therapist the event represents a therapeutic activity that comes to some closure in the hour. The event is like a short incident in a novel or drama. It is intrinsically complex and composed of interconnected activities in a changing pattérn, but it occurs within a continuous period of time and comes to some closure within the session.

Experienced therapists have some implicit or explicit guidelines concerning recurring events. They are alert for particular client performance patterns that signal the presence of an affective issue needing to be resolved, which can be worked on in a particular fashion. These situations were termed "when-then" performance events (Rice & Greenberg, 1974), to capture the way in which therapeutic interactions can be characterized by statements such as "*When* the client did this *then* the therapist did that." Therapists, we are suggesting, are continually making "process diagnoses" of client process that suggests to them some particular intervention. In any particular approach some client performance pattern (the "when" of the event) acts as a marker that there is some affective issue needing to be resolved and that the client is presently amenable to intervention (the "then" of the event). The marker, the therapist interventions, and the subsequent client process make up a discriminable event in the therapy with an identifiable beginning and end. These events appear to have sufficient structural similarity to warrant detailed study.

AFFECTIVE TASKS

Certain client therapeutic performance, we are suggesting, can be viewed as the unfolding of attempts by the client at solving problems of an affective rather than a primarily cognitive nature. These client performance patterns can therefore be regarded as indicators or "markers" of the affective tasks on which the client is engaged, and the appearance of these markers indicates the client's readiness to work on the particular task. Many of the "markers" from potent events in therapy can be seen to possess task-like characteristics. These markers have similar recurring structures, which are expressions by clients about situations in which they need to discover solutions in order to attain some goal. Certain types of client problem statements appear to recur within and across clients when one describes the problems in terms of the structure of the client's in-therapy performance and the underlying phenomenological experience. These functional problems, such as the experience of conflict, problematic reactions, or states of being confused or wanting understanding, can be construed as affective tasks to which the client is actively seeking resolution (Greenberg, 1975).

Affective tasks can be thought of as overall goal-directed attempts to reach affective objectives in the face of particular problematic aspects of experience. A person engaged in one of these tasks appears to be working toward an affective resolution to some issue of concern or toward some personally desirable affective goal. These "tasks" possess a subjective quality similar to those problems which may be colloquially described as "nagging" or "teasing" at a person. They seem to call for attention. They are incomplete tasks or unfinished business in the affective realm that pushes for resolution.

The description of a task and situation in the cognitive area is relatively simple compared to the complexity of the description required for a therapeutic event. There are at least three ways in which an affective task in therapy is more difficult to describe. The primary difference between studying cognitive and affective problem solving is that in the latter the final outcome is often less defined and the correct solution is not generally known. Affective problems are more like "ill-defined" problems, such as the composition of a fugue or the writing of a computer program, in which the problem solver contributes to the definition of the problem and in which there is, therefore, no one correct solution (Reitman, 1965; Simon & Hayes, 1976). Once resolution is achieved, it is implicitly recognized by the quality of completion that the person experiences. It is as if the individual possesses a tacit test of when the answer to the problem has been found, and when this state is reached the problem seems no longer to exist, because a pathway out of the dilemma has been found. The resulting resolution is marked by feelings of calmness, relief, decisiveness, firmness, and a sense of direction. These characteristics of resolution enable us to recognize when a problem has been solved and to study how resolution is achieved.

In the second place, the task environment in the therapeutic event is more complex in that it contains the therapist as part of the task environment, whereas in the cognitive area a second person is typically not involved in the task. In the analysis of affective tasks we must therefore define the therapist's effect on task performance, that is, whether client task resolution is facilitated or retarded. The therapist's role or task is, among other things, to keep the person in a productive psychological problem space. Simon and Newell's (1970) definition of problem space is the way a particular subject represents the task in order to work on it. Thus, a productive problem space in therapy is one that keeps the client working on the task in a fashion likely to lead to resolution.

In the third place, the therapeutic subtask is ill defined in the sense that a clear starting point for the task is not specified. Yet we need to ensure that we can *select* behavior segments or protocols for study which do represent problem situations. To do this we need to build strong definitions or understanding of the task situation so that we can identify problems clearly. This is where our procedure differs radically from that of the study of cognitive problem solving. In studying a therapeutic task performance we do not present a subject with a problem, but recognize when the subject's own functional processes are in a problem state. The description of this initial client state is therefore the beginning of a study of the task and in fact provides us with a description of the task.

This view of the therapeutic interaction as consisting of events in which the client, facilitated by the therapist, is engaged in a task directed toward affective resolution enables us to study complex therapeutic performances using the process–structural methods of task analysis. Task analysis allows us to study the moment-by-moment performance of an active construing being engaged in a complex goal-directed activity. The client's goal can be identified in terms of his or her stated or implied desire to resolve a specific issue or to find an emotional solution to a particular affective problem. The structure of the task environment can be carefully defined and partially controlled, as it is largely created by the therapist interventions performed during the task performance.

TASK ANALYTIC STRATEGIES FOR MODELING AFFECTIVE TASKS

The task analysis of therapeutic events suggested here and used in the research described in Chapters 2 and 3 involves five basic strategies from the task analytic literature for representing data and structuring it in a way that will aid the intensive analysis of affective task performance. These strategies are (1) the description of the task, (2) the specification of the task environment, (3) the rational task analysis, (4) the empirical task analysis, and (5) model construction.

The task description involves selecting and describing, clearly and completely, the client task to be performed. Recurrent problems or issues that are troublesome to clients must therefore be identified. Precise behavioral definitions of these task markers are made by specifying the distinctive features of the markers and any subtypes or exceptions to the general definitions. An inductive procedure for constructing definitions based on distinctive feature analysis has been developed for this purpose (Greenberg, 1975).

The second procedure in the task analysis of therapeutic events is the specification of the task environment. This amounts to the writing of a manual of suitable therapist interventions for facilitating task resolution. The therapist interventions, construed as task instructions, must be clear and understandable to both the client and the investigator, for they form an integral part of the task and task performance. Although the therapist might at any time use one of a number of interventions, the function of the intervention in relation to task resolution must always be clearly understood by the investigator in order for subsequent client responses to be meaningful.

The third procedure, the rational task analysis, is performed by the investigator running through the task mentally, repeatedly asking himself or herself "How could this be solved?" This provides an initial understanding of possible resolution strategies and components of resolution performances. Such possible performances are generated using what the observer would ideally do if he or she were in the subject's place. The investigator is thus conducting a kind of thought experiment (Husserl, 1939/1973) in which possible performances are varied freely in imagination to extract the essential nature of resolution performances and the fundamental strategy underlying these performances. Husserl refers to this "intuition of essences" as the core mental operation in discovery.

Task analysis, therefore, goes beyond performance analysis in which the subject's behavioral performance is the only data. In this rational analysis the observer's mental performance of the task is also part of the data. The purpose of the rational analysis is to provide a framework for understanding the client performance to be studied. Although Newell and Simon's (1972) construction of the problem space is an aspect of the rational analysis, such an analysis goes beyond the specification of strategies toward a description of possible client performances in sequential detail. Once the investigator has a representation of how the subject might perform in solving the problem, that is, an idealized model representing his or her best guess regarding the strategies involved, he or she can progress to a description of the client's actual performance and determine how it compares with the best guess.

Generation of idealized possibilities is an aspect of all creative scientific thinking. This approach is clearly not "induction by abstraction," in which by considering the facts one abstracts their common character. It is more like the method of a "reading of essences," as proposed by Husserl (1939/1973) in his eidetic psychology. As Merleau Ponty (1964) points out, an intuition of essences, like induction, is based on facts. The difference in the methods is that the former involves the "imaginary free variation" of aspects of certain facts in order to grasp the essence represented by these facts. To do this we consider a concrete experience, for example, that of a lamp, and then change it in our thought, trying to imagine it as effectively modified in all respects. That which remains constant or invariant throughout these changes is the essence of the phenomena in question.

According to Husserl (1939/1973), Galileo used this method in abstracting from certain impure and imperfect concrete phenomena the free fall of a body. He forged with his intellect this essence, an idealized fiction that was nevertheless founded on the facts. He conceived of the pure case of a freely falling body, of which there is no example in human experience, and verified this idea by showing how the empirical facts, often unclear and containing anomalies, could be understood through the introduction of additional conditions (such as friction and resistance) which explained differences between the facts and the pure concept. We see therefore how Husserl argues that the observation of concrete events is guided by an intuition of essences. These essences in effect are constructed by the investigator who freely varys the facts possessed in order to read the essential invariants. The model constructed in this manner is then used to provide explanations and make predictions which are tested against reality.

In the task analytic procedure proposed in this chapter, the investigator explicitly used this type of "thought experiment" prior to description of actual performances in order to inform and clarify the observational attempt. The thought experiment makes explicit that which guides the empirical investigator in his or her observations and makes each observational description a test of the idealized formulation, by either supporting or refuting certain possibilities. Any concrete performance which is focused upon is enveloped by the idealized framework already spelled out. It is also true, however, that the essential insight or intuition of a performance possibility can incorporate the concrete instance only because it was based on prior observation or experience with similar instances. Although inductive findings are often claimed to have been arrived at by abstraction, model construction actually proceeds by a type of factually based inductive–reflective spiraling in which one moves in circular fashion from the data to reflection on the invariance in the data back to the data. The investigator, in actuality, iteratively constructs essences based on prior observation and experience and then, guided by this "intuition of essences," observes reality more closely, thereby gaining more data to inform the constructions.

The fourth procedure, the empirical task analysis, is the most complex strategy and involves the description of the actual moment-by-moment performance of the individual engaged in the task. This is done by generating a client performance diagram, analogous to the problem behavior graph in the information-processing area, to track the sequence of experiential states clients go through in the actual task performance. This procedure separates and identifies in sequence each discrete state and diagrams the progression from one state to another.

In the rational analysis the investigator first infers the set of possible performances that a human being could generate in the therapeutic situation. The presupposition here is that the constraints imposed by the task and task situation limit the set of performances that any human of the client's personality type could possibly produce. To the extent then that the investigator is able to generate a nearly complete set of possible performances in the rational analysis the actual performance used by the client will have been anticipated. Once the type of performances generated by clients are fairly well known, more detailed possible performance diagrams are constructed on primarily rational grounds. The empirical task analysis then serves to correct any mistakes in the performance description generated in the rational analysis. In addition, any behavior from the empirical description of the actual performance becomes in and of itself interesting when viewed in the light of the rational analysis because it automatically confirms, broadens, or radically changes the assumptions underlying the thought experiments of the rational analysis. In this fashion, detailed descriptions of client and therapist behaviors are carried out on a number of events, and a successive reworking of the client performance diagram takes place. It would only be after substantial looping through the rational and empirical analyses that the investigator would have any faith in the performance model and use it in attempts to predict the performance of a client dealing with a particular type of task.

A task analysis of affective tasks using the five strategies discussed leads to the construction of two possible types of models, with each type representing an important research thrust. The detailed description of human behavior finally results in the construction of client and therapist *performance* models, the first type of model. A research thrust in this direction is consistent with Fiske's (1977) recommendation to study acts rather than people in order to arrive at rules that govern behavior. This type of detailed model of observable client and therapist performance would greatly enhance our understanding of what occurs in therapy. The second type of model, an information-processing model, comes out of a research thrust designed to understand human information processing (Neisser, 1967). In this approach the investigator attempts to construct a model of the psychological system that would have generated a change performance. Using observable performance as a base, the investigator attempts to understand and model the covert mental processes underlying these performances in a fashion similar to Newell and Simon's (1972) and the neo-Piagetians' (Pascual-Leone, 1976a, 1976b) attempts to understand cognitive problem-solving performances.

VERIFICATION OF MODELS

After constructing models of one form or another, it is necessary to explore the generalizability of the models and test their validity. This is done by testing the model on new cases and by relating the process suggested by the model to therapeutic outcome.

In order to test a newly constructed performance model derived from the task analysis, the investigator advances hypotheses concerning client performance on the task. Resolution and nonresolution performances on the task are then collected and compared to see if the specified components of resolution performance discriminate between the successful and unsuccessful performances. If the predicted patterns and components are indeed found to discriminate between resolution and nonresolution performance, credibility is added to the performance model. In addition, hypothesized and observed resolution performances can be compared, using statistical tests appropriate to the data, to refute or add confidence to the hypothesized model.

Similarly, once an information-processing model of the psychological system has been constructed, many predictions about psychological functioning could be generated from the model. Of particular interest would be hypotheses concerning the mechanisms of client change. These predictions would then be tested on further instances of the same task, on other tasks, or by some laboratory experiments.

As a final verification step in a research program using a task analytic approach, more traditional outcome-effects studies would be done in which the relationship between the proposed successful client performances and long-term outcome are studied. In these studies the links between the therapeutic methods that lead to these client performances and outcome would also need to be demonstrated. The advantage of verification studies coming at this stage of a research program is that a hypothesized causal link between specified client processes and outcome provides an increase in control on client performance variance. Client performance is usually a source of great variance in a study attempting to link therapeutic method to outcome and often obscures method effects. This approach of intensively analyzing successful client performances in order to construct a model therefore holds promise of improved prediction and control as well as improved explanation of client mechanisms of change.

THE UTILITY OF TASK ANALYSIS
IN THE STUDY OF PSYCHOTHERAPY

What can the application of the intuitions and methods of task analysis offer to the study of psychotherapeutic events?: The long-range contribution of task analysis would be the specification of client mechanisms of change in the actual conduct of psychotherapy. The specification of client and therapist performances is the major short-term contribution of task analysis. This specification of behavior will provide a clear definition of what the treatment is and what client performance effects it has, that is, the nature of the immediate effects of the treatment. Task analysis works directly on identifying and describing the step-by-step components of the change process and thereby provides a detailed description of what actually occurs in therapy. In so doing it also provides an important set of new dependent measures—the successful performance outcomes achieved—by which the impact of therapist characteristics, new therapist interventions, and other situational variables can be tested. It is in this way, by the provision of clear dependent variables, that task analysis can greatly enhance existing psychotherapy practice. If we have a clear definition of desired therapy performance outcomes we could learn more about how to bring these short-term outcomes about and how to relate them to long-term outcome. In addition, the task analytic approach would fill a gap pointed out by Orlinsky and Howard's (1978) categorization of existing research. No research has been done on the transactional strategies and task performances of therapists and clients in therapy and how these relate to outcome.

Task analysis has been pervasive in psychological research in implicit form for a long time: In psychotherapy implicit task analyses were used by most theorists in building their theories. In considering what kinds of explicit task analyses could be useful in psychotherapy research, several broad criteria can be set up to view the potential contributions of task analysis of psychotherapeutic events.

1. *Relevance to change.* Are the tasks analyzed ones that will lead to change? Are the tasks studied because they are active ingredients of therapy or possibly because they are theoretically interesting, are easy to study, or have a history of past research? A criterion of relevance to therapeutic change means that most tasks analyzed will be more complex than many laboratory experiments related to dysfunction or change.

2. *Description of change.* Does the task analysis describe performance components of the process of change or does it describe components of competent social behavior? Therapeutic task analysis, at its best, will elucidate the actual process of change, spelling out the relationship between performance during therapy and the competence or outcome that results from therapy. Another form of task analysis (Schwartz & Gottman, 1976) delineates the components of competence of socially competent behavior by comparing the composition of the repertoire of competent and incompetent populations. This is a useful but more static form of task analysis. Ideally, task analysis should suggest methods for change and investigators should recognize that the components of change performances may be different from the components of competence utilized by individuals who are expert in a particular performance.

3. *Treatment enhancement.* An obvious concern in psychotherapy research is whether the results of a particular analysis are usable in therapeutic practice. The task analysis that examines complex performances is useful inasmuch as it reveals a substructure of the task that is amenable to psychotherapeutic intervention of some type. A task analysis should result in an understanding of a task that makes its resolution more "instructable" in the sense that the therapist can intervene so as to increase the probability of resolution.

4. *General theory formulation.* Does the task analysis yield descriptions of the task in a general psychological language that goes beyond a particular therapeutic school or approach? Task analysis is a method of analyzing ecologically valid tasks by means of existing psychological concepts and theories so that therapeutic practice can benefit from the scientific findings of psychology. An integration is being sought between the general findings of psychological science (especially cognitive psychology) and the specific wisdom of a particular therapeutic approach to delineate therapeutic change principles.

REFERENCES

Bacon, F. *Bacon's "Novum organum"* (Thomas Fowler, Ed.). Oxford: Clarendon Press, 1899.

Bateson, G. *Steps to an ecology of mind.* New York: Ballantine Books, 1972.

Baylor, G., & Lemoyne, G. Experiments in a seriation with children: Towards an information processing exploration of horizontal decalage. *Canadian Journal of Behavioural Science*, 1975, *7*, 4-29.

Bernard, C. *An introduction to the study of experimental medicine.* New York: Dover, 1957. (Originally published, 1865.)

Bower, G. Contacts of cognitive psychology with social learning theory. *Cognitive Therapy and Research*, 1978, *2*, 123-146.

Burks, A. Van Neumann's self-producing automatia. In A. Burks (Ed.), *Essays on cellular automata.* Urbana: University of Illinois Press, 1970.

Byrne, R. Planning meals: Problem solving on a real data-base. *Cognition*, 1977, *5*, 287-332.

Case, R. Structures and strictures: Some functional limitations on the course of cognitive growth. *Cognitive Psychology*, 1974, *6*, 554-573.

Case, R. Gearing the demands of instruction to the developmental capacities of the learner. *Review of Educational Research*, 1975, *45*, 59-87.

Chomsky, N. *Language and mind.* New York: Harcourt, Brace & World, 1968.

Farnham Diggory, S. (Ed.). *Information processing in children.* New York: Academic Press, 1972.

Fiske, D. Methodological issues in research on the psychotherapist. In A. Gurman and A. Razin (Eds.), *Effective psychotherapy.* New York: Pergamon Press, 1977.

Gagné, R. Contributions of learning to human development. *Psychological Review*, 1968, *75*, 177-191.

Gagné, R. Task analysis: Its relation to content analysis. *Educational Psychologist*, 1974, *11*, 11–18.

Gottman, J., & Markman, H. Experimental designs in psychotherapy research. In S. L. Garfield & A. E. Bergin (Eds.), *Handbook of psychotherapy and behavior change*. New York: Wiley, 1978.

Greenberg, L. S. *Task analytic approach to the study of psychotherapeutic events*. Unpublished doctoral disseration, York University, 1975.

Gregg, L. Methods and models. In D. Klahr (Ed.), *Cognition and instruction*. Hillsdale, N.J.: Erlbaum, 1976.

Horowitz, M. *States of mind*. New York: Plenum Press, 1979.

Husserl, E. *Experience and judgment* (L. Landgrebe, Ed.; J. Churchill & K. Ameriks, Trans.). Evanston, Ill.: Northwestern University Press, 1973. (Originally published, 1939).

Kiesler, D. *The process of psychotherapy: Empirical foundations and systems of analysis*. Chicago: Aldine, 1973.

Klahr, D. Cognition and instruction. In D. Klahr (Ed.), *Cognition and instruction*. Hillsdale, N.J.: Erlbaum, 1976.

Lindsay, P., & Norman D. *Human information processing*. New York: Academic Press, 1972.

Merleau Ponty, M. The primacy of perception. In M. Natanson (Ed.), *Phenomenology and the social sciences*. Evanston, Ill.: Northwestern University Press, 1973. (Originally published, 1964).

Miller, R. Analysis and specification of behavior for training. In R. Miller (Ed.), *Training research and education*. New York: Basic Books, 1955.

Morris, W. On the art of modeling. *Management Science*, 1967, *13*(12), 77–114.

Neisser, U. *Cognitive psychology*. New York: Appleton-Century-Crofts, 1967.

Newell, A. Protocol analysis. In P. Johnson-Laird & P. Wason (Eds.), *Thinking: Readings in cognitive science*. New York: Cambridge University Press, 1977.

Newell, A., & Simon, H. *Human problem solving*. New York: Prentice-Hall, 1972.

Orlinsky, D., & Howard, K. The relation of process to outcome in psychotherapy. In S. L. Garfield & A. E. Bergin (Eds.), *Handbook of psychotherapy and behavior change*. New York: Wiley, 1978.

Pascual-Leone, J. Metasubjective problems of constructive cognition: Forms of knowing and their psychological mechanisms. *Canadian Psychological Review*, 1976, *17*, 110–122. (a).

Pascual-Leone, J. A view of cognition from a formalist's perspective. In K. Riegel & J. Meacham (Eds.), *The developing individual in a changing world* (Vol. 1). The Hague: Mouton, 1976. (b)

Piaget, J. *The construction of reality in the child*. New York: Basic Books, 1954.

Piaget, J. *Structuralism*. New York: Basic Books, 1970.

Pylyshyn, Z. Computational models and empirical constraints. *The Behavioural and Brain Sciences*, 1978, *1*, 93–127.

Reber, A., & Lewis, S. Implicit learning: An analysis of the form and structure of a body of tacit knowledge. *Cognition*, 1977, *5*, 333–361.

Reitman, W. *Cognition and thought*. New York: Wiley, 1965.

Resnick, L. Task analysis in instructional design: Some cases from mathematics. In D. Klahr (Ed.), *Cognition and instruction*. Hillsdale, N.J.: Erlbaum, 1976.

Rice, L., & Greenberg, L. S. *A method for studying the active ingredients in psychotherapy*. Paper presented to the Society for Psychotherapy Research, Denver, 1974.

Schwartz, R., & Gottman, J. Toward a task analysis of assertive behavior. *Journal of Consulting and Clinical Psychology*, 1976, *44*, 910–920.

Sidman, M. *Tactics of scientific research: Evaluating experimental data in psychology*. New York: Basic Books, 1960.

Simon, H. Information processing models of cognition. In M. Rosenzweig & L. Porter (Eds.), *Annual Review of Psychology*, 1979, *30*, 363–396.

Simon, H. & Hayes, J. Understanding complex task instructions. In D. Klahr (Ed.), *Cognition and instruction*. Hillsdale, N.J.: Erlbaum, 1976.

Simon, H., & Newell, A. Human problem solving. *American Psychologist*, 1970, *25*, 191–199.

von Neumann, J. *Collected works*. (A. Traub, Ed.) New York: Pergamon Press, 1961.

Winograd, T. *Understanding natural language*. New York: Academic Press, 1972.

Ysseldyke, J., & Salvia, J. Diagnostic-prescriptive teaching: Two models. *Exceptional Children*, 1974, *41*, 181–185.

DISTINCTIVE APPROACHES IN THE NEW PARADIGM

In the present section four different research approaches are illustrated. All of them share the same goal of describing process patterns and understanding some of the basic mechanisms underlying client change, as well as sharing the principles and strategy decisions discussed in the first chapter. Each one of them follows a different approach, however, and each makes a distinctive contribution to the field. Some promising directions for future research are spelled out in each chapter. The four approaches described and illustrated in this section are the symptom-context method, configurational analysis, analysis of transitions between levels of experiencing, and interpersonal process recall and comprehensive process analysis.

THE FOUR RESEARCH APPROACHES

In the following overview of these approaches we will attempt to place each of them in the context of the larger research program of which it is a part, pointing out the features that characterize each of them as a rigorous creative-inductive strategy within the new paradigm presented in this volume.

In Chapter 5 Luborsky and his associates apply the symptom-context method to gain an understanding of some of the client mechanisms that underlie entry into states of depression. The symptom-context method grew out of the wedding of the clinical method of observing the patient's flow of thoughts with the scientific method, in which categories are defined precisely, qualities are quantified, and measurement is made reliable. This marriage provides a rigorous clinical research method.

For the symptom-context method to be applied effectively, a number of conditions should hold (Luborsky, 1967). First the patient must report, in therapy, the occurrence of the symptom, as in the report of a feeling of depression, or the symptom must make itself directly known to the therapist, as in a petit mal attack. This permits one to pinpoint the onset and duration of the symptom to be studied. In addition, the patient must be reporting his or her thoughts as they are occurring before and possibly after the symptom onset, and these must be recorded. Finally, a sufficient number of instances of the symptomatic behavior should be available, together with a control sample of instances in which the symptom does not occur, to permit formal statistical analysis. Given these conditions, a symptom of some theoretical and/or clinical relevance is selected for study, the occurrence of the symptom is identified, and the relevant transcript is divided into three sections: the symptom statement and the immediate contexts before and after the symptom. The crucial advantage of this procedure is that one can study the symptom and its context just as it is occurring, rather than having to depend on the usual retrospective accounts.

The approach of Luborsky and his associates appears to be the most extensively applied example of the rational–empirical method underlying the new approach to research suggested in this book. Before studying the symptom-related performances, they make preliminary descriptions of possible patient performances that might precede symptom occurrence. These notions of possible performances guide them in their selection and invention of measurement instruments to be used to describe actual performances. They then examine a series of instances, usually starting with a sample of incidents from a single patient, in order to compare actual performances with the possible performances of their theoretical models.

This approach has all the hallmarks of a creative–inductive procedure in which each new step is informed by the findings from the earlier observation of the data. They study cases individually in a rigorous fashion in order to guide the study of further cases, adding instruments to measure further aspects of the process that emerge as relevant. The procedure of moving from theory to data and from data to theory to enrich one's model of clinical change phenomena is well exemplified by the symptom-context work. Finally, they have utilized across-subject, group verification studies to validate models they have constructed for momentary forgetting (Luborsky, 1967) and the emergence of somatic symptoms (Luborksy & Auerbach, 1969), thus demonstrating the place of verification after the creative–inductive clarification of the phenomena. Although Luborsky and his associates have concentrated on the study of symptom occurrence, this approach can also be used to study the context of positive therapeutic change. In the present section they point in that direction when they describe things learned about the interaction context that precedes shifts out of depression as well as into it.

In Chapter 6, Marmar, Wilner, and Horowitz report on a study of "states" and the patterns of transition between states. In Chapter 7 Mathieu-Coughlan and Klein describe essential transitions between different levels of "experiencing." Both of these research programs are focused on gaining a deeper understanding of the essential mechanisms of change in psychotherapy by dividing the complex stream of an ongoing therapy into a series of separate ways of being in the therapy encounter and describing them in a rigorous and reliable fashion. A central focus of both research programs has been their focus on the development of a limited number of descriptive categories within which one can classify the quality of the client's engagement in therapy at any given moment. Both behavior and reported internal experience are used in making these classifications. By means of these categories, they map the client's engagement in the therapy process from moment to moment, focusing on the patterns within a single interview or a series of interviews. They look intensively at a fine-grained descriptive level at the stages thus identified, attempting to understand their essential nature. An especially interesting feature of both these programs is their focus on the transitions between categories, an attempt to understand the client operations underlying these particular change episodes. These two programs are quite different from each other in a number of important respects, however.

Horowitz and his associates have designed a method called "configurational analysis" for mapping a therapy according to clients' states of mind, role-relationship models, and information processing. In this chapter they focus on the important transition points by means of segmentation into states of mind, where a state is defined as "a recurrent pattern of experience and behavior that is both verbal and non-verbal" (Horowitz, 1979, p. 31). For each new client one first identifies the various states that appear, focusing first on problem states, and then on other recurrent states, including those appearing seldom but thought to be potentially significant. Once these states have been tentatively identified, one goes back to the videotaped interview as many times as necessary, verifying the presence of each state and obtaining a more and more fine-grained feel for each. Then the nature of each state is further illuminated by identifying the kinds of relationships to self and others and the modes of thinking or information processing that characterize that state.

The approach of Horowitz and his associates sharply exemplifies the iterative nature of creative–inductive methods in research. The following statement by Horowitz (1979) has clearly stated the basic assumption of their research program:

> Repetition is a vital aspect of this method and results in a gradual clarification of interactive patterns; each clarification, in sequence is essential in a complex human field wherein definitive statement by means of a single-stage analysis of evidence is impossible. The avoidance of rigid classifications or preformed definitions allows individual qualities to emerge and determine labels. (pp. vii–viii)

An important feature of their method is the reliable recognition not only of the states themselves but of the moment when a given state shifts to another one. Thus they are able to pinpoint times of state transitions and to draw diagrams showing the patterning of states and the pattern of transitions between them that seems to characterize the individual at a particular stage of therapy. It is this process of establishing the reliability and relevance of the observational categories and the transitions between them that is the central focus for Marmar, Wilner, and Horowitz in Chapter 6.

The analysis of states and state transitions is fundamentally empirical, although grounded in theory that is essentially psychoanalytic. As Horowitz (1979) states, "The energic point of view is replaced by a modified ego psychology that emphasizes information processing and the structural aspects of self and object representations" (p. ix). The emphasis of the research is clearly on letting the formulation for each new client emerge from steeping oneself in the characteristics of the interactions of that particular client with that particular therapist, thus staying descriptively close to the phenomena. The basic observational categories, the states, are not inherently determined by the underlying theory. Although the usefulness of their method has been tested mainly in therapies within a general psychoanalytic orientation, this approach to intensive analysis would be applicable to therapies grounded in other theoretical systems. In fact, they view this extension of the method as an important future step.

Their method is at present applied in an idiographic fashion. New state categories are established for each new client to be studied. The definitions for each new state must grow out of an intensive study of that particular client and should be uniquely useful for understanding the progression of that particular therapy. In formulating and testing predictions generated by the state transition models it is possible therefore to verify predictions across a range of different situations for this particular client. Some states are viewed as "working" states, potentially productive of change, while others are more representative of the basic pathology involved, and one can test predictions concerning their relative frequency and or duration as therapy progresses. Inasmuch as the state transitions can be precisely pinpointed, one can develop hypotheses concerning effective or ineffective therapist interventions for promoting these transactions.

The state categories and the relationships among them do not constitute a measure that can be applied to new therapy situations. It is the methodological and heuristic structure of configurational analysis that is transferable to new situations. Configurational analysis constitutes a tool for research and clinical understanding by means of which one can identify the crucial recurring patterns among the complexities of each new therapy. The authors have, however, begun to explore the possibility of the development of a "state dictionary" which would provide a list of general states and provide possibilities for moving toward classification and comparison of different cases on the basis of the occurrence of particular states and state transitions.

The research program described by Mathieu-Coughlan and Klein in Chapter 7 is directed toward understanding the transitions between levels of "experiencing" in psychotherapy. The experiencing construct is central to the theory of experiential psychotherapy, an approach that has developed from, and has in turn strongly influenced, client-centered therapy (Gendlin, 1973). The authors begin their chapter by providing perspective on the rational–empirical process of cycling between intensive observation and theory from which the Experiencing Scale emerged (Klein, Mathieu, Gendlin, & Kiesler, 1969).

The level of experiencing of a client at any point in therapy can be assessed by means of the Patient Experiencing Scale, a set of categories used for rating therapy transcripts and/or tapes. The categories are seen as constituting a scale ranging from remote, impersonal reporting of events to peak moments in which there is "felt shift" and resolution. The measurement stage of this research has received a great deal of attention in earlier studies, and the reliability and relevance of these observational categories has been extensively investigated. A new measure, the Therapist Experiencing Scale, consisting of categories for rating two dimensions of therapist participation, is also described here.

The approach of Mathieu-Coughlan and Klein is clearly nomothetic, leading to the construction of measures applicable across clients and therapists and even across a variety of therapy orientations. Even the assumed relationships between categories is invariant across situations, with a transition to a higher stage considered to be a favorable sign. The experiencing model makes the assumption that certain levels of experiencing must be reached if therapeutic change is to take place. The focus of the present study is on the four crucial change episodes identified by shifts in level on the Patient Experiencing Scale from Stage 3 to 4, from 4 to 5, from 5 to 6, and 6 to 7.

The authors' approach to studying the crucial transition points is to specify some expected relationships between these transition points and the level of the preceding therapist interventions as assessed on the two dimensions of the Therapist Experiencing Scale. Although they do not actually test their predictions concerning optimal therapist interventions at potential transition points, they suggest a number of interesting hypotheses which could be investigated by means of sequential designs involving client–therapist–client interaction sequences. They are clearly implying an alternative research strategy, one that might bring clarity and direction to the chaotic and controversial research area concerning the effectiveness of therapist "conditions." They point out that it is meaningless to view therapist conditions as "operating independently from client process qualities and skills," and that in both research and training we need to understand the interactional or process context in which the techniques are applied.

The continued work over the years with the experiencing construct and its measurement is an excellent example of the procedure of repeated cycles from theory to data and from data to theory, and the construction of a more and more refined performance model based on the increased understanding gained from the process of intensive observation guided by a rational framework. This process seems to have operated without the guidelines of a formal creative–inductive method and can be regarded rather as the creative process of the individuals involved. We are suggesting that the process individuals engage in to arrive at models of what people actually do in therapy and to construct systems for measuring these performances are characterized by a cycling between theory and data which can profitably be formalized as an important method for research in psychotherapy, one that combines clinical observation with rigorous description in order to build models that can be tested.

In Chapter 8 Elliott uses interpersonal process recall (IPR) in order to discover significant moments in therapy. Once some class of recurrent significant events is discovered, the moments and their surrounding interactional context are described by means of an extensive battery of process measures. Two characteristics of his approach set it apart from the others in this volume. The first is the use of the client's perspective in the selection of episodes for study. In Elliott's procedure clients are asked to identify events that have been significantly helpful, and then the client (and therapist) is asked to describe his or her fleeting impressions and reactions as the event unfolds, things which would ordinarily be forgotten or incorporated into more global memories of the session. Client recall statements are then used as data for understanding the processes of change in that type of significant event. In addition to the use of recall material, comprehensive process ratings of the therapy segments before, during, and after the significant moments are made in order to obtain observer descriptions of the client process during the event. These are used in conjunction with the IPR material to describe and explain the change episode.

The second major difference from the other approaches is the emphasis on the empirical discovery rather than the selection of the classes of change phenomena to be studied. One of the strengths of Elliott's method is its potential for providing for the study of new phenomena that might well not have been identified from the clinician's map alone.

It is important to recognize that in this approach, starting with an empirical procedure in which a phenomenon is selected for study, a rational or intuitive process guides the questions which are asked of the data. In this approach to the creative–inductive cycle of clinical theorizing, the inductive aspects are primary in that the investigator starts with an empirical step which leads to the generation of tentative hypotheses about the performance. Guided by these empirically induced hypotheses, further observations and measurements are made. Formal rational analysis takes place only after the gathering of data, although the investigator's implicit map is evident in the selection of instruments for the process analysis.

Inasmuch as Elliott's study of insight events is in its first stages, it is appropriate that no validation studies have yet been attempted. It is clear, however, that once a model such as the one he proposes is constructed it will lend itself to a variety of validation procedures. Studies comparing reported insight events with noninsight events could be undertaken in order to validate ideas about the necessary components of the model, while studies relating process to outcome would provide predictive validity.

Although these four research programs are very different from each other, all of them share the basic goal of attaining a fundamental understanding of some of the essential client mechanisms of change within one or more classes of change episodes. Viewed in conjunction with the previous section on task analysis, they provide a perspective on the possibilities of intensive analysis for helping to illuminate therapeutic change.

REFERENCES

Gendlin, E. T. Experiential psychotherapy. In R. Corsini (Ed.), *Current psychotherapies.* Itasca, Ill.: F. E. Peacock, 1973.

Horowitz, M. J. *States of mind: Analysis of change in psychotherapy.* New York: Plenum Press, 1979.

Klein, M., Mathieu, P., Gendlin, E., & Kiesler, D. *The experiencing scale.* Madison: Wisconsin Psychiatric Institute, 1969.

Luborsky, L. Momentary forgetting during psychotherapy and psychoanalysis: A theory and research method. *Psychological Issues*, 1967, *5*(2–3), Monograph 18/19, pp. 177–217.

Luborsky, L., & Auerbach, A. The symptom-context method: Quantitative studies of symptom formation in psychotherapy. *Journal of American Psychoanalytic Association*, 1969, *17*, 68–99.

5

Shifts in Depressive State during Psychotherapy: Which Concepts of Depression Fit the Context of Mr. Q's Shifts?

LESTER LUBORSKY
University of Pennsylvania

BARTON SINGER
Rutgers University

JOHN HARTKE
The Fairmount Institute

PAUL CRITS-CHRISTOPH
Yale University

MARJORIE COHEN
University of Pennsylvania

It has been hard to achieve consensus on some basic concepts of the sequence of states leading to depression. For example, Dr. George Engel, at a symposium of the American Psychoanalytic Association on symptom formation, described a state preceding depression and other symptoms as "the giving-up–given-up complex" because of the underlying affects of helplessness–hopelessness (Engel & Schmale, 1967). In discussing the paper, Dr. Max Schur expressed the opinion that the helplessness state might be indistinguishable from depression rather than antecedent to it. A similar idea was accorded a similar reception when Dr. Martin Seligman presented his work on learned helplessness in dogs to a conference of the Department of Psychiatry at the University of Pennsylvania (Seligman, Maier, & Geer, 1968). He suggested that learned helplessness was an antecedent to depression-like behavior in certain dogs who had been taught "helplessness" by being subjected to inescapable shock. Several discussants questioned his ability to distinguish the two affects, helplessness, and depression, and whether they were, in fact, distinguishable.

One straightforward way of establishing the relationship of the two states—if they are truly two separate or partially separate states—is to look at what happens just before a depression, as we will do in this chapter. By continuous observation of patients who have shifts into or out of depression, one can examine the sequence of states prior to the depression or the lifting of the depression. Psychotherapy is an excellent medium for this type of study since the patient is under continuous observation and often makes a great effort to say much of what he is experiencing. If sessions are tape-recorded, then not only the therapist but independent observers as well can estimate the temporal course of the affects to determine whether helplessness tended to precede depression, was concurrent with it, or could not be distinguished from it.

Other controlled conditions can also be instituted. After having located the instances of the nodal symptom, the data can then be segmented into three main divisions: (1) the words and other behaviors before the symptom; (2) the selected nodal event, the symptom itself; and (3) the words and other behaviors subsequent to the symptom. These three divisions can then be compared with similarly divided material from the same patient around selected control points, such as points that do not contain the symptom or points that contain other nodal behaviors. These control segments provide a baseline for comparison with the segments containing the nodal symptom. This method may sound somewhat like the same old clinical approach, for it is in part, but there are significant added ingredients—the application of the types of controls just described, which were developed as the "symptom-context methods" (Luborsky, 1964, 1967, 1970; Luborsky & Auerbach, 1969).

The symptom-context methods have advantages over more conventional methods. They permit more exact determination of the degree of fit of different theories of symptom formation to the data of each patient. Furthermore, the symptoms and other behaviors can be studied at the moment they appear rather than, as is usually done, depending upon patients' retrospective accounts of them. A review of psychosomatic research on onset conditions, for example, revealed that few studies (up to 1971) had been based upon symptoms that were observed at the time of their appearance rather than retrospectively described (Luborsky, Docherty, & Penick, 1973).

Since the development of the symptom-context method, about 30 of such observation studies have been completed or are in progress. Among the first psychological symptoms studied by this method was momentary forgetting (Luborsky, 1964, 1967). Other somatic symptoms investigated were migraine headaches (Luborsky & Auerbach, 1969); petit mal epileptic attacks (Luborsky, Docherty, Todd, Knapp, Mirsky, & Gottschalk, 1975); and premature ventricular contractions, a disorder of the heart rhythm (Docherty, Leigh, & David, 1974). Of the many context qualities which have been examined in these varied symptoms, helplessness is the one that has appeared most consistently (Luborsky, 1970).

Two main contributions to knowledge about depression were expected from the research described in this chapter: (1) an exploration of which concepts of depression fit the contexts for shifts in depressive mood, and (2) an examination of the applicability of the symptom-context method to the understanding of mood shifts.

BACKGROUND OF RESEARCH
ON SHIFTS IN DEPRESSION

A focus on the exact time of shift points into and out of depression has never been accomplished in research on depression. Such research has been based mainly upon patients who were already depressed or had already recovered from depression (e.g., Beck, 1967; Mendels, 1970; Mendelson, 1974). Bunney, Murphy, Goodwin, & Borge (1972) studied gross shifts in depression in single patients. They investigated shifts in manic–depressive patients from mania to depression or from depression to mania in terms of gross comparisons of daily measures of psycho-endocrine functioning. One limitation of such studies has been that they may not reveal much about the conditions that influenced the shift from one state to another. Furthermore, most of what is known depends upon the patient's retrospective account of what made him or her depressed rather than upon observations by the patient and by others as the transition occurred. An exception to the trend was the studies (Engel & Reichsman, 1956) that demonstrated that Monica, a child with a gastric fistula, abruptly went into a withdrawal state very much like a depressive state whenever a stranger entered the room. Concomitantly, she also showed decreased hydrochloric acid secretion in her stomach.

THE SYMPTOM-CONTEXT METHOD APPLIED TO
A PATIENT WITH DEPRESSIVE MOOD SHIFTS

The present research analyzes the psychological concomitants of a patient, Mr. Q, who experienced shifts in depressive mood, some of which occurred during psychotherapy. The special symptom-context method employed was a comparison between those instances in which depression increased versus those in which depression decreased.

The methods of analysis developed for these data will be given in detail in the hope that it will serve as a model for further research on the depressions of similar patients. We obtained the tape recordings of the psychotherapy of this patient who occasionally rapidly shifted his mood either towards depression or out of depression during the sessions. Of the 244 sessions, all but the first 41 were tape-recorded, and brief process notes were available for those 41. It was not necessary to transcribe or even to listen to all of these sessions because, conveniently, the therapist had completed a brief checksheet (Luborsky, 1971) at the end of each session. The postsession checksheet provided space to rate a set of variables for each session and to note mood shifts. We needed only to cull the checksheets to locate the sessions in which mood shifts occurred; only these sessions, a total of ten, were then transcribed.

The postsession checksheet also contained a space for brief process notes which served to summarize each session. Review of these notes suggested hypotheses about the nature of the context for each mood shift. The hypotheses were then checked by the more precise symptom-context analyses based on the transcripts.

CRITERIA FOR SELECTING SHIFTS IN "DEPRESSION"

The primary criterion for selecting a shift in "depression" for study was the patient's report of a shift in mood, for example, "My mood just went down." The suddenness of some shifts in this patient's mood was convenient for our method since it helped us to locate the exact moment of the shift. Whenever patient-reported mood shifts occurred, they were noted by the therapist on the postsession checksheet. (The shifts were 1 of 45 aspects of the session on the checksheet.) To further objectify the selection of the instances to be examined, two independent judges read the transcripts. For an instance to be usable both judges had to agree that the patient was, in fact, saying that a mood shift had *just* occurred. The shift had to be more than slight, that is, more than 1.0 on a 5-point depressive mood scale. The majority of the shifts were around 2.0 on the scale, which would make them of moderate size.

We chose those shifts that were within a reasonably long sample of the patient's speech, a context containing 400 words before and 400 words after the shift. (For this patient, 800 words typically took about 15 minutes.) Therefore, when shifts occurred in close proximity—as they tended to do—usually the first shift was selected or, occasionally, the one which occurred in the longer uninterrupted context of the patient's speech. In the ten sessions selected by the postsession checksheet method for transcription because they contained shifts, fourteen shifts were located, eight in which depression increased and six in which depression decreased. After excluding some instances on the basis of overlap, only nine of the original fourteen remained as the final selections, four in which increases in depression occurred and five in which decreases occurred.

We will briefly indicate here, and elaborate more fully later, the three ways in which we determined that the shifts involved depression.

1. For the nine selected segments of transcripts two independent judges rated the affective quality of the voice in terms of the degree of depressive mood that was conveyed in it. Their judg-

ments tended to be consistent with increased depressive affect when the patient was becoming increasingly depressed and somewhat consistent with decreased depressive affect when the reverse was true (p. 182).

2. The other independent judges rated the degree of depression before and after the shift. Again, their ratings were consistent with the patient's and the judges' classification of the direction of the shift (p. 171).

3. Other independent judges applied the depression component of the Gottschalk–Gleser (1969) Hostility-Inward Scale to each segment. Again, their scorings were consistent with the directions of the shift (p. 181).

THEORIES OF DEPRESSION AND THE VARIABLES RELATED TO THEM

Much consideration went into deciding which variables would be measured before and after the mood shifts. These variables were derived from three main sources:

1. Three of the psychological theories of depression reviewed by Beck (1967) and Mendelson (1974). Those variables related to each theory are noted in the list of variables on p. 173 by the notation "see Theory # _____."

2. The variables tried in other symptom-context studies* because of their relevance to theories of symptom formation. These formed the bulk of the variables in the list on p. 173.

3. From our reading and rereading of the process notes and transcripts of the sessions. The one additional variable derived from this source was Oedipal conflict.

The main psychological theories of depression agree that it is multifaceted and even tend to agree about many of the facets, but they differ about which are central. We will consider three theories of depression reviewed by Beck (1967) and Mendelson (1974) and some measures which we derived from them.

Theory #1: This theory is the specific Freudian theory of depression as stated in "Mourning and Melancholia" (1917/1957), which has as its core concept aggression turned inward in the form of anger at oneself,

---

*The following variables are excepted: "lack of control," because it was so similar to helplessness; "new attitude," because it would be so difficult for a judge to know which attitudes are "new" unless he knew much more about the treatment; "tired," because it appears so rarely; and "attention difficulty," because there was relatively little of it.

guilt, and self-blame. Measures derived from the theory include judges' ratings and the Gottschalk–Gleser (1969) Hostility-Inward Scale.

Theory #2: This theory is the general Freudian theory of the onset of psychological symptoms. According to this theory the patient evaluates his or her strength to deal with a potential danger situation defined in terms of expected or remembered situations of helplessness. It is the anticipation of becoming helpless which triggers the symptoms, including the depression. A number of theorists, including Horney (1957) and Goldstein (1939), have developed similar formulations. As we mentioned at the outset, there is some controversy over whether helplessness actually precedes depression or is coincident with it. Beck's cognitive theory (1967, 1972) emphasizes helplessness (Theory #2), but also involves "loss of self-esteem" (Theory #3) as well as other facets, such as "loss of supplies." Each of these involves a negative view of the self and of the future which, in turn, is related to "feeling blocked" (Beck refers to this as "feeling thwarted," implying both an affective and cognitive component). Measures derived from the theory include judges' ratings and the scale for scoring "helplessness" (see Table 5-1).

Theory #3: This theory holds that loss of self-esteem may be the main precursor of depression (as well as helplessness). Bibring's (1968) theory, which is representative of this view, stresses that "Depression can be defined as the emotional expression (indication) of a state of helplessness and powerlessness of the ego" (p. 163) and that "Depression can be defined as the emotional correlate of a partial or complete collapse of the self-esteem of the ego since it feels unable to live up to its aspirations (ego ideal, superego) while they are strongly maintained" (p. 164). Measures derived from this theory are judges' ratings.

Theory #4: Another theory, based on learned helplessness, has a large array of research to support it (Seligman, 1975). In brief, the theory holds that when a person finds he or she is helpless, the causal attribution he or she makes determines both the generality and chronicity of the helplessness deficits as well as his or her later self-esteem and possible depression. That theory will be briefly examined with the present data but presented elsewhere because of its length (Peterson, Luborsky, & Seligman, 1983).

VARIABLES TO BE MEASURED

Our principal approach toward understanding the patient's depression was to examine the context for the patient's shifts in mood toward increased or decreased depression during psychotherapy sessions. Typically, we began the analysis by a clinical review of the context for the shifts, then rated the contexts, then applied scoring systems to the contexts. Each 100-word unit of the patient's speech was rated for 17 variables:

TABLE 5-1. Helplessness versus Capability Scoring Manual

NEGATIVE POLE		POSITIVE POLE	
CATEGORIES	EXAMPLES	CATEGORIES	EXAMPLES
a– *Feeling helpless* (Feels unable to function and not confident of own ability)	I am not performing well. I don't know anything. I am unsure of myself. I can't do, respond, think. I feel inadequate. I feel ineffectual. I don't know what to do. I screwed everything up.	a+ *Feeling able to cope and not helpless*	I am doing well.
b– *Describing the situation as "too much"*	I am victimized or manipulated by _____. Things are too difficult to deal with.	b+ *Describing the situation as one which is not too much*	The job is one I can handle.
c– *Believing that relationships can give no help or gratification*	Nobody helps. You can't or aren't helping me. I'm wasting time in treatment. I don't get enjoyment from it anymore.	c+ *Believing that relationships can give help and gratification* (Affiliative behaviors shown by relationships within treatment and outside of treatment; feels he or she is benefiting from treatment)	You [therapist] are able to help me.
d– *Feeling hopeless and giving up efforts to cope*	I have given up. What's the difference? What's the use? It's useless to try. There's no sense in doing anything. Nothing is worth it. Nothing works. I can't change.	d+ *Feeling hopeful and making efforts to cope* (Initiates activities)	I suppose if I keep going things will get better.

concern about getting supplies and loss of supplies (rated as single variable), anxiety, separation anxiety, helplessness, hopelessness, blocked, blocked by therapist, guilt, hostility, hostility to therapist, depression, reflective, reference to therapist, involvement with therapist, hostility to self, loss of self-esteem or wounded self-esteem (rated as single variable), and Oedipal conflict.

We tried four scoring systems. The first three were based upon a count of the number of phrases containing the variable being examined within each 100-word unit. For scoring helplessness, we developed our own Helplessness Manual (see Table 5-1). For scoring hostility-inward we used the Gottschalk–Gleser Manual (Gottschalk & Gleser, 1969). The fourth scoring system is described on pp. 189–190 and in Peterson *et al.* (1983).

METHODS OF DETERMINING CONSISTENCY OF VARIABLES WITH THEORIES

The logic of our research approach entails examining the applicability of the measures associated with the first three theories of depression to the contexts of the depressive shifts. Since data from only one patient is presented, we cannot claim that we are testing the theories of depression; rather, we are asking only whether the shifts are consistent with what the theories would claim. For example, if, as Theory #1 states, inverted hostility was an important precursor for depression, then it should gradually increase at the moment of the shift and rise concurrently with the rise in depression. When the patient becomes less depressed, inverted hostility should begin to decrease at the shift point and continue to decrease as depression decreases. Consistency with Theory #2, the general theory of symptom formation, would require helplessness to be temporarily associated with the shift point for increased depression. When depression decreases, helplessness should decrease. The prediction for Theory #3 would be expressed similarly. It is possible that none of these theory-related variables would be associated with shifts in depression, and, therefore, we added a number of variables derived from other symptom-context studies, and one suggested by reading the transcripts.

BRIEF HISTORY OF THE PATIENT'S DEPRESSION

The treatment began just after this bright, 22-year-old man (Mr. Q) started veterinary school in a large midwestern city. The treatment was expressive–supportive psychoanalytically oriented psychotherapy. In view of the precariousness of his functioning, especially in the first year of the treatment, he did not seem a suitable candidate for psychoanalysis. In the first 3 years of the treatment there were two sessions per week and in the fourth year only one session per week.

During the year prior to starting veterinary school, his senior year at a university, he had become severely depressed, so severely that at times he found it difficult to function. He said that it started with the preoccupying thought that his girlfriend was not going to give him what he wanted—either as a friend or as a sex partner. In that period he had several months of psychotherapy with Dr. _____. According to the patient, in that treatment there was no change in the general level of his depression.

For about the first 2 years of the present treatment, severe ups and downs of depression persisted. Along with these there were also sleep disturbances, interferences with ability to concentrate, and frequent self-castigations. He seemed, to himself, to have no way of controlling the onset or termination of the depressions, nor was he even able at the beginning of the present treatment to identify the nature of his affect as being depression. Toward the end of the first 2 years of the treatment, he began to label his state more clearly as depression and to recognize its onset and termination. In the last 2 years of the treatment, the patient showed only relatively mild and brief depressions and more general equanimity in the face of severe external difficulties—such as the necessity of dealing with the depression of the woman he had married during the last 6 months of his treatment. He was functioning better in school and planning on his practicum with a relatively high degree of anticipatory confidence and satisfaction.

Diagnostically, in terms of DSM-III, the patient would be considered a dysthymic disorder with depressive-neurosis (300.40), meaning that these diagnostic criteria were fulfilled:

1. During the past two years he has been bothered most of the time by symptoms characteristic of the depressive syndrome.
2. The syndrome has been separated by periods of normal mood lasting a few days to a few weeks, but no more than a few months at a time.
3. During the depressive periods, there was prominent depressed mood with marked loss of interest in almost all of the usual activities.
4. During the depressed periods, these symptoms were present: insomnia; low energy level; feelings of inadequacy; decreased effectiveness in school work; decreased attention, concentration, or ability to think clearly, especially concentrational difficulty; social withdrawal; loss of interest in or enjoyment of pleasurable activities; inability to respond with pleasure to praise; less active or talkative than usual; pessimistic attitude toward the future, brooding about past events and feeling sorry for himself.
5. Absence of psychotic features.

METHODS FOR UNDERSTANDING SHIFTS IN DEPRESSION DURING SESSIONS

Understanding the context of the patient's repeated mood shifts was achieved by applying successive methods of analysis with the increased rigor of measurement in each. We began with clinical inspection and reinspection of the contexts (Method 1); then we derived categories for rating the contexts and added some from other symptom-context research (Method 2); finally we fashioned or selected process scoring systems for some of the categories to be rated (Method 3).

METHOD 1: CLINICAL INSPECTION OF CONTEXT

Method 1 consisted of a clinical analysis of the context of each depressive shift. The simplest way to give the reader a sense of what the depressive shifts were about is to present a précis of the context of each patient–therapist exchange at the time of the shift, especially just before it, for each of the nine shifts, and then to perform the clinical exercise of finding the main themes across instances (as in Luborsky, 1977).

Shifts toward Decreased Depression

Session #60 (p. 7 of transcript): The therapist interpreted the reason for the patient's depression as wanting the therapist to shove him out of the depression. The patient agreed and then snapped out of his depression.

Session #77 (p. 14 of transcript): The therapist made a long interpretation about the patient's relationship with him: "When you want to get closer and you're not getting the response you want, then you fall into depression." The patient agreed and then snapped out of his depression, but explained his decreased depression on the basis of having just looked at a note in his hand, which he had brought with him to the session, reminding him that the *Merck Manual* says that depression is due to lots of things and, therefore, was not due to the "total abject hopelessness of the real facts."

Session #144 (p. 17 of transcript): The patient was very angry at the therapist and felt like "ripping out your [the therapist's] bookshelf." His depression then lifted.

Session #172 (pp. 14–15 of transcript): The therapist said, "You were in a lost state and all alone in relation to me," and the patient then asked, "What do you want me to do?" The therapist replied, "Pull out of the depression." The patient did. The technique here involved both interpreting the conflict specifically in terms of relationship to the therapist and then using the patient's accessibility by directing him to pull out of his depression. A brief excerpt from the transcript of about 200 patient words before and 200 words after the shift illustrates the technique.

P: . . . longer ago than I thought. It's been bad since the last pharmacology exam which I didn't do well in. I mean I did all right but I didn't take it feeling well.

T: Oh, you did all right and it sounds like ever since this uh . . .

P: Well . . .

T: . . . new girlfriend that you've been getting more worried.

P: Probably that's where it starts but, but—I—you know, what am I gonna do? I mean . . .

T: Well apparently the first thing is to see if you, you can't get out of this state you're in. The state in which you feel . . .

P: Well, sure.

T: . . . that nothing I say and nothing you say can be heard.

P: Yeah.

T: All that can be heard is this cry for help, kind of, thing: "There is nothing I can do." You've sort of given up almost.

P: Well, I don't know. I th—it's like I've been trying to forg—all this time and I—for two years and then I—I still don't seem to have the tools to be able to do anything about it.

T: It varies. It varies very much.

P: Hm. Yeah, but, I know it varies. For four months [300-word point] I could do what I wanted but then all of a sudden . . . May—I mean maybe I wasn't doing what I was wanted. I was messing around with some chick who meant nothing to me and, and who was just a good lay.

T: Well, once you get in this state then everything gets interpreted in terms of it. You say . . .

P: I know.

T: . . . everything!

P: Well, I don't, I don't know what to do. I'm lost. I really feel . . .

T: That's what I'm reacting to. You're in this kind of lost state where somehow you feel out of reach. You're crying all alone a lot.

P: Yeah. I am. I—I don't know that anyone can do anything. I mean I'm, I'm, I'm at a lo—I uh—I feel like going now. I mean I don't know what to do. I mean I'm really not—I don't know. (*pause*) Okay. What do you want me to do?

T: See if you can't get this state under control so we can start to go over what's happening.

P: Okay. What do you want me to do? I'll stop it. **(SHIFT POINT)** What? [400-word point]

T: Well, now let's go over what it is and see if it has some meaning to you. That all these—about 20 minutes or so, 25 minutes or so—you've been saying a lot but you haven't been able to listen to any of it somehow.

P: No.

T: Y'know, both of us can agree about a lot of it but it isn't meaningful somehow . . .

P: Right.

T: And you're saying you just can't stop it. The state can be called, kind of, crying alone. I don't know whether that—*that* seems to describe it to me. You're not with yourself and you're not with me. Neither one.

P: Yeah.

T: What—suppose you try and describe it. Does it say—it sounds like you're alone and it sounds like you're crying and you're saying someone else has to do something. There's nothing *you* can do. Doesn't it feel that way, like you've sort of thrown in the towel you've given up?

P: Yeah, that's exactly what I'm doing. You see I'm—now I'm trying not to but I . . . I don't know.

T: I know you're trying not to and it felt to me like somehow that part of you which had been obliterated suddenly asserted itself again. It said, Okay, here I am . . .

P: No, it was there all the time. I just didn't feel I should show it then, or something.

T: Why not?

P: I don't . . . 'Cause I, I didn't ha—I don't know. Probably because I want to make you suffer or something like that. Because I'm trying to—to show you that you're no good or that I'm—that I'm right or something like that.

T: All right. And I'm no good because, because you're no good, why . . .

P: Yeah.

T: I'm no good because I can't help you out of that state . . .

P: Exactly. Right. I mean th—th—th—th—uh—uh you can be depressed an' it's a wonderful weapon. I mean like if I left here depressed I—I don't know. I—I'm sure you'd learn how to deal with it but, I mean, you know, at least to my untrained eye, looking at it from my prospective view, if a patient leaves a doctor and he's still terribly depressed it's an—and you're pissed off at him, too it's a good way of getting at 'im, I mean . . .

T: All right. Okay.

P: I mean, I should suspect, you know, you know how to deal with that but, but, eh, at least it'ssss a weapon but all right, see, I'm . . .

T: Okay, now that you know . . .

P: . . . it's just general hostility.

T: Okay, now that you're back with yourself it really begins to make sense . . .

P: I could hate you . . ."

Session #175 (p. 18 of transcript): The therapist told the patient that things were not bad; it was just the way he saw them when he was depressed. Then when the patient was more accessible, the therapist said, "Enough of this." The patient then pulled out of his depression.

Shifts toward Increased Depression

Session #135 (p. 5 of transcript): The patient referred to a dream of himself and a girl, a girl who could be gotten by a much stronger man than he. The patient then got depressed.

Session #135 (p. 11 of transcript): The therapist referred to the patient's conception of the role of a patient and the therapist as a situation involving one person being inferior to the other. The patient's depression then increased. He explained that he was going to talk about his relationship with a divorced woman, where he felt inadequate in relation to her greater experience.

Session #138 (p. 11 of transcript): The patient was thinking over whether he should or should not write to a girl that he wanted to write to. He found himself unable to speak to the therapist and then got depressed.

Session #144 (pp. 21–22 of transcript): The patient was speaking of hating his father. He began to get guilty and then depressed. The guilt was how the patient explained his depression just after it increased. A brief excerpt shows this very clearly.

P: . . . he [father] was poor, see, and I was always taught that they were kind of bad. I was. Really!

T: By whom?

P: Guys like Johnny, or Robert, and, and, and, and Jane. You know what it was, I mean, really. He spit, too. I remember they said, "Your father spits." And, I mean, I don't know. I've never know—I guess he does. But, I remember it, and I was a poor, and so was he. Well, I guess, that's something I could've forgiven him for maybe. Hated Sunday School. (*pause*)

T: It was too easy to forget that uh he was your father and that was too easy to think you could put *him* on his ass.

P: Well, I don't know. I probably just felt bad about it. I didn't want to fight [300-word point] with him.

T: That's exactly what you did. You felt that you had to feel bad everytime you thought of sticking him on his ass.

P: Yeah, but I never did.

T: You never did but you often wanted to.

P: Heh, no, I don't think I ever did wa—think of . . . Y'know, I don't—I mean—there was never anything to fight about. Well there was thing—reasons to fight—okay, I guess I am s . . . I hate 'im now sometimes but (*sigh*), I mean, he never did a damn thing. He was useless. He made money. I mean, all right, I will consider him within the—his historical milieu and, and, blah blah blah and Depressions and not having anything to eat and all that shit—But I—I—I don't know. (**SHIFT POINT**)

[400-word point] This—this just confuses me. This isn't doing me too much good.

T: Why not?

P: I don't know, 'cause I don't feel good now again.

T: Well what was—what did you say that made you not feel good right then?

P: 'Cause I just got all back and depressed again when I wasn't. I was out ten percent then.

T: That's right, you were. Then catch what made you feel all depressed again.

P: Something about my father, I guess.

T: Yes.

P: I don't know. I was fighting him or something.

T: Yes.

P: That I hated him.

T: Yes. Yes.

P: Why I had to feel guilty about . . .

T: Yes.

P: . . . hating him?

T: Yes.

P: Well, I guess you do. You have to love your father, and all that shit.

T: Right. Yeah. And so if you hate him and you feel like fighting him and setting him on his ass, then you have to feel depressed about the whole damn thing.

P: And it's therefore I feel that way with all males.

T: Honest to God you do."

One clinical generalization that fits all nine depressive shifts is that their context reflects stressful patient–therapist exchanges. Those five shifts in which the patient decreased his depression were ones involving an interpretation about the relationship by the therapist with which the patient agreed and which pulled him into a closer positive relationship with the therapist. The increased positive response derived either from the therapist's interpretation of the conflict in the relationship and/or through a fairly direct statement that the patient could or should put aside his depression.

The four instances in which the patient increased his depression were usually ones where the patient (rather than the therapist) was speaking before the shift. The immediate trigger for increased depression appears to be patient-determined—the patient came upon a theme that made him feel helpless. Usually the theme was comparing himself with another man and feeling inferior and inadequate. The two instances in Session #144 are good examples of what tipped the balance toward or away from depression. In the shift on page 17 of that session's transcript, the patient felt angry and spoke of wanting to rip out the therapist's bookshelf. Being able to speak in this way and to express his anger seemed to make him feel strong, so that his depression decreased—in Freud's terms, the hostility was not turned inward. In the other instance in the same session (p. 21 of the transcript) he had a similar thought, but involving anger at his father. He began to feel guilty, inferior, and helpless because he had such thoughts, and then felt more depressed. In terms of Freud's theory, hostility-inward is clearly expressed in this instance.*

After reading the same four examples of increases in depression, other clinicians, despite slightly different emphases, had a strong core of agreement about the issue of competition with men and resulting feelings of helplessness. These are examples of the comments by four outstanding psychoanalysts: (1) "He is mainly preoccupied with taking a woman from you; secondly, with helplessness." (2) "Whenever he feels hubris, he has a depressive shift, for example, in showing the therapist his wedding ring or speaking of throwing father on his ass." (3) "He has hostility to the therapist that threatens the narcissistic union with the therapist." (4) "Helplessness is outstanding in all the examples. Secondly, the pre-Oedipal level sets the stage for the response to frustration on the Oedipal level."

METHOD 2: RATINGS OF SEGMENTS
BEFORE VERSUS AFTER THE SYMPTOM

In Method 2, ratings of each of the nine segments—the five toward decreased depression and the four toward increased depression—were made independently by two clinically trained judges who had had some training in the rating of the 17 variables. Each rating was done on a graphic 5-point scale (with half-point divisions permitted). Both of these judges were aware of the hypotheses about depression in the published literature and of the point of the depressive mood shift in the segments.

Interjudge Reliability

Each judge rated the nine segments independently for each of the eight 100-word units of patient's speech, that is, the four 100-word units before the shift and the four 100-word units after the shift. The correlations were

---

*Freud's theory (1917/1957) involving hostility-inward is obviously much more complex than is represented by that one variable. For example, Freud also speaks about using the hostility to hurt the introjected object. This component of the theory seems to be represented in the patient's explanations after the instance in Session #172, p. 15 of transcript, where the patient speaks (p. 16) of using the depression "to make you suffer" and comments, "it's a wonderful weapon."

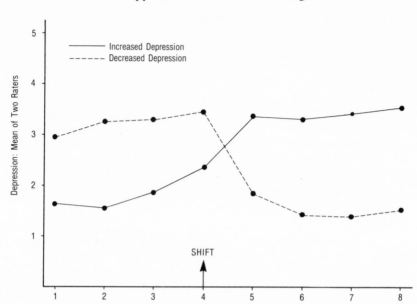

FIGURE 5-1. DEPRESSION RATINGS BEFORE AND AFTER THE SHIFT.

based on an *n* of 72. This appeared to be an adequate method since we wished only to know how these variables covaried. The loss of independence seemed preferable to the loss of information which would have resulted from combining all eight 100-word units for each segment. Therefore, we have not computed significance tests.

As shown in Table 5-2, the interjudge correlations were generally satisfactory in level and somewhat similar to the levels of reliability obtained for those variables in other symptom-context studies (e.g., Luborsky *et al.*, 1975). The highest of the reliabilities, .87, was for the criterion variable depression; helplessness was next highest, .81; concern about supplies was .77; hostility to self, .52; and loss of self-esteem, .51.

Depression Ratings and Other Correlated Variables before versus after the Point of the Depressive Mood Shifts

Now we are ready to present our main results—the kinds of changes which were associated with the patient's shift points. We begin by giving the results of ratings of depression before and after the shift points. Figure 5-1 shows the mean rating for the two judges over the eight 100-word units for the four segments with increased depression and the five segments with decreased depression. The shape of these curves turned out to be

TABLE 5-2. Reliability of Variables (Interjudge Agreement)

| | CORRELATIONS | |
VARIABLE	PER JUDGE	POOLED RATINGS[a]
RATINGS		
1. Concern about supplies	.77	.86
2. Anxiety	.44	.61
3. Separation anxiety	.26	.27
4. Helplessness	.81	.91
5. Hopelessness	.73	.84
6. Blocked	.70	.82
7. Blocked by therapist	.54	.67
8. Guilt	.43	.53
9. Hostility	.69	.82
10. Hostility to therapist	.67	.80
11. Depression	.87	.93
12. Reflective	.47	.64
13. Reference to therapist	.69	.72
14. Involvement with therapist	.63	.74
15. Hostility to self (see Theory 1)	.52	.56
16. Loss of self-esteem (see Theory 3)	.51	.66
17. Oedipal conflict	.50	.66
SCORINGS		
18. Hostility-inward (Total)[b] (see Theory 1)		
19. Hostility-inward ($a + b$) (see Theory 1)		
20. Hostility-inward (c) (see Theory 1)		
21. Helplessness Manual score (see Theory 2)		
22. Attributional style (see Theory 4)[c]		

[a]Judges BS and JH; [b]Gottschalk & Gleser (1969); [c]Peterson, Luborsky, & Seligman (1983).

what had been anticipated beforehand. The increased depression curve shoots up at the end of the fourth segment and remains up. The decreased depression curve drops down at the end of the fourth segment and remains down. The curves also reveal that in the segments in which the patient was most depressed, the ratings were just a little over "3.0," indicating moderate depression. The shifts to increased depression that we are dealing with, therefore, are not really marked shifts—they are shifts from a mean of about 1.5 to a little over 3.0; the same occurs in reverse for the shifts toward lessened depression.

Helplessness is the variable that is most similar to depression in the shape of its curve (Figure 5-2) and in its intercorrelations (Table 5-3). Higher intercorrelations are shown for depression and helplessness ratings than for any other pair of variables: .95 (before) and .99 (after) for pooled

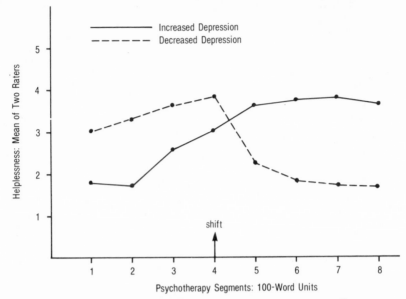

FIGURE 5-2. HELPLESSNESS RATINGS BEFORE AND AFTER THE SHIFT.

ratings. (As noted earlier, eight 100-word units were rated for each of the nine segments). Although the level of the helplessness curve happens to be slightly higher and its onset is slightly earlier than the curve for depression, the anticipation is not significant. Guilt, hostility-to-self, hopelessness, and loss of self-esteem (Figures 5-3–5-6) follow a pattern which is similar to depression, especially after the shift, as do the variables blocked and concern about supplies (Figures 5-7 and 5-8). Blocked by therapist (Figure 5-9) does not fit this pattern as clearly, however.

It is noteworthy, therefore, that the helplessness–hopelessness dimension is especially closely associated with the depression curve and also that every one of the variables which we listed as associated with the three concepts of depression have curves which are similar to the depression curves. The remaining variables are less correlated with the depression curves: anxiety, separation anxiety, hostility, hostility to therapist, reflective, reference to therapist, involvement with therapist, and Oedipal conflict.

In another analysis, significance tests were performed on the variables using a 2-factor analysis of variance in which type of segment (increasing vs. decreasing depression) was considered a between-subject factor and location (before vs. after the shift) was considered a repeated measures factor. (The data were averaged over the four 100-word units before the shift and over the four 100-word units after the shift.) The results indicated

TABLE 5-3. INTERCORRELATIONS OF VARIABLES

VARIABLES	1	2	3	4	5	6	7	8	9	10	11	12	13	14	15	16	17	18	19	20	21	22
Ratings																						
1. Concern about supplies		11	11	74	76	72	01	55	-69	-25	73	-57	02	-19	78	80	-22	58	11	59	62	-37
2. Anxiety	73		09	04	-28	-41	-38	-37	-49	-36	-10	29	-10	-50	09	-22	-01	-29	-01	-30	-14	50
3. Separation anxiety	07	-03		-16	-14	-11	-54	27	24	-43	-18	24	-36	-54	-07	14	79	-15	42	-21	-17	29
4. Helplessness	71	86	-19		92	78	11	58	-47	-09	99	-91	-08	-08	83	78	-46	88	22	89	97	-52
5. Hopelessness	77	83	-24	91		89	29	68	-40	02	95	-95	05	11	76	82	-45	94	19	96	93	-72
6. Blocked	83	90	-15	97	94		42	61	-20	31	84	-81	-05	35	62	77	-42	73	00	76	79	-80
7. Blocked by therapist	60	42	-59	65	66	64		-14	11	81	17	-22	26	92	-25	-20	-56	14	-58	22	16	-83
8. Guilt	74	82	-23	93	95	94	61		-04	-24	65	-60	02	-25	69	75	21	72	14	65	65	-28
9. Hostility	11	-38	-26	-15	-22	-21	40	-07		34	-40	30	10	28	-63	-44	49	-58	-62	-31	-29	01
10. Hostility to therapist	39	18	-52	25	22	28	82	23	60		-05	-05	11	94	-32	-26	-50	-10	05	-04	-04	-64
11. Depression	84	78	-14	95	93	97	70	95	-06	-05		-95	-20	-01	82	81	-05	92	23	93	99	-59
12. Reflective	33	05	23	-19	10	-03	-04	12	15	31	02		25	39	-74	-78	53	-97	-59	-98	-96	66
13. Reference to therapist	07	09	-61	-16	05	-05	26	02	10	11	-14	25		77	-34	-35	-55	-33	-62	-27	-28	-46
14. Involvement with therapist	57	46	-43	42	58	46	78	52	37	46	87	39	60		-35	-25	-58	75	49	05	-02	-72
15. Hostility to self	75	93	-11	89	94	93	49	95	-28	72	93	43	08	53		90	-28	77	75	72	77	-17
16. Loss of self-esteem	78	94	-06	96	89	98	52	93	-24	13	-10	19	-08	40	90		-21	66	74	75	76	-32
17. Oedipal conflict	08	-30	68	-24	-20	-18	-42	-30	-38	21	-05	-01	-61	-58	-28	-21		-32	47	40	41	56
Scorings																						
18. Hostility-Inward (Total)[a]	70	62	-38	69	89	73	76	81	06	46	77	38	31	81	79	66	-32		38	99	95	-58
19. Hostility-Inward (a + b)	49	79	02	69	81	70	26	79	-29	-06	65	32	02	46	89	74	-27	74		27	28	29
20. Hostility-Inward (c)	63	30	-56	46	65	52	89	56	30	69	61	30	42	81	46	38	-26	87	31		95	-64
21. Helplessness Manual score	74	79	-44	93	92	93	81	90	-05	43	91	-13	14	62	84	87	-38	79	59	68		-58
22. Attributional style[b]	66	86	29	82	79	83	18	82	-40	-20	78	08	-29	21	89	88	02	51	82	12	66	

(Upper triangle = AFTER; lower triangle = BEFORE)

Note. Intercorrelations of variables are based on nine segments, each with data averaged over four 100-word units before the shift and four 100-word units after the shift. Decimal points are omitted. Numbers below the diagonal were before the shift and those above the diagonal were after the shift. [a]Gottschalk & Gleser (1969); [b]Peterson, Luborsky, & Seligman (1983).

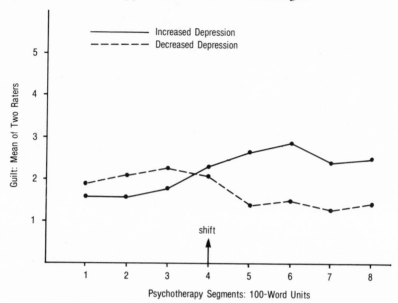

FIGURE 5-3. GUILT RATINGS BEFORE AND AFTER THE SHIFT.

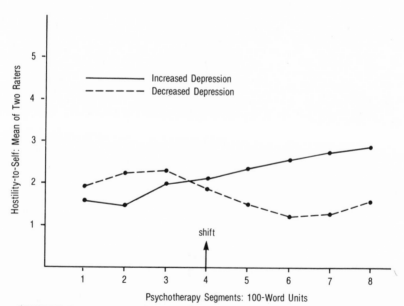

FIGURE 5-4. HOSTILITY-TO-SELF RATINGS BEFORE AND AFTER THE SHIFT.

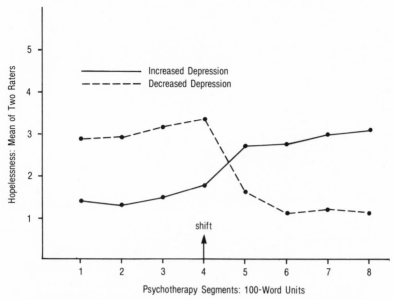

FIGURE 5-5. HOPELESSNESS RATINGS BEFORE AND AFTER THE SHIFT.

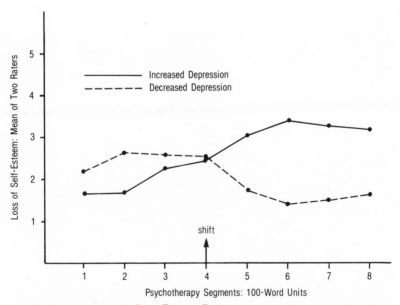

FIGURE 5-6. LOSS OF SELF-ESTEEM RATINGS BEFORE AND AFTER THE SHIFT.

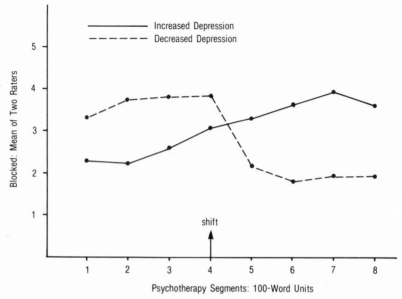

FIGURE 5-7. BLOCKED RATINGS BEFORE AND AFTER THE SHIFT.

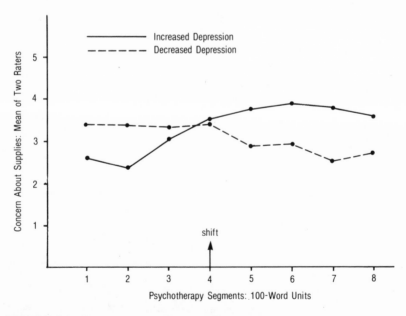

FIGURE 5-8. CONCERN ABOUT SUPPLIES RATINGS BEFORE AND AFTER THE SHIFT.

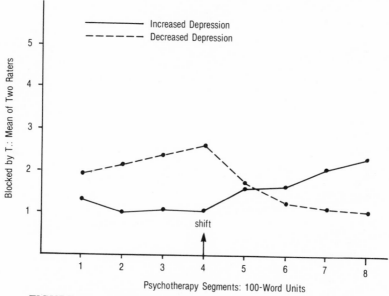

FIGURE 5-9. BLOCKED BY T RATINGS BEFORE AND AFTER THE SHIFT.

that five variables (anxiety, blocked, guilt, hostility to self, and loss of self-esteem) had significant ($p < .05$) F-ratios for type of segment, and one variable, hostility-inward ($a + b$), had a significant ($p < .05$) F-ratio for location. However, all six variables had significant ($p < .01$) type of segment by location interaction terms which qualify the interpretation of the main effects. In addition, several other variables (concern about supplies, helplessness, hopelessness, blocked by therapist, depression, hostility-inward (total), hostility-inward (c), Helplessness Manual scores) also yielded significant ($p < .05$, at least) type of segment by location interaction effects. In order to understand the nature of these interaction effects, separate analyses of variance were computed for the increased depression segments and also for the decreased depression segments using location (before vs. after the shift) as the only factor. The important changes can be discerned by a listing of those variables which significantly differ before versus after the shift in order of those with the highest F-ratios ranked first (Table 5-4). For the increased depression segments this is the order: increases in loss of self-esteem, helplessness, depression, hostility to self, Helplessness Manual score, hostility-inward (total), involvement with therapist, and blocked. For the decreased depression segments this is the order: decreases in blocked, guilt, hostility to self, depression, hopelessness, anxiety, Helplessness Manual score, loss of self-esteem.

TABLE 5-4. *F*-RATIOS FROM ANALYSES OF VARIANCE COMPARING FOUR 100-WORD UNITS BEFORE SHIFT VERSUS FOUR 100-WORD UNITS AFTER SHIFT

VARIABLES	4 INCREASED DEPRESSION SEGMENTS		5 DECREASED DEPRESSION SEGMENTS	
Ratings		*Rank*[a]		*Rank*
1. Concern about supplies	4.38		11.88*	
2. Anxiety	2.47		16.69*	(6)
3. Separation anxiety	4.42		< 1	
4. Helplessness	46.68**	(2)	12.47*	
5. Hopelessness	9.63		22.25**	(5)
6. Blocked	12.84*	(6)	132.26***	(1)
7. Blocked by therapist	6.40		3.46	
8. Guilt	9.64		52.07**	(2)
9. Hostility	< 1		< 1	
10. Hostility to therapist	5.87		1.30	
11. Depression	36.77**	(3)	30.89**	(4)
12. Reflective	1.18		3.17	
13. Reference to therapist	1.71		1.27	
14. Involvement with therapist	15.71*	(5)	1	
15. Hostility to self	20.50*	(4)	31.84**	(3)
16. Loss of self-esteem	54.98**	(1)	11.56*	
17. Oedipal conflict	2.78		1.15	
Scorings				
18. Hostility-Inward (Total)[b]	17.13*		4.73	
19. Hostility-Inward ($a + b$)	7.78		4.38	
20. Hostility-Inward (c)	6.68		6.31	
21. Helplessness Manual score	17.18*		13.02*	
22. Attributional style[c]				

[a]For example, from before to after the mood shift to increased depression, the loss of self-esteem was greatest of all the variables examined, that is, Rank (1).
[b]Gottschalk & Gleser (1969).
[c]Peterson, Luborsky, & Seligman (1983).
*$p < .05$, **$p < .01$, ***$p < .001$.

METHOD 3: ANALYSES BY SCORING SYSTEMS

Methods for analysis in addition to clinical review and ratings were needed to provide even more objective methods to deal with two problems: (1) measuring with still more precision some of the variables which we had estimated by ratings, and (2) lessening the possibility of contamination of judges with information about the point of the shifts. The results of two scoring systems will be given: a new system for scoring helplessness (Luborsky, 1976), a Hostility-Inward Scale (Gottschalk & Gleser, 1969), and, in addition, a third system, analyses of patient's voice and speech rate.

A Helplessness Manual Scoring System (see Table 5-1)

A scoring scale (Luborsky, 1976) was constructed for helplessness, one of the most theoretically central variables, and the related variable hopelessness. The scale contained four categories of items, some derived from Engel and Schmale's (1967) "giving-up–given-up" complex: (1) feeling helpless, (2) describing the situation as "too much," that is, too difficult to deal with, (3) believing that relationships can give no help or gratification, and (4) feeling hopeless and giving up efforts to cope. (The Helplessness Manual also has a positive pole which was not used for the analyses presented here.) The text was divided into phrases, then every phrase containing a scorable item was underlined and the scores noted in the margin. Only the main score given to each phrase was summed for the present analyses.

Interjudge reliability for scoring the Helplessness Manual was high, $r = .86$ for Judges BS versus JH. The curves for the Helplessness Manual scores (Figure 5-10), based on the sums of scores for the two judges, were very similar to those for ratings of helplessness. The correlation between the Helplessness Manual scores and the helplessness ratings was .83. These results, therefore, were helpful in providing more objective assessments for our previous observations about helplessness.

A Hostility-Inward Scoring System

This variable, crucial to Freud's theory (1917/1957) theory of depression, was independently scored on the Gottschalk and Gleser (1969) scoring system by Dr. Carolyn Winget, an expert on the scales. The value of these results was augmented by the fact that the expert only had the transcripts and knew nothing about our study. Her results (Figure 5-11) provided curves of the same shape as those from our ratings.

The items in the Gottschalk–Gleser Hostility-Inward Scale are composed of 11 subtypes. These, in turn, fit into three main subtypes, a, b, and c: a and b consist of items which refer explicitly to anger at the self, that is, they are more directly an estimate of hostility-inward, while c refers to "disappointment, loneliness, discouragement, giving up hope, despairing, grieving, being depressed, having no purpose in life." In other words, these c items are more related to depression than are the a and b items. Moderate correlations between their Hostility-Inward Scale (Total) and various depression scales are reported in Gottschalk and Gleser (1969): (1) for 19 patients on psychiatric wards, the Wittenborn (1955) subscale labeled "depressed state" (five items similar to hostility-inward) correlated .66, and the correlation with the total Wittenborn Depressed State Scale was .35; (2) for 24 depressed and nondepressed inpatients, the hostility-inward scores correlated .48 with the depression scale of the Adjective Checklist (Gleser, 1960) and .47 with the Beck Depression Inventory

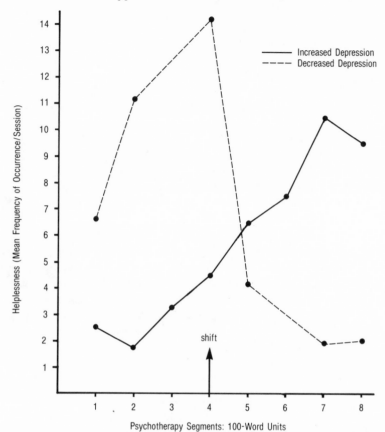

FIGURE 5-10. HELPLESSNESS MANUAL SCORES BEFORE AND AFTER THE SHIFT.

(Beck, 1967); (3) For 50 psychiatric outpatients in psychiatric treatment, the correlation with the Beck Depression Inventory was .34, and .52 with the depression score on the Adjective Checklist.

In our data, hostility-inward (*c*) score correlated .61 with depression ratings, while hostility-inward (*a* + *b*) items correlated only .31 with depression ratings. In sum, the hostility-inward scores, especially the subtype *c*, appear to reflect depression and show the same main trends in relation to the shift points. Since this hostility-inward depression measure is completely independently assessed, it serves to reduce the kind of contamination to which the ratings were vulnerable.

Analyses of Voice and Speech Rate

The Presence of Shifts in Affect Recognizable in Voice Quality
To further examine what is shifting, we decided to go beyond inferences from the transcript and reexamine the affect component of depression by

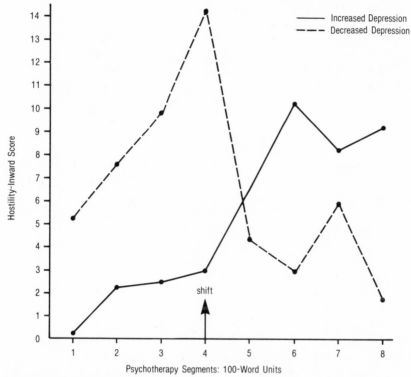

FIGURE 5-11. Hostility-Inward Scores (Total) before and after the Shift.

listening to the tape recordings. (A variety of emotions, such as grief and anger, have been shown to be judgeable from voice qualities; see, for example, Markel, Meisels, & Houck, 1964; Costanzo, Markel, & Costanzo, 1969). Two judges working independently listened to the tapes of the nine segments and rated the affect of depression. The first finding was that depressive tone in the voice could be recognized with a high degree of agreement by the two judges ($r = .89$, BS vs. JH). The next finding was that the depressive shifts were usually accompanied by recognizable shifts in depressive tone in the voice: For both judges the ratings for only two of the nine segments did not include a shift in depressive tone, and for three more, the shift was only moderate. For the other four segments, the shift in depressive tone was commensurate with what had been inferred from the transcript alone. This analysis suggested that transcript analysis restricts the judges' access to cues to affective tone. It may be, therefore, that the results of such analysis overplay the cognition of helplessness as a main component of depression ratings and somewhat underestimate the affective component of depression.

The Presence of Shifts in Rate of Speech
Coincident with Depression

We suspected that the patient's rate of speech slowed as he became more depressed and speeded up as he became less depressed. Since rate of speech, sometimes called fluency, is thought to change in relation to change in depressive mood (e.g., Cattell, 1950), Aronson & Weintraub (1967) compared improved depressed patients with unimproved depressed patients on a 10-minute sample of speech. As predicted, the improved patients spoke at a more normal rate of speech than the less improved patients.

Our own observations were based upon moment-to-moment shifts in depression in relation to the rate of speech and provided some evidence along the lines we expected. The curve for the eight 100-word units was examined for each of the nine segments in terms of the lowest point versus the highest point on the curve. Starting with the four increased depression segments, all four showed their lowest point of speech rate after the shift. For the five decreased depression segments, three of the five showed a point of increased speech rate after the shift. Taking the nine segments together, therefore, seven out of the nine showed consistency in these terms.

Another way to analyze the same data is in terms of the direction of the change in rate of speech. Of the four increased depression segments, all four showed a slowing in speech rate. The five decreased depression segments did not show the same consistency in terms of change in speech rate: from the third to the fourth 100-word unit, only one of the five showed increased speech rate, and from the third to the fifth, only two of the five showed an increase in speech rate.

WHAT HAS BEEN LEARNED ABOUT THE CONTEXT OF MR. Q'S SHIFTS IN DEPRESSION

In this section we will integrate what has been learned about the context for shifts in depression, how the main variables intercorrelated with each other, and especially the temporal correlation of helplessness and depression. Finally, we will try to synthesize the quantitative and clinical analyses with each other as well as with another perspective of depression, based upon attributional style.

THE CONTEXT VARIABLES FOR SHIFTS IN DEPRESSION

For this depression-prone patient, the context variables which changed most before and after the patient-identified shifts in depression were those related to the first three theories of depression. The variables included helplessness (related to Theory #2), hopelessness (related to Theory #2), loss of self-esteem (Theory #3), blocked, and blocked by therapist (probably related to helplessness and hopelessness), and guilt and hostility to self (both associated with Theory #1). The temporal associations of these variables with depression are obvious from inspection of the curves for these variables: They shift markedly in relation to the patient-identified shifts in depression, in the direction that would be expected from increased versus decreased depression segments. In essence, all the variables selected from the three theories were prominently represented in the symptom-onset context for this patient, even though each was chosen from a different theory of the onset of depression. This result is not entirely unexpected, since these multifaceted theories contain similar elements which receive differing degrees of emphasis in each theory.

So far we have discussed only theory-related variables. However, because our exploration was not limited to variables derived from these theories, we were open to the possibility of discovery of other shift-related concepts. But none of these appeared.

Helplessness and related variables are not only important for the shifts in depression of this patient but have been found to be prominent for other symptoms in other patients: for example, stomach pain report, migraine headache report, petit mal seizures as shown on the EEG, and others (Luborsky, 1967, 1970; Luborsky & Auerbach, 1969; Luborsky et al., 1975). It did not matter how a symptom was identified—the presence of stomach pain and migraine headache was established by the patient's report of the symptom while the petit mal seizures were identified in the objective EEG measures. In all of the single-case symptom-context studies (Luborsky, 1970), helplessness is a discriminating variable more often than other variables. Therefore, as Freud's general theory of symptom formation holds (1926/1959), helplessness is generally connected with the onset of symptoms and is not specific to the onset of depression.

THE INTERCORRELATIONS AMONG THE VARIABLES

The main variables which shift as the shift points are approached appear to be part of a global constellation, as revealed by their intercorrelations (Table 5-3). An even clearer view is presented in a cluster sketch of a few of the main theory-related variables (Figure 5-12). Ratings of depression and helplessness correlated very highly with each other (.95 before; .99 after). The other theory-related variables' ratings also correlated highly with the more objective Helplessness Manual scores, which suggests much overlap in what they measure.

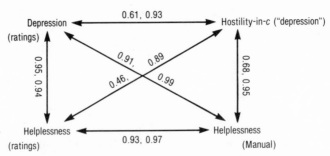

FIGURE 5-12. Cluster Sketch of Principal Intercorrelations. The First Correlation Is before the Shift, the Second is after.

The Temporal Coincidence of Helplessness and Depression

The high correlation level (Table 5-3) of .95 (before) and .99 (after) between helplessness and depression ratings supports the view of those who claim that judgments of helplessness and judgments of depression are almost indistinguishable. Nevertheless, the temporal relationships of helplessness and depression ratings as well as those of their more objective counterparts, the Helplessness Manual scores and hostility-inward (c) scores, may still show a slight prior slope of the onset for the helplessness curve (Figures 5-1, 5-2, 5-10, 5-11).

A new step will allow a closer comparison: The two rated measures and their two objective counterparts are converted to standard scores and replotted on the same graphs. The increased depression segments (Figure 5-13) are the ones of greatest interest only because theories of depression pay so much more attention to explaining increased depression than to explaining overcoming depression. We now can readily see (1) the considerable correspondence in the shape of the curves; (2) that the changes in mood and helplessness have already begun to occur between 100 to 200 words before the reported shift; (3) that the helplessness ratings do antecede the depression ratings at the 300- and 400-word units but nonsignificantly; and (4) that the Helplessness Manual scores antecede the hostility-inward (c) scores (depression) at the 400- and 500-word units, but nonsignificantly; however, they are reversed at the 200-word unit.

For the decreased depression segments (Figure 5-14), the curves are the reverse of the curves for the increased depression segments. There is considerable synchrony in the four measures; as a whole it is the agreement which is more impressive than the slight temporal differences. However, if the theory expects increased helplessness before increased depression, then the reverse should be true for decreased depression. In fact this is true; the Helplessness Manual score decreases *before* the depression score, that is, the hostility-inward (c) score, but nonsignificantly.

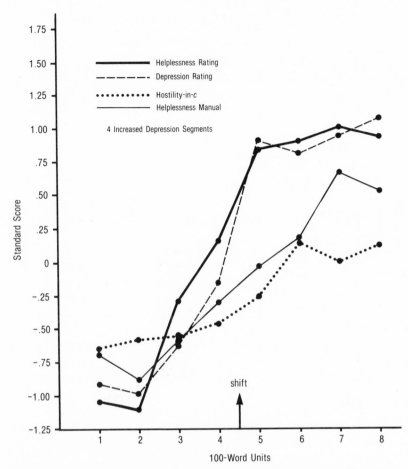

FIGURE 5-13. STANDARD SCORES PLOTTED OVER TIME FOR THE TWO RATED MEASURES OF HELPLESSNESS AND DEPRESSION, AND THE TWO SCORED MEASURES OF HELPLESSNESS AND DEPRESSION [HOSTILITY-INWARD (C)] FOR THE FOUR INCREASED DEPRESSION SEGMENTS.

INTEGRATING THE QUANTITATIVE ANALYSES WITH THE CLINICAL ANALYSES

We have presented inferences, derived from ratings and scores, about the context for Mr. Q's shifts in state. To achieve broader dimensions of understanding, these inferences have to be reembedded in the larger framework of the clinical analyses even though clinical analyses are not as easily subjected to reliability tests. For inference-making, a profitable mutual interaction should exist: The clinical analyses suggest variables which may be objectively measured; the quantitative results, in turn, derive added meaning from the clinical framework.

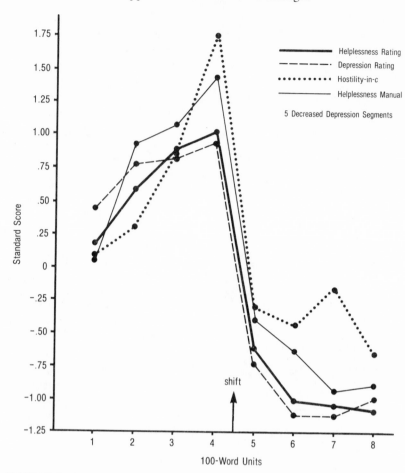

FIGURE 5-14. Standard Scores Plotted over Time for the Two Rated Measures of Helplessness and Depression, and the Two Scored Measures of Helplessness and Depression [Hostility-Inward (C)] for the Five Decreased Depression Segments.

Further inspection of the patient–therapist interactions around the shift point revealed.that the moments of shift in mood were embedded in moments of a shift in the patient–therapist relationship (see pp. 170–171). Some of the shifts in this relationship are reflected in a nonsignificant increase in explicit references to the therapist as the shift nears and just after the shift. The latter was also found to a significant degree in other symptom-context analyses (Luborsky, 1970). In instances with a shift to decreased depression, the patient came into a closer positive relationship with the therapist. He often expressed this by a greater inclination to agree with what the therapist had just said. Shifts toward increased depression revealed signs that the patient had become more negative toward the therapist. It was especially clear in three of the four instances (and maybe was implicit in the fourth as well) that the patient compared himself with another man, often the therapist, who seemed to him more capable in dealing with a woman, and then experienced low self-esteem and felt put down and helpless (the analysis of variance p-value was greatest for loss of self-esteem and increased helplessness). This theme probably also reflects Oedipal conflict (although the agreement of judges in rating Oedipal conflict was low, most likely because it was hard for the judges to recognize this variable in such small samples).

ANOTHER THEORY OF DEPRESSION: "BAD" ATTRIBUTIONAL STYLE

The first three theories of depression we have examined clearly do not exhaust even the most important theories available. We will, therefore, briefly present some data on an increasingly influential fourth theory, the reformulated learned helplessness theory. As hypothesized by Abramson, Seligman, and Teasdale (1978), internal, stable, and global attributions precede increased depressive symptoms, while external, unstable, and specific attributions precede decreased depressive symptoms. To test this theory, the same nine segments for Mr. Q were scored for attributional style by four other independent judges. Since the three attributional style dimensions were highly intercorrelated, a composite was used. The composite was reliably scored (.83) by the four judges. It is of interest that the attributional style composite before the shift is highly correlated with many of the variables including those with which it would be expected to correlate. These correlations above .80 are anxiety, .86; helplessness, .82; blocked, .83; guilt, .82; hostility-to-self, .89; loss of self-esteem, .88; Gottschalk–Gleser hostility-inward $(a + b)$, .82. After the shift the correlations tend to be negative. The two which are highest are blocked, $-.80$, and blocked-by-therapist, $-.83$.

Some differences predicted by the theory were, indeed, present by an unweighted means of analysis of variance (Winer, 1971) in which type of session (increased depression vs. decreased depression vs. control samples with no change in depression) was considered a between-subjects factor, and location (before vs. after shift) was considered a repeated-measures factor $(F(2,9) = 33.12, p < .001)$; this is reported more fully in Peterson et al., 1983. The significant effect was for type of session. Attributional style did not yield significant effects for location or type of session-by-location interaction. This is the major difference between the attributional style variable and the variables we used—attributional style distinguished the type of segment but changed little over the shift points. It appears to be a kind of background factor, while the variables we used are very sensitive to the shifts into and out of depression.

APPLICABILITY AND LIMITATIONS
OF THE SYMPTOM-CONTEXT METHOD

We will conclude by considering both the limits of the symptom-context method and its potential for further application in research on depression:

1. A possible limit to the method's applicability to depression research was discussed by Erik Erikson (1970): "It is not clear what the affect is even when the patient affirms it is depression and the observer believes it is depression . . . psychoanalytic research has a tendency to take a patient's description of an affect as a natural observation . . . How much true observation is there in his statement?" Fortunately, our method provides a positive answer to Erikson's question: There is evidence that the patient's statements are based upon some valid observations. First, the context for patient-identified shifts in "depression" were independently judged to show changes in the appropriate direction (as shown in Figure 5-1): When the patient made a statement that he was more depressed (the "shift point"), the observers rated the *subsequent* material as showing more depression; when the patient said he was "less depressed" (the "shift point"), the observers rated the *subsequent* material as reflecting less depression. Second, the related objectively scored measure, the Hostility-Inward Manual score (Gottschalk & Gleser, 1969), and its depression-related component c (Figure 5-11) also changed after the shift point in appropriate directions. Third, observers listening to tape recordings of sessions could identify the mood shifts in terms of voice quality as well as in the content of the statements. Fourth, the patient appeared to the therapist to be depressed at the time he said he was depressed, and less depressed when he said he was less depressed.

2. Not all forms of depression would necessarily show the same onset of conditions. Schmale (1972) emphasized the diversity of types of depression and attempted to integrate them into one dynamic schema. He stressed the importance of distinguishing the form of the depression in order to know whether it involves a "biological threshold phenomenon, an affect with somatic components, a character style, or a defensive symptom formation that protects with varying degrees of success against an unresolved deprivation with fixations related to repressed infantile separation or castration trauma" (p. 349). Mr. Q's depression is probably best described as a moderately severe neurotic depression. It should be valuable to see how general the onset conditions are. We have already begun studies using similar methods applied to other neurotic, depressed patients who showed shifts in depressive mood.

3. It is difficult to be precise about the time when a depressive mood shift occurs. We have taken the various precautions already described in order to be as exact as possible. Precision also increases with increasing precipitiousness of the patient's mood shifts; the larger the shifts, the easier it is to recognize them. Concurrent physiological indices might also be helpful as long as these can be shown in each patient to be depression-related.

4. Our study concerned the *immediate* psychological context of shifts in depressive mood and only tangentially touched upon any *background* factors that might be involved. In other studies we have dealt with some background factors which were revealed by taking much larger segments than we have done in the present study. Background factors are likely to be important; for example, Beck (1967) stresses as major background factors negative attitudes toward oneself, the outside world, and one's future. These negative attitudes, which often begin early in the person's development, are set off by specific stresses, which is what we are catching in the analyses presented in this chapter. Such negative conceptions of one's worth are referred to by Beck (1967) as "idiosyncratic schemas." The general level of stress is another background factor that makes the individual more depression-prone at certain times than at others.

5. We have focused only on the psychological level of symptoms, in this study. We hope to find some patients with a high frequency of large precipitous depressive shifts so that they can be studied by concurrent psychophysiological measurements, especially psychoendocrine ones, to expand upon the work done by Bunney et al. (1972), who were only able to study shifts within hours of their occurrence.

In summary, the continued success of the applications of this research style to research on depression depends upon finding additional patients with clear depressive mood shifts, with enough instances to cross-validate within each patient. Then we will both expand our exploration into the broader background contributing factors for these shifts and expand our range of measures beyond the psychological to the psychophysiolog-ical. So far, the main benefits from the method have been derived from the high-powered focus on the context of actual current nodal events and behaviors, such as the precipitous shifts in depressive mood, as they wax and wane in the flux of a psychotherapy process. Consequently, the method serves to limit retrospective as well as current distortions of the meaning of such events and behaviors, and to increase our skill at estimating the fit of theoretical formulations.

ACKNOWLEDGMENTS

This study was supported in part by USPHS Research Scientist Award MH 40710 to Lester Luborsky.

The authors wish to acknowledge the assistance of Drs. Aaron T. Beck, George S. Klein, Carolyn Winget, Frederick J. Evans, Martin Seligman, and Christopher Peterson.

REFERENCES

Abramson, L. Y., Seligman, M. E. P., & Teasdale, J. D. Learned helplessness in humans: Critique and reformulation. *Journal of Abnormal Psychology*, 1978, *87*, 49–74.

Aronson, H., & Weintraub, N. Verbal productivity as a measure of change in affective status. *Psychological Reports*, 1967, *20*, 483–487.

Beck, A. T. *Depression: Clinical, experimental, and theoretical aspects.* New York: Harper & Row, 1967.

Beck, A. T. *Depression: Causes and treatment.* Philadelphia: Univ. of Pennsylvania Press, 1972.

Bibring, E. The mechanism of depression. In W. Gaylin (Ed.), *The meaning of despair.* New York: Aronson, 1968.

Bunney, W., Jr., Murphy, D., Goodwin, F., & Borge, G. The "switch process" in manic depressive illness: I. A systematic study of sequential behavioral changes. *Archives of General Psychiatry* 1972, *27*, 295–302.

Cattell, R. B. *Personality.* New York: McGraw-Hill, 1950.

Costanzo, F., Markel, N., & Costanzo, P. Voice quality profile and perceived emotion. *Journal of Counseling Psychology*, 1969, *16*, 267–270.

Docherty, J., Leigh, H., & David, T. The immediate psychological context of premature ventricular contractions. *Psychosomatic Medicine*, 1974, *36*, 461–462.

Engel, G., & Reichsman, F. Spontaneous and experimentally induced depression in an infant with fistula: A contribution to the problem of depression. *Journal of the American Psychoanalytic Association*, 1956, *4*, 428–452.

Engel, G. L., & Schmale, A. H. Psychoanalytic theory of somatic disorder: Conversion, specificity, and the disease onset situation. *Journal of the American Psychoanalytic Association*, 1967, *15*, 344–356.

Erikson, E. Personal communication, June 1970.

Freud, S. Mourning and melancholia. In J. Strachey (Ed.), *Standard Edition* (Vol. 14). London: Hogarth Press, 1957. (Originally published, 1917.)

Freud, S. Inhibitions, symptoms and anxiety. In J. Strachey (Ed.), *Standard Edition* (Vol. 20). London: Hogarth Press, 1959. (Originally published, 1926.)

Gleser, G. C. An adjective checklist for necessary affect. Unpublished manuscript, 1960.

Goldstein, K. *The organism.* New York: American Book, 1939.

Gottschalk, L., & Gleser, C. *The measurement of psychological states through the content analysis of verbal behavior.* Berkeley: University of California, 1969.

Horney, K. *The neurotic personality of our time.* New York: Norton, 1957.

Luborsky, L. A psychoanalytic research on momentary forgetting during free association. *Bulletin of the Philadelphia Association of Psychoanalysis*, 1964, 14, 119–137.

Luborsky, L. Momentary forgetting during psychotherapy and psychoanalysis: A theory and research method. In R. R. Holt (Ed.), *Motives and thought: Psychoanalytic essays in honor of David Rapaport.* New York: International Universities Press, 1967. Also in *Psychological Issues*, 1967, *5*(2–3), Monograph 18/19, pp. 177–217.

Luborsky, L. New directions in research on neurotic and psychosomatic symptoms. *American Scientist*, 1970, *58*, 661–668.

Luborsky, L. Perennial mystery of poor agreement among criteria for psychotherapy outcome. *Journal of Counseling and Clinical Psychology*, 1971, *37*, 316–319.

Luborsky, L. *A helplessness rating scale and manual for verbal samples.* Unpublished manuscript, 1976.

Luborsky, L. Measuring a pervasive psychic structure in psychotherapy: The core conflictual relationship theme. In N. Freedman & S. Grand (Eds.), *Communicative structures and psychic structures.* New York: Plenum, 1977.

Luborsky, L. & Auerbach, A. H. The symptom-context method: Quantitative studies of symptom formation in psychotherapy. *Journal of the American Psychoanalytic Association*, 1969, *17*, 68–99.

Luborsky, L., Docherty, J. P., & Penick, S. Onset conditions for psychosomatic symptoms: A comparative review of immediate observation with retrospective research. *Psychosomatic Medicine*, 1973, *35*, 187–204.

Luborsky, L., Docherty, J. P., Todd, T. C., Knapp, P. H., Mirsky, A. F., & Gottschalk, L. A. A context analysis of psychological states prior to petit mal EEG paroxysms. *Journal of Nervous and Mental Disease*, 1975, *160*, 282–298.

Markel, N., Meisels, M., & Houck, J. Judging personality from voice quality. *Journal of Abnormal and Social Psychology*, 1964, *69*, 458–463.

Mendels, J. *Concepts of depression.* New York: Wiley, 1970.

Mendelson, M. *Psychoanalytic concepts of depression* (2nd ed.). New York: S. P. Books 1974.

Peterson, C., Luborsky, L., & Seligman, M. E. P. Attributions and depressive mood shifts: A case study using the symptom-context method. *Journal of Abnormal Psychology,* 1983, *92*, 96–103.

Schmale, A. H. Depression as affect, character, style, and symptom formation. In R. Holt & E. Peterfreund (Eds.), *Psychoanalysis and contemporary science.* New York: International Universities Press, 1972.

Seligman, M. *Helplessness: On depression, development and death.* San Francisco: Freedman, 1975.

Seligman, M., Maier, J., & Geer, J. Alleviation of learned helplessness in the dog. *Journal of Abnormal Psychology*, 1968, *73*, 256–262.

Winer, B. J. *Statistical principles in experimental design* (2nd ed.). New York: McGraw-Hill, 1971.

Wittenborn psychiatric rating scales. New York: Psychological Corp., 1955.

6

Recurrent Client States in Psychotherapy: Segmentation and Quantification

CHARLES R. MARMAR

NANCY WILNER

MARDI J. HOROWITZ
University of California–San Francisco and
Langley Porter Psychiatric Institute

INTRODUCTION

Psychotherapy is a complex form of communication. Research exploring its process requires selection of a fundamental pattern of segmentation. Previous studies based on the counting of words, phrases, and vocal sounds have yielded few clinically useful results, primarily because such procedures mechanically group content, without regard for the flow of events that comprise the therapeutic interaction (Chance, 1966; Gottschalk & Gleser, 1969; Kiesler, 1973; Scheflen, 1966). In his work, Knapp (1974) indicated the difficulty in using sequential time periods as units for study. While this technique offered certain advantages for statistical analysis, the arbitrary fractioning of the fabric of therapy obscured important clinical sequences that did not fit the empirical demands of time sampling. As a better approach to this kind of research, he suggested demarcation according to changes in overall patterning, marked whenever they occurred. We have extended this concept by recognizing the need to specify what it was that changed and by using states and state transitions as the criteria for segmentation.

Careful case studies have shown that states, with their definitions anchored closely to observable behavior, are a useful concept. Clients frequently present their initial complaints as troublesome states of mind, such as anxiety, depression, or confusion. Clinicians tend to explore the nature of these problematic states, search for the interpersonal or intrapsychic triggers that cause them to occur, and review the developmental issues that determine susceptibilities to presenting complaints. For example, detailed inquiry about depressive states is followed by probes for recent or early object loss and prior regulation of self-esteem in the face of frustration or failure. It is less usual, however, to elucidate the relationship

194

between the presenting problem state and other recurrent states of mind. This is accomplished by inquiring about the behavior pattern and subjective experiences just before and immediately after an anxiety attack or the onset of a depressive mood. In addition, the clinician observes the transitions of states displayed by the client during a therapy session and from session to session. The potential of specific states for facilitating or hindering the working-through process in psychotherapy can then be evaluated and related to the underlying systems of meaning that explain why a given state recurs. This analysis can lead to therapeutic strategies to alter the patterning of state prevalence and transition in order to accelerate change.

States are observable recurrent patterns of behavior that have both verbal and nonverbal components. They are commonly recognized during a clinical interview because of changes in facial expression, posture, intonation and inflection in speech, focus and content of verbal reports, degree of self-reflective awareness, general arousal, shifts in degree and nature of empathy, and other communicative qualities. The information that indicates that this is a recurrence of a familiar state is not confined to any one system, but is a configuration of information in multiple systems. The change in states of a person in psychotherapy is recognizable in the same way as the change of atmosphere in a drama, from cheerful sunlight to thunder and lighting, or the shifts, in musical work, of the sounds of rhythm, harmony, timbre, and tonality.

Review of videotapes of over 20 brief psychotherapies of persons with neurotic-level reactions to stressful life events has indicated that a typical case contains an average of about seven states that occur with sufficient frequency and duration to bring them over the threshold of clinical significance.

The concept of states has been shown to have explanatory power in the clinical formulation of change processes in psychotherapy (Horowitz, 1979; Horowitz, Marmar, & Wilner, 1979). The germane research issue is to determine whether states can be assessed quantitatively in a manner that will yield consensus. Once reliability is confirmed, state analysis might be used in intensive case examinations, and generalized classifications of states early in a treatment process might be applied to see if they could serve as a predictor of the eventual outcome of psychotherapy. If particular state categories are predictive of successful or unsuccessful treatment outcomes, it would then follow that the therapeutic interventions that effect state stabilization or transition should be examined. The states of a client described elsewhere in detail (Horowitz, 1979; Horowitz, Marmar, & Wilner, 1979) will be presented here to illustrate the reliability of quantifying states and testing specific hypotheses about changes in state frequency and quality as a function of changes in the communicative pattern between the client and the therapist.

BACKGROUND

Dissociative states have been described by physicians for thousands of years (Veith, 1977). Breuer and Freud (1893–1895/1955) describe them and the reasons for entry into these states in terms of unconscious role-relationship fantasies or memories and the conflict between wishes, enduring attitudes of morality, and defenses. The separation of ideas, feelings, and modes of experience and expression during dissociative episodes was also described by Charcot (1877) and Janet (1901/1965).

Recently, several typologies of personality disorder have been described in terms of cyclical patterns between a limited number of states. These include the hysterical (Horowitz, 1977), the narcissistic (Kohut, 1971) and the borderline personality disorders (Hartocollis, 1977; Kernberg, 1975). While the characteristic pattern of state change is readily recognized in more severe forms of personality disorder, such as the narcissistic and borderline conditions, state transition can be noted in persons with every type of psychopathology. States common to most persons include those moments dominated by expression of strong emotions such as anxiety, anger, guilt, sadness, shame, excitement, and joy, affects that lead to universal phenomena (Darwin, 1872/1965; Ekman, 1973; Tomkins, 1962).

However, even these ubiquitous emotional states are experienced with idiosyncratic variations. Each person may cry—the tissue box is a common fixture in the psychotherapist's office—but each person has a unique way of crying, emitting sounds, contorting facial muscles, experiencing sadness, and so forth. An enormous quantity of work has been done on the general aspects of emotion; little has been done to describe unique variations on such universal themes.

The most spectacular state transitions and state variations are noted in persons with multiple personalities and other types of dissociative phenomena. Sudden episodes of strong emotions are also clear shifts in state. Somewhat more subtle state variations require description of introspective experience. Federn (1952) studied a variety of states that he felt could not be categorized as dissociative episodes or as episodes of specific emotions and called them "ego states." He found evidence that the ego states of earlier developmental periods remained throughout life as potentially recurrent in behavior and experience. These might emerge during pathological or normal regressions: For example, the phenomenon can be clearly elicited by hypnotic age regression in normal persons (Weiss, 1960).

Berne (1961, 1964) built upon Federn's work by developing a theory of child, parent, and adult ego states and game-like transactional sequences based upon the interplay of these states. He pointed out that each person possessed these potential ego states and could recognize his or her characteristic patterns of feelings in each state. Every event or choice faced by the person was simultaneously interpreted according to the intrinsic patterns of each ego state, although action was largely determined by the dominant state for that situation.

Berne and his coworkers (Dusay, 1972) found that the system was easily understood, but they found it necessary to add additional subclassifications. For example, each person might be characterized according to his or her typical self-concept and view of others as determined by these ego states: the critical parent, the nurturing parent, the adult, the adapted child, the "little professor" (a scientifically inquiring child), and the "natural child."

The transactional analysis approach to ego states devised by Berne has several advantages. It deals with observable phenomena in a clear way. It provides a classification system that encourages the clinician to seek information about other states and about how a problem state, such as the intrusion of a "child state," might influence transitions to and from other states. Of course, the disadvantage of a predefined classification system is that relevant states are too numerous to be contained by available categories. States such as "good," "bad," and "real" ego states, defined by other theorists (Biddle, 1969), are also too circumscribed to permit sufficiently individualized state description. What is needed are some loosely articulated guidelines or sets of procedures for state analysis that do not artificially compress an individual's experience into categories that are predetermined and excessively limited.

Another procedure similar to state analysis has developed in research addressing role playing aspects of Gestalt therapy technique. Greenberg (1979, 1980) describes an intensive process analysis of the resolution of conflict utilizing the two-chair technique developed by Perls (1969). In the technique, the client carries out a dialogue which is partitioned according to the therapist's instructions to change chairs and to speak as if he or she were the person just addressed. Role exchange continues as conflict is first clarified and then resolved. The Patient Experiencing Scale of Klein, Mathieu, Kiesler, and Gendlen (1969) and the rating of voice quality and expressive style following the methods of Rice and Wagstaff (1967) and Rice, Koke, Greenberg, and Wagstaff (1978) are applied to the phases of conflict clarification ("preresolution") and conflict resolution. As work progresses to repair conflictual splits, a differential pattern of depth of experiencing and quality of voice contact is reported across the phases of conflict resolution.

Greenberg's analysis also follows our own formats for defining self and object schemata for each separately described state of mind (Horowitz, 1979). The client's behavior in the "experiencing chair", representing acceptable aspects of the self, shows a progression of gradually increasing depth of inward exploration. The client's behavior in the "other chair" is defined by Greenberg (1979) as representing disavowed aspects of the self, frequently internalized critical parental part-objects experienced as self-condemnations or projected onto external figures. The voice qualities of the client while in the "other chair" are initially characterized by a harsh lecturing indignation and later, during the resolution phase, by a softening of criticism and a feeling tone of compassionate acceptance. These shifts in client behavior are similar to the kinds of changes in experiential state described in our own research.

STRATEGY

Our aim has been to arrive at an operational definition of a state of mind in a manner that would allow individualized description as well as an opportunity to determine if a reliable consensus of judgment could be reached. To achieve this aim we (1) defined states as units, (2) defined states for a single case, and (3) determined if independent raters could agree when a given state was manifest in video recordings of psychotherapy sessions.

DEFINITION OF A STATE AS A STRUCTURAL UNIT

The unit of study for content analysis in this procedure is defined as a discrete state with its confluent behavioral form, verbal content, and various congruities or incongruities. "Behavioral form" is defined as the posture, facial expression, tone of voice, gestures, hand and foot positioning, flow of speech, and deployment of attention. "Verbal content" refers to the reported thoughts, feelings, and behavior of the person. "Congruence" and "incongruence" refer to the degree of synergy between the behavioral form and the verbal content.

Table 6-1 describes the research criteria for the five states present during therapy in the client used here as a case example. These research criteria were elaborated from the therapist's initial descriptions. It was the therapist's impression that two states were most prevalent during the therapy interviews: an *artificial and engaging* state in which the client was cheerful, lighthearted, and entertaining, with a variant of angry mimicry, and seemed to be pretending to have real feelings, and a contrasting *hurt but working* state in which the client seemed somewhat deflated and was actually experiencing "hurt feelings," but went on with the tasks of therapy.

Three other states were present: a *hurt and not working* state, in which the client appeared withdrawn, insulated, or aloof, stopped the task of therapy, withdrew from communication with the therapist, and felt depressed and sullen; a *self-disgust* state, in which the client was markedly distraught about an unpleasant self-realization; and finally, a *competitive–angry* state, which ranged from a covert struggle for one-up position with the therapist to open anger and blaming directed toward others.

RELIABILITY OF STATE JUDGMENTS

The task, then, was to determine whether independent judges could reliably score the occurrence of these states as identified by the therapist and operationally defined by the research team. The goal was to arrive at a measure that would meaningfully segment interview data, using a method superior to standard clock-time intervals. The problem, therefore, was not only to identify the occurrence of a particular state at a specified time, but to designate the points of state transition as well.

METHODS

EXPERIMENT 1: PILOT RELIABILITY STUDY

Prediction: States and state transitions can be recognized by persons other than the therapist. To test this prediction, four video segments, each 10 minutes in length, were randomly selected from the 600 minutes available from the therapy of a single client seen in a special clinic for the brief therapy (12 sessions) of stress response syndromes. A detailed analysis of this case has already been published (Horowitz, 1979). The client gave written informed consent to the research aspects of her treatment. The four segments, one from each of four therapy hours, were presented to two raters (CM and NW) who were blind to the treatment hour of each segment and to the time of occurrence within the hour. Using the operational definitions of Table 6-1, they independently scored the segments for states and state transition points, using synchronized stopwatches to record the state transitions. In order to eliminate fleeting and fragmentary excursions into states, they were instructed to only score those states that lasted more than 10 seconds. Agreement was said to occur when the two judges identified the same state and the state transition points within ±7.5 seconds of each other. This qualification was necessary because transition from one state to another was not always instantaneous, and required an interval of several seconds for stabilization as one state terminated and a second clearly established itself.

This design demanded that the judges determine both the client's state and the point of transition from one state to another. It differed from the procedure of asking raters to make statements at fixed intervals of time, such as every 10 seconds. This latter method of fixed time

TABLE 6-1. Description of Patient States

ARTIFICIAL AND ENGAGING

Behavioral Form: Engaging, perky, has histrionic verbalization and gestures, deploys attention on others, smiles, makes faces, speaks quickly, interrupts, raises voice, gestures outward, sits forward, is highly animated.

Verbal Content: Often angry, competitive, flirtatious; uses mimicry to express hostile, contemptuous feelings.

Incongruent: Playacts or exaggerates ideals and feelings while at a distance from them; wishes to feel mutually and actively creative, but is inwardly at a distance from these ideals.

HURT BUT WORKING

Behavioral Form: Head down, hands held together, rubbing and picking at self, slow, soft speech, sad or hurt look, attention turned inward, bodily stillness.

Verbal Content: Reflective comments on self, comments or thoughts turned inward, analytic about self and others.

Congruent: Behavioral form and verbal content are congruent.

HURT AND NOT WORKING

Behavioral Form: Withdrawn, attention directed inward, may throw head back or downward in despair, speaks slowly, mumbles, trails off.

Verbal Content: Comments reflect hopelessness, demoralization, sadness, loneliness, depression. Reports feeling foggy and unreal. Expresses bodily concerns. Does not have ready access to thoughts and feelings available in other states.

Congruent: Form and content express and demonstrate helplessness.

SELF-DISGUST

Behavioral Form: Looks away, lowers voice, half-smiles, speaks slowly, plays with hair, raises eyebrows, repeats key word several times ("demand," "suck," "give me").

Verbal Content: Feelings of self-contempt, self-hatred, shame, guilt, negative body images (fat, ugly, hairy), passivity, defective feminine self-image, unaccomplished.

Congruent: Experiences and communicates self-disgust.

COMPETITIVE-ANGRY

Behavioral Form: Attention directed outward to involve other. Challenging or contemptuous edge to voice, which may be raised, usually with increased flow of speech. Occasional pounding of chair arm, direct eye contact; chin out, arms occasionally extended.

Verbal Content: Struggle for control of situation; challenging and critical of the worth of others, concerned with blame, expresses feelings of contempt, indignation, and anger. Can escalate to temper outburst.

Congruent: Expresses and demonstrates competitiveness and hostility.

---

sampling would have simplified the rating task (by requiring one judgment of state rather than two judgments, of state and state transition), but was rejected because it did not conform to the real-life experience in which the observing clinician's mental set is aimed at recognition of the moment of change, that is, upon the occurrence of a discontinuity in the flow of the client's experience. For example, if the therapist makes an intervention and the client, who has been earnestly and cooperatively engaged in the treatment process for the previous few moments, abruptly withdraws or lashes out at the therapist, the shift in the client's state registers for the therapist as one of the most relevant bits of information for understanding the therapeutic interaction.

Results

The results of Experiment 1 are presented in Table 6-2. There was 74% agreement between the two judges for both the artificial and engaging state ($n = 24$ segments) and the hurt but working state ($n = 28$ segments). Agreement was good for the other states as well (83% for both hurt and not working and self-disgust), although the small samples necessitate cautious interpretation. The one exception was the competitive–angry state, where agreement was only 46%. Review of this finding resulted in a redefinition for more precise descrimination between authentic expressions of anger and mimicry of it in the artificial and engaging state.

Discussion

While the results of the pilot study were encouraging, considering the complexity of the clinical phenomena that were rated, it suffered from several methodological limitations. First, the two raters (CM and NW) were already familiar with some of the clinical material. Second, there was great variability in the base rate of occurrence of the states. Artificial and engaging and hurt but working appear most often; the remaining three states occur with relative infrequency. This might inflate the agreement for the more common states and understate the agreement for the states that occur less often. It was not possible, given the design just described, to apply the rigorous statistical tests that would take the base rates of occurrence into account. This led to the design of Experiment 2.

TABLE 6-2. EXPERIMENT 1—INTERRATER AGREEMENT: FREQUENCY OF AGREEMENT ON JUDGMENT OF STATES AND STATE TRANSITIONS (MEAN OF TWO JUDGES) ON A SAMPLE OF FOUR 10-MINUTE SEGMENTS

STATE ENTERED	EPISODES	MEAN DURATION OF EPISODES (SEC)	AGREEMENT
Artificial and engaging	24	42 (10–175)	74%
Hurt but working	28	35 (10–120)	74%
Hurt and not working	4	28 (10–55)	83%
Self-disgust	2	23 (15–30)	83%
Competitive–angry	4	22 (10–40)	46%
TOTAL	62	30 (10–175)	73%

EXPERIMENT 2: RELIABILITY STUDY

Prediction: States and state transitions can be recognized by persons other than the therapist. Minutes 15 to 25 of each of the 12 treatment hours were selected for this study, a time interval most likely to be representative of the therapeutic interaction and less influenced by idiosyncratic events of the opening and closing moments of each treatment hour. The two judges of Experiment 1 now identified states and the moment of transitions (using the time indicated on time code generator markings on the videotaped segments). Meanwhile, the two new clinician judges (BH and RJ), who had no previous experience in rating tasks for state identification and no knowledge of this client, were trained to recognize states on separate material. They then judged each state of the excerpted videotapes, accepting as units the time between transition points agreed upon by the first two judges.

Procedures

The new judges were first provided with the written criteria for the states (Table 6-1). They were then shown several video excerpts illustrative of each state (taken from other sections of the therapy), and subsequently asked to call out states on their own. Discussion clarified criteria for ratings. When this part of the training was satisfactorily completed, they were asked to write down their independent identification of states from a tape containing randomized samples of preselected segments of the five states. Through this progression of increasingly difficult judgments, the second two judges were calibrated to an acceptable level of reliability of agreement with the first two judges (80% agreement for one rater, 82% for the other).

They then independently scored minutes 15 to 25 of each of the 12 therapy hours. Their task was only to label the predominant state between each of these preestablished sets of state transition points. This design for agreement on the states alone controlled for the effects of variable base rates of different states. (It is not possible to do this and at the same time determine agreement on both states and state transitions.)

Results

Table 6-3 shows the results of using this second set of judges on the new material. Agreements occur along the diagonal, all other cells representing disagreements. The simple percent agreement was 71%. Cohen's κ (a coefficient of agreement for categorical data which corrects for distortions related to varying base rates of occurrence; Cohen, 1960; Fleiss, Cohen, &

TABLE 6-3. RELIABILITY RATINGS OF STATE IDENTIFICATION

JUDGE 2	JUDGE 1					
	HBW	AAE	SD	CA	HANW	ROW TOTAL
Hurt but working (HBW)	36			2	6	44
Artificial and engaging (AAE)	1	30	2	3		36
Self-disgust (SD)	2	1	2		1	6
Competitive–angry (CA)		3	1	2	2	8
Hurt and not working (HANW)	2		2	1	2	7
COLUMN TOTAL	41	34	7	8	11	

Note. Percent agreement = .71; adjusted agreement: Cohen's κ = .59.

Everitt, 1979) was .59. These results indicate adequate agreement in judging, comparable to other reliabilities reported for psychiatric diagnoses (Spitzer, Endicott, & Robins, 1978).

One source of disagreement was again between the artificial and engaging state and the competitive–angry state. As already noted, this client would at times express hostility through mimicry in the artificial and engaging state, leading one or another judge to confuse this hostile variant of the state with the angry content of the competitive state. A second source of rating difficulty was presented by the task of discriminating the hurt but working from the hurt and not working state. This required careful attention to the quality of patient engagement with the therapist during moments of hurtful self-exploration.

EXPERIMENT 3: LEVEL OF JUDGE EXPERIENCE STUDY

Prediction: Recognition of states is based largely on observable phenomena rather than clinical inference, and therefore can be achieved by nonclinicians as well as clinicians. This reliability rating task was repeated a second time with first-year medical students (JK and TB) rather than mental health clinicians as judges. The purpose of this effort was to determine whether state identification was based on observable phenomena needing little clinical experience. The κ coefficient for the two medical students was .63, a level of agreement closely similar to that of the previous two clinician judges. The success of these students supports the assumption that the capacity to recognize client states is not restricted to clinicians alone, and that judgments of states rest on clearly observable phenomena.

EXPERIMENT 4: PATTERN OF STATE FREQUENCY
AND QUALITY DURING THERAPY

Frequency of States

The establishment of adequate interrater agreement for state judgments makes it possible to study the pattern of state changes during therapy. The clinical impressions of the therapist, upon review of the treatment through configurational analysis (Horowitz, 1979), was that critical work on the alliance occurred in hours 4 and 5, followed by an increase in the hurt but working state and a decrease in the artificial and engaging state. Therefore, this experiment tested the following prediction: *The frequency of the hurt but working state will increase as the therapy progresses, and the frequency of the artificial and engaging state will decrease.*

Procedures

States and state transition points for minutes 15 to 25 of each of 12 therapy hours had already been scored in Experiment 2. The scores of the first two judges were graphed (Figure 6-1) and confirmed the clinical impressions of the therapist. There was an increase in hurt but working and a decrease in artificial and engaging states after the fifth hour of therapy.

As a replication study, the same research team judges scored minutes 30 to 40 of each of the 12 therapy hours. First, these segments were randomized by a technician and then presented to them. Analysis of the judges' best guesses of the hours indicated that they did not know this accurately. The judgments were again made by consensus. The results are shown in Figure 6-2 and replicate the findings of the other time frame (Figure 6-1). The shift from artificial and engaging state predominance before hour 5 to the hurt but working state thereafter is a representative result, not a sampling artifact.

EXPERIMENT 5: STATE QUALITY STUDY

In addition to the previously predicted change in the frequency of states during therapy, it was hypothesized that the quality of the two most frequent states would change with time. Specifically, it was assumed that the intensity of "hurt feelings" in the hurt but working state and the degree of exaggeration in the artificial and engaging state would diminish as therapy progressed. Therefore, the experiment tested the following prediction: *The intensity of the hurtful aspect of the hurt but working state will decrease over the therapy period, as will the exaggerated component in the artificial and engaging states.*

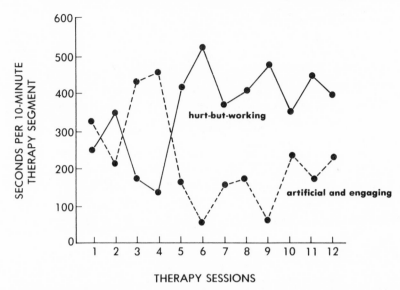

FIGURE 6-1. Experiment 4: Minutes 15–25 of Each of 12 Therapy Sessions. Scored by Two Judges.

Procedures

Three-point rating scales with anchoring descriptors for each point were developed for the central quality of these two states and are shown in Table 6-4. The twelve 10-minute segments (minutes 30 to 40 of each treatment hour) previously scored for state and state transitions (see Figure 6-2) were scored independently by the two judges (CM and NW) using the state quality rating scale. The judges based their scores on their global impressions of the predominant quality of each state as it occurred, even though the quality might fluctuate to some degree within a state.

Results

The judges achieved satisfactory reliability on the state quality ratings. The level of agreement was 81% for a sample of 43 artificial and engaging states, and 74.5% for 59 hurt but working states. There was a tendency for both the degree of hurt feelings and the degree of exaggeration to increase during the first third of the treatment, and reach a maximum between the fourth and the sixth hours. In the second half of therapy there was a diminution in the degree of exaggeration of the artificial and engaging states and a stabilization of a mild to moderate degree of hurtfulness in

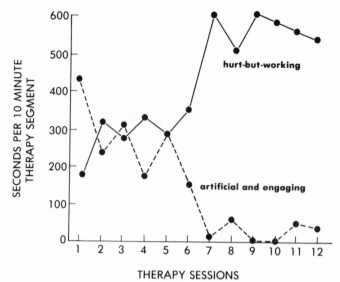

THERAPY SESSIONS

FIGURE 6-2. EXPERIMENT 4: MINUTES 30–40 OF EACH OF 12 THERAPY SESSIONS. SCORED BY TWO JUDGES.

the hurt but working state, until the last few hours, when an increase in the intensity of hurt feelings occurred.

Interpretation of the State Quality Changes

During the period of confrontation that occurred between the fourth and sixth hours, there was an intensification of both hurt feelings and exaggeration of artificiality. During the seventh to tenth hours, a period the therapist had previously described as one of cooperation and authentic involvement in the therapeutic process, there was little exaggeration and a degree of hurt feelings that suggests real but not overwhelming recognition of personal difficulties. It appears, for this client, that affect varies according to specific phases of the treatment and that level of affect optimal for therapeutic work occurred in those hours that the therapist felt provided the most substantial working through of the client's conflicts.

DISCUSSION

This work indicates that states originally described by the therapist and subsequently elaborated into research criteria could be reliably rated along the dimension of transition points, frequency, and quality. The

TABLE 6-4. EXPERIMENT 5—STATE QUALITY PARAMETERS

1 MILD	2 MODERATE	3 SEVERE
HURT BUT WORKING—DEGREE OF "HURT FEELINGS"		
Self-aware Reflective Authentic Working Minimally hurt	Somewhat hurt, as evidenced by downcast look Slowed speech Some self-searching Picks at self and touches self in comforting gesture	Markedly hurt, concerned with losses Self-critical Many pauses, speaks slowly Still willing to work and not withdraw
ARTIFICIAL AND ENGAGING—DEGREE OF EXAGGERATION OF ARTIFICIALITY		
Social chit-chat, without the other features	Some hand gestures outward Some head movement Some animation and mimicry	Gestures widely Speaks quickly with a singsong quality to voice Highly animated May use mimicry to express hostility

demonstration of state frequency and quality change in the predicted direction following clinically identified shifts in the client–therapist relationship, such as the establishment of a working alliance, is evidence for the usefulness of states as content analysis units for the study of the change process in psychotherapy.

RELATIONSHIP OF STATE ANALYSIS
TO OTHER DESCRIPTORS

While it is encouraging to demonstrate reliability in state judgments in this preliminary study, it remains to show how this construct relates to other relevant dimensions of personality description. Horowitz (1979), using a conceptual system he calls configurational analysis, articulates states of mind with two other descriptive organizers: role relationship models and information processing. Role relationship models refers to the schematization of the self-concept, concepts of others, and the relationships between self and others. Such models of relationships are instances of what Piaget (1954) has defined as higher-order schemata, that is, organized, enduring mental representations which guide perception and the attribution of meaning.

Such schemata guide the assimilation of new knowledge about the interpersonal world according to existing models of relationships. The models themselves are subject to change in the process of accommodation to changing experience. There is the explicit theoretical assumption that for every individual there are multiple self-concepts and a multiplicity of corresponding concepts of others. These are formed across a developmental history which, even for people whose lives have been relatively nontraumatic, is checkered by the ordinary vicissitudes of success and failure, closeness and loneliness, activity and passivity, the sense of the self as good and bad, and so on.

The models of self and others formed in early experiences are subject to the distortions of formation during periods of cognitive immaturity. These representations do not disappear in adulthood despite replacements by more realistic models. Early models may be reactivated following losses (Horowitz, Wilner, Marmar, & Krupnick, 1980) and by such techniques as hypnotic age regression (Weiss, 1960). Support for the multiplicity of self-concepts and role-relationship models is found in the clinical work of Knapp (1969), Arlow (1969), and Jacobson (1964) and in the empirical application of the repertory grid technique of Kelly (1955).

The traffic back and forth among adult, adolescent, and childhood models of the self and others is characteristic of epigenetic systems. Momentary shifts in states, such as those described in this chapter, reflect changing conceptions of the self in relationship to others. Role-relationship models serve as cognitive underpinnings guiding sequential shifts in experiential state. The linkages between these two conceptual sets is illustrated for this client in Table 6-5.

The explanation for the shifts among recurrent self-images and complementary images of others anchored to the specific states rests upon an understanding of how constellations of meanings about persons and events are processed. The third broad conceptual area in the configurational analysis technique, information processing, describes changes in role structures and the associated sequencing of various states of mind by the examination of the relationship between environmental and internal sets of information and emotion, controls and actions. In describing the pattern of information processing for an individual, the central constellations of experienced and warded-off ideas and emotions are modeled, as are habitual defenses against experiencing conflictual feelings and affect-laden thoughts. Events which carry for an individual real or imagined threats of activation of negative self-concepts or unacceptable views of others, with associated painful states, will motivate controls to interrupt the chain of implied meanings in order to protect against entry into unpleasant states. As an example, when the client described in this chapter tried to contemplate themes of procrastination in pursuing her career, she was prone to experiencing herself as a lazy, defective wrongdoer. At the same time she experienced the therapist as a haughty, righteous critic, and entered the self-disgust state. She would then initiate a defensive reevaluation of her procrastination, minimize its importance or counter this defective image by switching to a recent accomplishment, feel as if competent, and enter the artificial and engaging state. She had not authentically

TABLE 6-5. COMPLEMENTARY ROLES OF SELF AND OTHER AS THEY RELATE TO
OBSERVED STATES

STATE	RECURRENT SELF-IMAGES	COMPLEMENTARY IMAGES OF OTHER
Artificial and engaging	As if competent	Competent
Hurt but working	Impaired but learning student	Teacher
Hurt and not working	Needy but self-sufficient and self-feeding	Lost, worthless, or remote
Competitive	Wrongly accused, critic	Wrongdoer or defective
Self-disgust	Defective extension of another	Supplier of identity
	Wrongdoer	Superior critic
	Greedy, selfish	Depleted and misused
	Depleted and misused	Greedy, selfish
	Depleted and helpless	Lost

resolved the problem of procrastination, which would have contributed to a real rather than mimicked sense of competence, but for the moment she escaped the pangs of self-disgust.

The description of states, role-relationship models, and information processing in an interactive conceptual model provides useful configurations which shed light on symptom formation and change processes in psychotherapy. These range from the molecular level of description involving micromomentary shifts in communication to the molar level of the description of structural personality change.

CONCLUSION AND DIRECTION OF FUTURE WORK

Through a series of small-scale but additive studies we have developed a plan for segmentation of psychotherapy sessions based upon identification of points of transition between one state of mind and another. By examining state patterns within these demarcation points, a set of prototype states can be individually defined. Descriptors of these sets of states can lead to reliable judgments by a variety of raters. Since reliable judgments can be obtained, it is possible to quantify state frequency in a given client and thus examine changes in state over the course of a therapy.

We believe this type of methdology may be extremely useful in intensive studies of individual cases and in such investigations of small sets of typologically similar cases. It is an approach sensitive to specific manifestations and to identification of points when salient changes occur, including the emergence of new behavior as well as the cessation of earlier ones. It has a great advantage in terms of relating symptoms to a matrix of other experiences.

The next steps, as we see it, are to continue the state analytic effort on an expanding variety of cases. Redundancies in states, state sets, and state transition patterns could thus be observed. Some such repetitive patterns across a set of cases have already been observed at a descriptive level for variations of pathological grief (Horowitz *et al.*, 1980) and for persons prone to attacks of narcissistic rage (Horowitz, 1981). These sets of state decriptions and state transition patterns could then be studied in an advance toward the demonstration of reliability and validity using the segmentation and quantification methods discussed in this chapter.

These methods may be utilized for examination of the process over a sequence of hours, as shown in Figures 6-1 and 6-2. While we have not yet done so, these methods could also be coupled with the symptom-context method developed by Luborsky (1962). That is, entry into a given state of mind can be selected as a marker event. Precursor communications, including therapist actions and emergence of conflict, could be contrasted for a period before this marker and contrasted with control markers, such as entry into a different state of mind. Either an untoward state of mind, such as a confusion, or an unusual advance, such as a moment of decision and conflict resolution, could serve as the marker state transition point.

We believe such an approach might free process research from the limitations of segmentations by clock time, allowing segmentation by event time with new observations as a potential research outcome.

ACKNOWLEDGMENTS

Research on which this chapter was based is from the Center for the Study of Neuroses, Langley Porter Psychiatric Institute, University of California–San Francisco, and was supported in part by NIMH Clinical Research Center Grant MH 30899. The authors wish to acknowledge the help of the four raters, Rachel Jenkins, DMH, Bruce Heller, PhD, James Kahn, and Terry Becker, and of Lola Faye Coyne, PhD, Daniel Weiss, PhD, and Anthony Leong, MS, who served as statistical consultants.

REFERENCES

Arlow, J. Unconscious fantasy and disturbances of conscious experience. *Psychoanalytic Quarterly*, 1969, *38*, 1–27.

Berne, E. *Transactional analyses in psychotherapy*. New York: Grove Press, 1961.

Berne, E. *Games people play*. New York: Grove Press, 1964.

Biddle, W. E. Image therapy. *American Journal of Psychiatry*, 1969, *126*, 408–412.

Breuer, J., & Freud, S. *Studies on hysteria*. In J. Strachey (Ed.), *Standard edition* (Vol. 2). London: Hogarth Press, 1955. (Originally published, 1893–1895.)

Chance, E. Content analysis of verbalizations about interpersonal experience. In L. Gottschalk & A. Auerbach (Eds.), *Methods of research in psychotherapy*. New York: Appleton-Century-Crofts, 1966.

Charcot, J. M. *Lectures on diseases of the nervous system* (G. Sigerson, trans.) London: New Sydenham Society, 1877.

Cohen, J. A coefficient of agreement for nominal scales. *Educational Psychology Measures*, 1960, *20*, 37–46.

Darwin, C. *Expression of the emotions in man and animal.* Chicago: University of Chicago Press, 1965. (Originally published, 1872.)

Dusay, J. Egograms and the constancy hypotheses. *Transactional Analysis Journal*, 1972, *2*, 37–41.

Ekman, P. (Ed.). *Darwin and facial expression.* New York: Academic Press, 1973.

Federn, P. *Ego psychology and the psychoses.* New York: Basic Books, 1952.

Fleiss, J. L., Cohen, J., & Everitt, B. S. Large sample standard errors of kappa and weighted kappa. *Psychological Bulletin*, 1969, *72*, 323–327.

Gottschalk, L., & Gleser, G. *The measurement of psychological states through the content analysis of verbal behavior.* Berkeley: University of California Press, 1969.

Greenberg, L. Resolving splits: Use of the two-chair technique. *Psychotherapy: Theory, Research and Practice*, 1979, *16*, 316–324.

Greenberg, L. The intensive analyses of recurring events from the practice of Gestalt therapy. *Psychotherapy, Theory, Research and Practice*, 1980, *17*, 143–152.

Hartocollis, P. (Ed.). *Borderline personality disorders.* New York: International Universities Press, 1977.

Horowitz, M. J. Structure and the process of change. In M. J. Horowitz (Ed.), *Hysterical personality.* New York: Aronson, 1977.

Horowitz, M. J. *States of mind.* New York: Plenum Press, 1979.

Horowitz, M. J. Self-righteous rage and the attribution of blame. *Archives of General Psychiatry*, 1981, *38*, 1233–1238.

Horowitz, M. J., Marmar, C., & Wilner, N. Analysis of patient states and state transitions. *Journal of Nervous and Mental Diseases*, 1979, *167*, 91–99.

Horowitz, M. J., Wilner, N., Marmar, C., & Krupnick, J. Pathological grief and the activation of latent self images. *American Journal of Psychiatry*, 1980, *137*, 1157–1162.

Janet, P. *The major symptoms of hysteria.* New York: Hafner, 1965. (Originally published, 1901.)

Jacobson, E. *The self and object world.* New York: International Universities Press, 1964.

Kelly, G. A. *The psychology of personal constructs.* New York: Norton, 1955.

Kernberg, O. *Borderline conditions and pathological narcissism.* New York: Aronson, 1975.

Kiesler, D. J. *The process of psychotherapy.* Chicago: Aldine, 1973.

Klein, M., Mathieu, P., Kiesler, D., & Gendlin, E. *The experiencing scale.* Madison: Wisconsin Psychoanalytic Institute, 1969.

Knapp, P. H. Image, symbol and person. *Archives of General Psychiatry*, 1969, *21*, 392–406.

Knapp, P. H. Segmentation and structure in psychoanalysis. *Journal of American Psychoanalytic Association*, 1974, *22*, 14–36.

Kohut, H. *Analysis of the self.* New York: International Universities Press, 1971.

Luborsky, L. Clinician judgment of mental health. *Archives of General Psychiatry*, 1962, *7*, 407.

Perls, F. *Gestalt therapy.* Lafayette, Calif.: Real People Press, 1969.

Piaget, J. *The construction of reality in the child.* New York: Basic Books, 1954.

Rice, L., Koke, C., Greenberg, L., & Wagstaff, A. *Voice quality training manual.* Toronto: York University (Counseling and Development Centre), 1978.

Rice, L., & Wagstaff, A. Client voice quality and expressive style as indices of productive psychotherapy. *Journal of Consulting Psychology*, 1967, *31*, 557–563.

Scheflen, A. E. Natural history method in psychotherapy. In L. Gottschalk & A. Auerbach. (Eds.), *Methods of research in psychotherapy.* New York: Appleton-Century-Crofts, 1966.

Spitzer, R. L., Endicott, J., & Robins, E. Research diagnostic criteria: Rationale and reliability. *Archives of General Psychiatry*, 1978, *35*, 773–782.

Tomkins, S. *Affect, imagery, and consciousness.* New York: Springer, 1962.

Veith, I. Four thousand years of hysteria. In M. J. Horowitz (Ed.), *Hysterical personality.* New York: Aronson, 1977.

Weiss, E. *The structure and dynamics of the human mind.* New York: Grune & Stratton, 1960.

7

Experiential Psychotherapy: Key Events in Client–Therapist Interaction

PHILIPPA MATHIEU-COUGHLAN
Wesleyan University

MARJORIE H. KLEIN
University of Wisconsin

INTRODUCTION

This chapter will present the "experiencing" construct and its impact on psychotherapy theory, research, and practice. After a review of the significant history of the construct, we will show how the experiential theory of therapy can be used to define critical moments of change and progress in therapy. Along the way we will also indicate how the Patient and Therapist Experiencing Scales, developed to measure verbal behavior in the therapy, can be used to define these key events. Examples from therapy hours will be provided of client experiential progress and therapist influence on this process. Finally, we will discuss how two familiar therapeutic impasses can be resolved by using experiential theory and the principles articulated in the Therapist Experiencing Scale. Throughout, we make recommendations for therapist behavior which are expected to facilitate client process movement along the experiencing dimension.

The experiencing dimension refers to the extent to which the ongoing, bodily, felt flow of experiencing is the basic datum of an individual's awareness and communications about the self and the extent to which this inner datum is integral to action and thought. At the low level on the continuum of experiencing, discourse is markedly impersonal or superficial. Moving up the scale, there is progression from simple, limited, or externalized self-references to inwardly elaborated descriptions of feelings. At higher experiencing levels, feelings are explored. Then, new aspects of experiencing emerge from what is directly sensed but at first unclear. This implicitly complex referent is basic for problem resolution and self-understanding (Klein, Mathieu, Gendlin, & Kiesler, 1969; Gendlin, 1979, 1981).

213

THE HISTORY OF THE EXPERIENCING CONSTRUCT
IN PSYCHOTHERAPY

THE CLIENT'S PERSPECTIVE

The history of the experiencing construct forms an interesting lattice between the work of Rogers and Gendlin within the client-centered framework, being developed and refined at each new crossover. Rogers perceived "experiencing" from a clinical–observational perspective, abstracting from client-in-therapy statements. He saw experiencing as a lawful process and he developed his observations into a general theory of therapy and personality (Rogers, 1959b). Gendlin, on the other hand, had a theoretical perspective arising from an interest in the phenomenological philosophers, including Merleau-Ponty and Husserl, and applied these ideas to a better understanding of the in-therapy behavior of clients (Gendlin, 1958, 1962b).

Chronologically, Rogers first identified the process of exploration and reference to self as significant in "good therapy." In 1950, at a meeting of the Chicago chapter of the American Association of Social Workers, he referred to the process of psychotherapy as "rich and complex" and described a phenomenon of client-centered therapy that he called "the client's experience of exploration." This experience progresses in steps by which the client explores his or her perceptual field. The first stage involves the client talking about things that are relatively remote from the "organization of self"—about others, job, environment, and so forth. In successive stages the client talks more about the self, tending to discuss those experiences which had not been "owned" or which had been denied to awareness. More and more this therapeutic experience centers around the self and its relationship to those denied or distorted experiences. In general, the exploration of the perceptual field tends to move from others to self, from symptoms to self, from surface concerns to deeper concerns, from past to present, from negative to positive, and from experiences in awareness to experiences that have been denied to awareness. Thus Rogers had identified an ongoing process in the client which would seem to have a positive progress or sequencing and be a verbal manifestation of an inner process (Rogers, 1950).

In 1954–1955 Gendlin, working with Zimring, studied characteristics of the client's expression and behavior (i.e., attention to an at first unclear "direct referent," richness of detail) that are indicative of the experiencing phenomenon. This represents the earliest attempt to state specific verbal and expressive indices or correlates of the internal process (Gendlin & Zimring, 1955). In 1956, Gendlin, Jenney, and Shlien published research based on counselors' estimates, on a 9-point scale, of the extent of client "immediate experiencing." The results indicated that immediate experiencing was correlated with success measures whereas other content scales were not. Success was not related to what clients discussed, but rather to the manner of the process (Gendlin, Jenney, & Shlien, 1960).

Meanwhile, Rogers defined pathology as "incongruence" between awareness and experience, but he lacked a way to define the term "experience" in observable terms, so that "congruence" with it could be measured. The hidden storehouse could not be observed and compared with aware experience. This problem was solved by Gendlin's definition of implicitly complex experiencing as the basic felt datum or referent of awareness; "congruence" can therefore be defined as one's direct sensing of this implicitly complex referent which can be observed and measured. Self-descriptions without this direct referent are then "incongruent."

By 1962 Gendlin had changed his understanding of what constituted client-centered therapy, as a function of having applied the method to psychotics. He maintained that therapeutic attitudes manifest themselves in interactive behaviors through genuine therapist self-expression and that this open interaction itself affects the nature of the client's present experiencing process. In spite of residual feelings (threat) and tendencies (withdrawal) the client finds experiencing occurring more spontaneously (Gendlin, 1962a).

The direction then was toward an interactive model where the therapist actually participates in an experiential sense and therefore impacts directly on the client's process. By 1969 there was a final version of the Patient Experiencing Scale (Klein *et al.*, 1969), with preliminary work by Rogers, Rablen, and Walker (Rogers, 1959a; Walker, Rablen, & Rogers, 1960) and Gendlin and Tomlinson (1962).

In 1966 several studies showed that clients who were initially low in experiencing were more likely to fail in therapy. Gendlin introduced a therapeutic procedure called "focusing" to teach such failure-predicted clients to attend to a direct referent. Focusing by itself is not sufficient for psychotherapy, but it can be used and taught in the context of any therapeutic orientation. Gendlin describes this procedure extensively in theoretical terms, provides technical methods for eliciting focusing in therapy clients or research subjects, and reports research results (Gendlin, 1969; Gendlin, Beebe, Cassens, Klein, & Oberlander, 1968). Focusing is seen as the fundamental skill for the kind of attention necessary in effective therapy and basic to the experiential exploration that the Experiencing Scale measures at higher stages. Research and clinical applications describe this sharp and complete shift in client attention. The client must cease talking at the self and must instead ask, "What's the crux of it?" The client should keep quiet and refrain from answering: After a moment of waiting a bodily sense of "the whole problem or feeling" arises. Next, the client moves to letting the "main thing" about the feeling come up more specifically, first in bodily terms, then by taking the words that come from it. The words, even if they don't make any sense, are checked against the bodily feelings; the problem area will unfold, open up, and a felt shift occurs. Along with the felt shift there is tension release (Gendlin, 1969). Thus, Gendlin moved from the finding that clients who are unable to "focus" early in therapy are failure-predicted to the development of focusing as a well-defined skill which can be taught to clients and others (Gendlin, 1974a, 1981).

THE THERAPIST'S PERSPECTIVE

Although the main focus of experiential psychotherapy is on the client's engagement in a process of experiential change, the therapist clearly has an important role to play (Gendlin, 1967, 1968, 1974a, 1974b, 1979). There are two aspects to this contribution: First, the therapist responsively "listens" to every bit of communication, and also teaches focusing, a little bit at a time, during therapy hours. In this way the therapist helps to draw out the client's experiencing and carry it forward to felt shift and resolution. Second, the therapist's presence and responses as an experiencing person have an inescapable influence on the interaction and thus also on the client's phenomenology. These two therapeutic forces or vectors, while distinct, have a common impact or a final common pathway in that each can initiate and sustain (or deter and interfere with) the key client processes of personality change, felt referent, focusing, exploration, struggle, and resolution through felt shift. These two therapist contributions are the basis for the two strands of the Therapist Experiencing Scale that will be described in this chapter (Klein et al., 1969).

Although Rogers's process conception depended heavily on the theoretical formulations of Gendlin, his attitudinal "conditions" variables were his own development. He explicated the core constructs of unconditional positive regard, accurate empathy, and genuineness as the major therapist variables (Rogers, 1957). In many subsequent theoretical and empirical presentations these therapist qualities have been viewed as operating independently of client process qualities and skills, thus as constituting the essential ingredients of therapist efficacy (Bergin & Lambert, 1978; Mitchell, Bozarth, & Krauft, 1977; Truax & Mitchell, 1971). It can be argued that this perspective vests a great deal of power in the therapist and places an undue influence on the therapist's performance as the major agent of change. While Rogers has continued to recognize the importance of the counterpart client processes, some of his colleagues, and the field in general, have tended to place more theoretical weight and research attention on the therapist variables. Where client process skills have been deemphasized in favor of therapist conditions, training programs have run the risk of stressing technique without concurrent learning and understanding of the client process at which the therapist techniques are aimed.

It would appear that "the essence of client centered therapy has not yet been learned by the field" (Gendlin, 1974a, p. 213). This essence is not a set of therapist responses, but a manner of listening in which the therapist always strives for and responds to experiential concreteness and specificity. The baseline from which genuine client-centered therapy takes off is thus the therapist constantly being experientially "in touch with what is occurring in the person (client)" (Gendlin, 1974a, p. 216).

This formulation of the therapist's contribution to therapy was always basic for Rogers and can be found also in his elaboration of therapist conditions. When viewed from an experiential perspective it becomes clear that to limit the so-called conditions concepts to therapist techniques and responses is to miss the more essential and the more basic experiential core of each. Thus, Gendlin's experiential, process view of psychotherapy was always consistent with Rogers's conditions (Rogers, Gendlin, Kiesler, & Truax, 1967). For example, let us review Rogers's definition of one of the core therapeutic conditions, "empathy," and indicate how it can be clearly defined and conceived in experiential terms, that is, as a description of the therapist's experiencing of self and client in the interaction. This kind of analysis can also be applied to the concepts of "congruence" and "unconditional positive regard."

Empathy, which is the core concept in Rogers's conditions triad, can be conceived as the *manner* in which the therapist experiences the client in the same moment. To quote Rogers:

> Accurate empathic understanding means that the therapist is completely at home in the universe of the patient. It is a moment-to-moment sensitivity that is in the "here and now," the immediate present. It is the sensing of the client's inner world of private personal meanings "as if" it were the therapist's own, but without ever losing the "as if" quality. (Rogers *et al.*, 1967, p. 104)

Further, Rogers (1967) states, "The ability and sensitivity required to communicate these inner meanings back to the client in a way that allows these experiences to be 'his' is the other major part of accurate empathic understanding" (p. 104). Thus, "at a high level of accurate empathy the message "I am with you" is unmistakably clear so that the therapist's remarks fit the client's mood and content" (p. 105).

This definition does not differ from Gendlin's more specific conceptions of the therapist's role in the client's change process. The therapist's task is to carry the client's experiencing forward. This necessitates the therapist's attaining an experiential grasp of the client's communication and requires ongoing efforts to present the client with feedback in experiential form (Gendlin, 1964; Gendlin & Zimring, 1955). The therapist's understanding of the client must be experiential rather than intellectual.

The therapist's aim is not to distract the client with ideas but to carry the experiential process forward. In addition to responding to every communication, the therapist also refers to the individual's felt referent, which is at first unclear. This creates in turn a reconstituted, fresh, or immediate experiencing between client and therapist and leads to resolution and change. At the highest levels of empathy in Rogers *et al.*'s (1967) description this dovetailing of client and therapist experiencing is apparent:

> The therapist's responses move, with sensitivity and accuracy, into the feelings and experiences that are only hinted at by the client. At this level underlying feelings and experiences are specifically identified so that the content that comes to light may be new but it is not alien. (p. 106)

MEASUREMENT

PATIENT EXPERIENCING SCALE

The present form of the Experiencing Scale preserves the integral progression as evolved by Gendlin and Tomlinson (1962). Changes were made to increase the scale's reliability and consequent utility; the changes direct the rater's attention to the client's manifest verbalizations and reduce the need for inferences. This approach increased rater reliability (Klein et al., 1969).

Independent of specific pathology or problem content, and apart from therapist technique, the scale assesses the degree to which the client communicates a personal, phenomenological perspective and employs referents to what is directly sensed but not yet clear (see Table 7-1).

Stage 4 defines the theoretically pivotal point where the client changes perspective from referring outwardly to referring inwardly. Focusing is the essential element for Stages 5–7, with qualitative differences at each— the directly sensed but unclear referent at Stage 5; the felt shift and emergent experiencing with a step of resolution of an issue at Stage 6, culminating in Stage 7, where focusing comes readily and provides the connections for all discourse.

The Experiencing Scale is relevant to both therapy and research. Experiencing should be important for all therapies where self-attitudes and expressive behavior are in any way used. As a research tool, the scale has been designed to serve a variety of needs. It is sensitive to shifts in client involvement, even within a single interview session (Kiesler, Klein, & Mathieu, 1965), making it useful for microscopic process studies, such as evaluating the effectiveness of therapist interventions, assessing the productivity of different topics, appraising different patterns of interaction between clients and therapists, or establishing a profile of client performance within the therapy hour. Sampling segments over a broader span of

TABLE 7-1. Short Form of (Patient) Experiencing Scale (Klein, Mathieu-Coughlan, Gendlin, & Kiesler, 1969)

STAGE	CONTENT	TREATMENT
1	External events; refusal to participate.	Impersonal, detached.
2	External events; behavioral or intellectual self-description.	Interested, personal, self-participation.
3	Personal reactions to external events; limited self-descriptions; behavioral descriptions of feelings.	Reactive, emotionally involved.
4	Descriptions of feelings and personal experiences.	Self-descriptive, associative.
5	Problems or propositions about feelings and personal experiences.	Exploratory, elaborative, hypothetical.
6	Direct sense of emergent feelings and their impact.	Feelings vividly expressed, spontaneous or affirmative.
7	Easy presentation of experiencing; elements confidently integrated.	Expansive, illuminating, confident, buoyant.

Note. Copyright © 1970 by the Regents of the University of Wisconsin. Revised, 1983. Reprinted by permission.

time could identify trends of involvement during treatment or pinpoint special moments or phases in therapy (e.g., when work was very good or resistance was high). To the extent that experiencing is relevant in non-therapeutic settings, the scale may also be used to evaluate other kinds of interviews.

The training techniques for the scale have been constructed so that nonprofessional, clinically naive people can serve as raters (Klein et al., 1969; Schoeninger, Klein, & Mathieu, 1968). This has been done not only because it is economical, but also because nonprofessionals are likely to be freer than professionals from biases concerning client types, therapeutic techniques, or research goals (Kiesler, 1970). Even more important, the training procedure has been standardized, so that ratings can be replicated with different judges and comparable research can be carried out in different settings.

Since its inception this scale has been used in over 30 studies. Most typically, segments ranging from 2 to 8 minutes in length are drawn from various points in the course of therapy for rating by trained raters. Longer segments and running ratings of entire sessions have also been done. Aside from tapes or transcripts of individual therapy, the scale has been adapted for use in diaries (Gruver, 1971), interviews, open-ended questions (Gorney, 1968), and dream reports. Group process (Lewis & Beck, 1980) and Gestalt two-chair interactions (Greenberg, 1980) have been rated, as well as more traditional individual therapy.

The training manual which accompanies the scale has been used in many settings to train raters, with excellent reliabilities: The average for nine studies are .75 and .81 for mode and peak ratings, respectively (Klein *et al.*, 1969). A study specifically addressed to rater selection and training found no difference in the performance of naive undergraduates versus clinical psychologists as raters (Kiesler, 1970). Group and individual methods of rater training were also found to be equivalent (Schoeninger, Klein, & Mathieu, 1968).

Methodological studies have considered issues such as segment length (Kiesler, Mathieu, & Klein, 1964) and segment location within sessions (Kiesler *et al.*, 1965). When form of data presentation was considered it was found that ratings were independent of the presence of therapist speech cues (Schoeninger, Klein, & Mathieu, 1967) and equivalent for audio versus transcript rating materials (Klein, 1971).

Studies of the relationship of experiencing to other session process variables suggest that experiencing is independent of speech patterns such as client and therapist speech rates (Kiesler, Mathieu, & Klein, 1967), but related to verbal response modes of "first person disclosure and disclosure intent" (Stiles, McDaniel, & McGaughey, 1979). Patient scale ratings are also independent of therapist speech content (Schoeninger *et al.*, 1967). Finally, experiencing ratings are independent of the specific affect state described, while consistently related to other indices of depth and richness (Wexler, 1974).

Results when the Patient Experiencing Scale has been used in psychotherapy outcome studies fall into several patterns. In general, experiencing has quite consistently been associated with diagnosis, being generally higher in neurotics than schizophrenics (Kiesler, 1969; Kiesler *et al.*, 1965; Rogers *et al.*, 1967). Subjects in treatment (clients) or interested in seeking treatment are also higher in experiencing than nonclients (Rogers *et al.*, 1967), indicating that experiencing may also reflect motivation or readiness for therapy (Rogers *et al.*, 1967; Ryan, 1966; Schoeninger, 1965). When considered in relation to therapy outcome, experiencing seems to operate in at least two ways: (1) More successful clients are consistently higher in experiencing throughout therapy than less successful clients (Gendlin *et al.*, 1968; Rogers *et al.*, 1967) and (2) more successful clients show more overall improvement, or more peak moments (Gendlin *et al.*, 1968; Karon & VandenBos, 1970; Rogers *et al.*, 1967; Ryan, 1966).

In our view, these two trends suggest that some individuals enter therapy with the preexisting expressive and reflective skills necessary to benefit, while others need to develop the skill through the learning, modeling, support, and other facilitative therapy conditions.

THE THERAPIST EXPERIENCING SCALE

The Therapist Experiencing Scale is a new formulation of the therapist's role in the treatment process which deals more directly with the experiential aspect of the therapist's participation than the Rogerian conditions concepts. It provides both an overview of and a context in which to anchor the key aspects of the therapist's experiential participation, which are described and illustrated in the clinical material that appears later. The scale is grounded in Gendlin's increasingly detailed writings about the role of the therapist in experiential therapy (Gendlin, 1962b, 1964, 1967, 1968, 1974a, 1974b, 1979).

The conception of the therapist's role which is basic to the scale delineates two aspects of experiential engagement: referent and manner. Referent is that aspect of the client's experiencing that is touched upon by the therapist's words. Manner is the quality or level of the therapist's own experiencing—how experientially involved the therapist is in the interchange. The manner dimension, as outlined in the right-hand column of Table 7-2, closely parallels the treatment dimension of the Patient Scale as presented in Table 7-1. In application, however, the requirements for judging the therapist's manner at Stages 1-3 are somewhat less stringent than the requirements for client experiencing. While the client must make his or her experiencing explicit, therapist manner may be inferred (i.e., the therapist need not say he or she is "interested" to be rated at Stage 2 for manner; to seem interested intellectually is sufficient). Like the client scale, Stage 4 is an important shift in perspective, where the therapist's experiencing is *explicitly* introduced into the dialogue as a focus.

The referent dimension, outlined on the left-hand side of the table, is the major "working" dimension of the scheme. The verbal behavior and attentional focus described in each stage represent the essence of the

TABLE 7-2. THERAPIST EXPERIENCING SCALE (KLEIN & MATHIEU-COUGHLAN, IN PRESS)

STAGE	PATIENT (P) CONTENT REFERENT	THERAPIST'S (T) MANNER
1	External events not including P.	Impersonal, detached.
2	External events including P; behavioral or intellectual elaboration of P's thoughts or activities.	Interested, intellectual self-referents.
3	P's reactions to external events; limited or behavioral description of P's feelings.	Reactive, T clearly expresses or refers to T's feelings.
4	Description of P's feelings and personal experiences.	Empathically involved, T elaborates or intensifies feelings and/or associations in this context.
5	P's problems or propositions about feelings and personal experiences.	T uses own feelings to explore P's feelings.
6	Focus on P's emergent feelings and their impact.	Uses own emergent feelings to affirm P's feelings.
7	P's facility to move from one inner referent to another with authenticity.	Expansive, with integration of all elements of the interaction, including P's feelings, T's feelings, and the explicit content.

therapist's contribution to the client's therapeutic experience. From the perspective of experiential theory it is the therapist's job to move the client progressively higher on the client experiential dimension. Thus, the referent dimension defines the major stages of the therapist's efforts. Implicit in this dimension is the assumption that it is important and necessary for the therapist to be mainly focused on and concerned with the client's phenomenology in order for the experience to be helpful to the client. This is not to say that clients cannot move therapeutically on their own. Quite the contrary, on occasions when the client is experiencing fluently the therapist's best choice is not to interfere with the process. But when it is necessary for the therapist to assist in the process, the therapist's proper role is to stay focused on the *client's* experience. Thus, the referent dimension is the major channel of experiential therapy (e.g., Gendlin, 1968, 1974a). The manner dimension, which is always present, also provides the affective tone in the interaction (much as the left hand of a piano score adds depth and dimension to the melody articulated by the right). Ideally, in good therapy, manner and referent are generally consistent.

KEY EVENTS IN THERAPY
ACCORDING TO EXPERIENTIAL THEORY

Experiential theory defines the key events of therapy in terms of a sequence of experiential stages and transitions between stages. The core or keystone event is the client's engagement in the basic and necessary process of experiential focus on a "felt referent," which is defined as a person's bodily felt, concrete sense of whatever is going on—the touchstone or reference point for words, ideas, affect, change (Gendlin, 1968). Without this referent, subsequent steps of struggle, shift, and resolution are meaningless and impossible. The Patient and Therapist Experiencing Scales provide a means to describe and analyze these key events.

Theoretically and clinically four key events can be specified which represent important *transitions* between stages of the scale.

1. The emergence of the client's ability to refer experientially (Stage 3 to 4).
2. The ability to hold on to a felt referent in order to focus on problems and areas of vagueness, struggle, and uncertainty (Stage 4 to 5).
3. The experience of the felt shift or "carrying forward" which follows from the ability to refer inward steadily (Stage 5 to 6).
4. The experience of new, autonomous, and more positive feelings that follow the resolution made possible by the felt shift (Stage 6 to 7).

These key events are transitions and processes that must take place in the client's phenomenology if good experiential therapy is to occur. There is *no substitute* for the client's process. If therapy does not include at least some of these key events or processes it is probably not adequate or helpful.

The client is the essential participant in therapy. It is theoretically possible that "therapy" could take place without a therapist present. Indeed, many such sequences of experiential depth that are very similar to therapeutic moments take place in the day-to-day life of the experientially well-functioning person. Nonetheless, the interpersonal relationship is also irreplaceable, and the therapeutic manner of relating is rare in ordinary life.

In the sections that follow we will use clinical material to illustrate these key events. Some moments when the client is doing well alone will be contrasted with examples where the therapist is either helping and facilitating or impeding the process. In each case we will use the Patient and Therapist Scales as the descriptive–analytic tool.

EMERGENT ABILITY OF THE CLIENT TO FOCUS AND DEVELOP AN EXPERIENTIAL REFERENT

Experiential psychotherapy is predicated upon the client's ability to work and speak from a personal awareness of an inner experiential process, something that he or she "knows" was experienced: Examples of this would be "I was angry!" or "I knew at the time I wanted to defend myself." Some persons start therapy with this capacity, but others lack such a personal sense. Theoretically, people pass through stages of experiencing in the process of personality change, most often in the context of participation in psychotherapy (see Table 7-1 and Klein *et al.*, 1969). While persons may enter the therapeutic dialogue at different stages, very often the progression follows the following sequence:

1. The content is either intrinsically impersonal, being very abstract, general, and superficial and having a journalistic quality, where events are presented with no personal referent, *or* in other instances, when there is a personal nature to the content, the involvement is impersonal and reveals nothing, so that the remarks could as well be about a stranger (Stage 1).

2. From the straight, detached narrative or depersonalized account the person advances to expressed association with the content. Here, the speaker is either the central character in the narrative or his or her interest is clear. But the client's involvement does not go beyond the specific situation or content. Any comments, associations, reactions, and remarks serve to get the story or idea across but do not refer to or define the client's feelings in any explicit way (although there may be an implicit referent). Unelaborated dreams, fantasies, hallucinations, and free associations belong to this stage (Stage 2).

3. As the client begins to "own" his or her association to the content there often follows a stage at which the speaker adds comments on feelings or private experiences to a narrative or a description. These remarks are limited to the event or situation described (Stage 3). It is as if the personal referent were parenthetical to the narrative or content and yet provides a clear sense of any one of the following:

- The client's feelings at the time of the event or in retrospect.
- The personal significance or implications of the situation (by relating it to the client's private experience).
- The client's state of awareness at the time of the event.

By the time the client has reached Stage 3, either after progression through Stages 1 and 2, or by direct entry level, he or she is on the brink of referring inward. This mode of self-awareness is akin to what Rogers has described as the shift from self-as-object to self-as-subject, which is the basic modality of client-centered therapy (Rogers, 1958). In some sense this ability "to be" is the first task of client-centered therapy and the first sign of a productive therapeutic alliance.

FOCUSING ON THE FELT REFERENT

The client's achievement of the ability to focus experientially, is the main "event" of experiential psychotherapy. Everything else flows from, builds on, is grounded in, and is validated by the client's capacity for felt referent. This capacity starts at Stage 5 but is grounded in the capacity for inner referent that will be described here and is defined as Stage 4 on the scale. It must be understood that focusing is a *sine qua non* at all of the higher experiential stages. What varies from one stage to another is the quality of the experience.

The client's content at Stage 4 on the Patient Experiencing Scale is a clear presentation of feelings; the perspective is personal and internal. It is the person, as the one who feels or experiences events, rather than the events themselves, that is the subject of the discourse. By attending to and presenting this experiencing, the speaker communicates what it is like to be him or her. These interior views are presented, listed, or described, but their "edges" and wider, more complex, unclear quality are not used as the basis for self-examination or change. There are different ways in which a person evidences Stage 4: (1) an initial content that is a specific situation is extended by self-references to show what the client is like more generally or more personally; (2) the content is a story told completely from a personal point of view; or (3) the content is a self-characterization from a personal perspective.

When the client has developed his or her ability to focus and to have ready access to the felt referent, movement is in the direction of a type of content which makes it possible for purposeful exploration of the speaker's conflicts, feelings, and experiencing to take place. There are two components to this stage. First, the client must pose or define a problem or proposition about the self in explicit experiential terms, that is, the client must adopt a questioning attitude. The problem or proposition may involve the origin, sequence, or implications of feelings or relate feelings to other private processes. Second, the client must explore, elaborate, or probe the problem in an experiential way—there must be an awareness of the problematic aspect of the content and a commitment to struggle with it. The exploration or elaboration must be clearly related to the initial proposition and must contain inner references so that it expands the speaker's awareness. *Both* components, the problem (i.e., question) and the probing or struggle, must be present.

At Stage 5 the speaker is exploring or testing the limits of his or her experiencing. While the client must define this clearly with inner references, the manner may be conditional, tentative, hesitant, or searching. An experiencing statement at Stage 5 will most probably be introduced by, or follow from, a fourth stage expression. Since Stage 4 very often represents the client's "laying out" of or "in-depth" assessment of familiar ways of experiencing, it follows from experiential theory that positive client movement will be toward less familiar territory. Thus, the problematic formulations or hypotheses at Stage 5 tend to further reveal heretofore inaccessible aspects of the self.

The therapist's most important role, according to Gendlin (1968), is to respond to the client's felt implicit meaning, to "point at a felt sense (of whatever is of concern) that is really more complex. . . , and . . . always involves many implicit aspects and complex reactions" (p. 210). What is required is client-centered "listening," in which the therapist is constantly trying to accurately grasp and recognize the meanings the clients conveys, as well as directly pointing to what is sensed and can be referred to. As the "listening" proceeds, the client "checks" the therapist's statements against the experiential referent and corrects the therapist, thereby also again referring and sensing freshly what is inwardly present. This is the essence of "empathy" as described earlier and the experiential bridge between client and therapist, the very key to the relationship and the achievement of the therapeutic alliance (Gendlin, 1974a).

The therapist's theoretical conceptions, formulations, and external information about the client are secondary to this quality of listening and responding. Therapist constructions must be brief and point to experiential referents. Concepts are useful therapeutically only insofar as they open up a sense of how the client feels or provide clues to fruitful areas of focusing. In this regard "wrong" conceptions can help if, in the process of experiential reference and checking, the valid felt referent unfolds; "right" conceptions can be unhelpful if they become the primary focus, obscuring the client's experiential referent (Gendlin, 1974b).

The therapist's contribution to client focusing is important, but not always necessary. This principle and some important corollaries can be stated as follows:

1. Therapy has not begun until the client refers and focuses experientially.
2. The more readily the client can check with and focus on experiential referents, the greater the therapeutic potential.
3. With respect to the therapist:
   a. It is the therapist's job to facilitate the client's ability to refer and focus experientially.
   b. The therapist should not interfere with the client's felt reference, such as by imposing conceptions on the client that do not "check out" experientially.
4. If the client cannot focus experientially, then the therapist can make the task easier in several ways:
   a. The therapist can encourage the client to focus—directly by means of focusing instructions, less directly by questioning, encouraging, focusing, and following the client's track.
   b. The therapist can "listen" experientially and respond with reflections of the client's experience, trying to point to the felt meaning.
   c. The therapist can use his or her own experiential focusing to provide a model for or stimulus to the client.
   d. Given that the therapist's presence in the interaction has an experiential effect, the therapist can use the relationship, particularly the here-and-now relationship, as a focus.

Blocking of Client Experiencing

Therapists can block or interfere with client experiencing. Some therapists and therapies are concerned with questions such as What really happened? or Did it really happen as reported? Such therapies are in danger of focusing on the events rather than on the essential experiential point of how the events were experienced by the person. As Gendlin (1974b) explains, "What people do to themselves because of what happened is more important than what happened. The more personal account of the events is as useful as a factual one" (p. 273).

Concepts and knowledge of events, as well as theoretical formulations, are more likely to be therapeutic when they are used experientially, as, for example, when they point to places where experiential steps rather than logical or factual steps provide the links between words and topics. Therapy is replete with examples of how the therapist's concern with facts or ideas gets in the way of or blocks both the client's and therapist's experiential grasp of what is going on. The following excerpt provides just such as example of a client being held back from Stage 4 on the Patient Experiencing Scale by the therapist's concern with circumstantial details (particularly statements T1 and T6–11). Although therapist remarks T2 through T5 do open up the client's feelings as a possible topic, the therapist's persistent concern with the wife's and mother's reactions to the client's feelings of nervousness is clearly at the expense of the client's focus.

	EXPERIENCING SCALE (EXP) STAGE*
C1: I know, I know. I gave up everything. I had my own plumbing business and um.	P2
T1: Did your wife feel as strongly as your sisters do?	TR1 TM2
C2: She seemed to. She seemed to think I should—When she did get there, she was a lot better and uh and I can't deny her that.	P2
T2: You had to give up a lot of things to go.	TR2 TM2
C3: Gave up my home, my business, everything I owned.	P2
T3: How did it go?	TR2 TM2
C4: I didn't like it but I felt it was the only thing to do. Then when I got there my—started bothering me more and more.	P2 (starting to move forward to P3)
T4: You needed to get some things out. What did you expect in return?	TR2 TM2
C5: Just for her to get better, which we were doing. I had a wonderful job. I got a job for a whole year, then they let me go because they said I wasn't fast enough. That kind of upset me. Then I got a job at a big high-rise office building. Then it just kept getting worse and worse.	P2 (again starting with P3)
T5: How did you feel leaving your parents?	TR3 TM2
C6: Well, I miss them but had an obligation to my wife to go.	P2 (more concerned with obligation)
T6: How did your parents feel about your going?	TR1 TM2

*P = Patient; TR = Therapist Referent; TM = Therapist Manner.

	EXP STAGE
C7: My mother was quite upset, but my father thought it was the right thing to do.	P2
T7: Your mother was upset. Could you explain what happened.	TR1 TM2
C8: Yeah. Well, she always thought that my wife's colitis was more emotionally than physically. They've never gotten along too good.	P2
T8: Your wife and your mother did not. What's been the trouble between them?	TR1 TM2
C9: Oh, my wife thinks that, my mother thinks that all my nerves is just because of all the trouble that I've had with my wife from her colitis and everything and carrying on. She doesn't get along at all with my mother.	P2
T9: That's the problem with your wife, and mother.	TR1 TM2
C10: Well, she knows how my mother feels and um . . .	P2
T10: And she perceives that your mother blames your nervousness on her colitis.	TR2 TM2
C11: Yeah, I think so.	P2
T11: What does your wife think about your colitis, about your nervousness?	TR2 TM2
C12: Well, she's glad that I'm better now and she seemed enthused about us getting a little apartment down there.	P2

The experientially inhibiting effect of the same therapist is even more apparent in another excerpt from the same case. Here the client clearly manifests the capacity to refer inwardly in a description of his feelings of nervousness.

	EXP STAGE
C1: I used to work; maybe try and get in a few small plumbing jobs on the side. Do something to bring in a little extra money, but I think I could manage . . . It's funny. I don't know if I told you, but about two weeks on my lunch hour, I usually just walk. I get awful nervous and (*pause*) I just walk around for an hour or so and it helps to calm me down a little. (*pause*) For two minutes once there I didn't know where I was. Scared the living daylights out of me. But it only lasted about a minute and I was right next to the office. It was maybe two weeks ago. [*T:* Uh huh.] And I was right on the next street from the office and that's before I had to go back just walking around and stuff, trying to re-	P2 P3 P4

lax. But gee, for about a minute I didn't
know where I was, gee that's the first time
that ever happened to me. It scared me.
Then after a minute I got all my senses
back, I mean, it kind of bothered me a
little, because it happened before. Well,
it did happen once when we were in California. My wife had come back from the
hospital. And I came home one night and
didn't recognize her, the children, or anything. Went down to the hospital, talked
to the doctor for awhile, and came home.
He said something on the line, battle fatigue,
working too hard. That was over two weeks
ago.

T1: Was this before we started or after we   TR2
started?   TM2

C2: Gee, I dunno. I suppose it was just be-   P2
fore we started or just afterwards.

Some available clinical notes on this case suggest that the therapist
had a very negative conception of the client as a "constantly complaining,
polysymptomatic, passive–aggressive character . . . , perhaps borderline
who had failed at previous therapy and was frustrating both the therapist
and significant other with his relentless complaining." The clinical com-
mentator felt that the therapist was overwhelmed by the client's symptoms. Our analysis of the excerpt in experiential terms is consistent with
this view in that the therapist was consistently backing off from or
blocking the client's clear capacity to focus (albeit complainingly and
repetitively) on his feelings. Thus, these excerpts illustrate a kind of
negative event in therapy whereby a potentially productive experiential
event is stopped or blocked.

Facilitation of Focusing through Good Listening

Therapists can facilitate focusing by good listening. Moments when clients
have difficulty focusing are important openings for a range of therapist
responses which directly encourage it. The most basic, and in some
respects the most natural, way that this is done is by the therapist's
attending to, tracking, "listening" to the client. This mode of the therapist's
being-with-the-client is described in Gendlin, 1969, 1974a, 1979, and in
great detail in Gendlin, 1981. Gendlin (1979) summarizes the essential
ingredient of such listening:

> The therapist must attend not only to the client's words, but to how they are
> said, and to how the client is living right in this moment, in saying this. This
> means observing the person's face, body, voice, gestures, and taking the
> person in much more broadly than verbally. (p. 338)

The purpose is to get at the directly sensed crux, the experienced core, from which the content arises. This mode of attending must be complemented by a mode of "responding in a listening way [which] is a baseline prerequisite for any other modes of responding that are helpful, such as experiential encouragement or reflection" (Gendlin, 1974a, p. 217). It is not enough for a therapist just to "be" in a listening mode: listening must be expressed or conveyed in some way to have the desired experiential effect.

> Listening [is] a baseline requirement making all other forms of interaction safer and more effective. Listening . . . does not mean some round restatement, but a very exact set of steps wherein the listener states exactly what the person said, and the person being listened to is expected then to correct the response, or to move another step. Without doing this fairly continually, no other methods of therapy are likely to provide a continuous therapy process, or to be very effective. (Gendlin, 1974a, p. 226)

In addition to listening, the therapist can facilitate focusing. The most direct method is for the therapist to use explicit focusing instructions (Gendlin, 1974a, 1981). The therapist can also promote focusing by responding with an experientially phrased pointing to the client's referent. As with concepts, it is crucial that this is offered tentatively. The validation and endorsement must come from the client's own experiential checking and felt shift. The following brief excerpt from experiential therapy illustrates this kind of facilitation.

	EXP STAGE
T1: Hello! (*silence 18 seconds*)	TR2
	TM2
C1: It's going to be hard for me to sit here.	P2
T2: Are you saying you want to sit somewhere else or that it's hard to sit?	TR3
	TM2
C2: It's hard to sit with this restless feeling.	P3
T3: It's hard to sit . . . sit still with this jumpy restlessness inside.	TR4
	TM3
C3: (*45-second silence*) It's like nervous.	P4
T4: Mhm. Mhm. It's nervous. (*45 seconds*)	TR4
	TM3
C4: It's like I *need* to stand still, though. I'm just keeping myself busy or something since Monday.	P4
T5: You do need to stand still and see how you feel. [*C:* Yea.] Not keep yourself running so you won't feel?	TR4
	TM3
C5: (*65 seconds*) It's like all I can feel is anxious.	P4

T6: Mhm. So it's hard to be with that, be-   TR4
cause as you . . . pay attention to what's   TM4
there, all you get is anxious, and anxious is
hard to sit with. Is that right? [C: Mhm.]
Yea, anxious is hard to sit with.

In the following excerpt a different therapist progressively reflects the client's experiential perspective, even though the therapist is working within a more interpretive framework.

	EXP STAGE
C1: I had forgotten to make a phone call to New York that I was supposed to make that had something to do with the program that had to be done, and so, you know, I, she asked me to stay. She didn't say, well, I know you're in a hurry. Well not only I felt guilty because I was leaving her early, and I knew I should have made this phone call before, but we were bus—, it wasn't that I was goofing off. We were doing something else all afternoon. But she said, "Well, I really think he ought to be called," she said, "Well, I'll do it since you're in such a hurry." You know, and right away I and right away I imagined that she was angry with me for having left her— blamed me for . . .	P2 P3 P2
T1: You know, this is a good example, I think. Here was the setup. You asked for something, which was what? You wanted to leave a couple hours early, one day a week. And she said no?	TR3 TM2
C2: Not in—she didn't say no emphatically. She said no in so many words.	P2
T2: Well, what did she say?	TR2 TM2
C3: She said that well, uh, uh, something to the effect that we get off at 4 o'clock in the afternoon during the summer anyway, and there are things to be done, and maybe in September you can work something out when you've been here longer. This type of thing.	P2
T3: OK. So she said no. And—how—how how did you react to that?	TR3 TM2
C4: Well, I just felt miserable because I thought I had asked for something that I didn't deserve, or you know, that I had asked	P4

for favors that I didn't—hadn't actually earned, y'know, at that point.

T4a: You asked them, right? You didn't— didn't steal—didn't sneak it when you said can I have this—   TR2 TM3

C4a: Yes.   C2

T4a: She said no, and—and then you started saying, oh aren't you a bad—You expected too much, and who are you to ask itself, y'know.   TR4 TM4

C4b: Uh huh.

T4b: Putting yourself down. Right away instead of saying well, I guess I'll have to wait. Guess she's a little on the—doesn't want to give me time or whatever. So you blame yourself for asking. It wasn't such a unreasonable request. You asked for it. You didn't take it without asking.   TR4 TM4

C4c: Right.   C3

Later on in the same session the therapist uses direct questions for the same purpose.

C1: But then when somebody turns me down, I feel like I really stepped on their toes, y'know.   P4 (in the context of the previous client statement)

T1: What was your thought you had when she turned you down? What ran through your mind?   TR4 TM2

C2: Well, I was angry first of all because I didn't think it was an unreasonable request.   P4

T2: OK. But then the anger somehow dissipated, right?   TR4 TM3

C3: Right.   P4

T3: Then what came next?   TR4 TM3

Another example of a therapist's experiential restatement:

C1: These [financial planning] are things that there isn't time to do, or if there is, the time to do them, you can make the time, but I don't have enough time to do them well.   P1

T1: Uh, I sense the pressure of the other things demanding to be done, even though.   TR4 TM4

C2: Yeah. I'm doing that at the expense of something else, and no matter what it is,   P3

when it's done, when it's done, either I know
he's going to thank me for it 'cause it's late
and they're a little pissed off, or they're going
to thank me for it and hit me with another
one right away, like a letter.

This eventually leads into a deeper level of experiencing:

Cl: And when I start to think that way, I   P4
think that I'm—my head's going to split and
the usual result of it is sitting at home
morose, or if it happens at work, sitting at my
desk with my stomach slightly nauseous and
absolutely no desire left in me. The only
thing I can imagine doing is kind of crawling
into a hole. Even if I get away from it, when
I come back it's not going to be solved.

In sum, the proof of the rightness of the therapist's responses must
come from the client. If the reflections have been on target, the client can
confirm them by a brief "checking" with his or her feelings. If the remarks
have encouraged focusing (i.e., attention to the "edges" of feelings), the
client should respond with some sort of experiential deepening (often
accompanied by a release of tension) which reveals more experiential detail
to the client and therapist. It is this release and movement that are basic to
the experiential levels characteristic of Stage 6 on the Patient Experiencing
Scale.

The therapist's activities that encourage focusing can be outlined:

1. The therapist may use explicit focusing instructions.
2. The therapist must attend to the client in a listening way and be
   experientially open to the client.
3. The therapist may try to give the client feedback in the form of a
   "truthful" sense when he follows, and when he does not (Gendlin,
   1981).
4. The therapist may restate his or her understanding or reflect the
   client's own perspective using the client's own words and ask him
   or her to check.
5. It is best for the therapist to focus on what is understood (the
   positive) on the assumption that what is not clear will unfold.
6. The client is the guide. The therapist's remarks should be considered tentative, as approximations that need to be re-formed.
7. The therapist's own words and own ideas should not be imposed.
   If tried out, they are quickly dropped if they do not fit.

Pointing to Focusing

Therapists can point the way to focusing. In therapy the client inevitably focuses on problems, troubles, and areas of conflict or confusion which, by definition, cannot be easily faced. "One cannot expect to grasp clearly what the trouble is while it troubles . . . grasping clearly is possible only as one experiences fully, and for that one must experience beyond the hang-up which constitutes a problem or difficulty" (Gendlin, 1968, p. 222). Both the client and the therapist must develop the capacity to sustain their focus on problems and stay with areas of pain, vagueness, confusion. These moments of problematic focusing are critical events in therapy because they provide the openings for unfolding, shift, and resolution: "Yet it's just where feelings and situations aren't clear, that a good process needs to happen. It can happen, if people will first *make a place* out of what's unclear, or unresolved, and then feel their way into that" (Gendlin, 1974a, p. 231).

By definition, focusing does not come easily. The therapist's efforts are particularly important in helping clients get through being stuck, but these efforts have to be of a special kind. The focus must be on the client, specifically on that "place" in his or her experience where things are vague and troubled. By an attitude of open interest, even shared struggle, the therapist can model the desired exploration. The therapist can often, preferably in the client's own words, ask tentative, open-ended questions that point to the yet unknown crux and thus sustain the process. Questions like "What really is this?", reference to the "whole thing," or acknowledgment of alternatives (i.e., "What might be different if it were all OK?") function to prevent closure and retreat. Pauses or moments for private focusing may be also needed (Gendlin, 1974a, 1981). Gendlin (1974a) summarizes the therapist's stance as follows:

> Especially when things are stuck, when a person goes round in circles and we have been around a circle many times, I feel quite free to try one thing after another. It is then best not to be too invested in any one way. Again, responding to the person's own sense between every two tries let one know that what one has tried has failed and enables one to return to the person's own process. (pp. 224–225)

The fact that within every problem and conflict there may be found a positive direction, a life-maintaining tendency that is being thwarted by the problem, also provides an important therapeutic opening. When the therapist can imagine, or better yet, authentically sense and respond to the positive side of the problem, the client's sense can be carried further to a new place. This may well include the therapist's sharing his or her own reactions to the struggle, his or her own desire for resolution. These points are illustrated in the following excerpt from experiential psychotherapy (Gendlin, 1982).

	EXP STAGE
C1: I've been looking forward to coming, much more than I did the other times, I've had a crummy week. My job is really bad, and I'm tired of my house, and everything seems flat like I'm just watching, I'm not in it. And I know it's me.	P3 P4 (peak)
T1: So everything seems flat and you're not involved in it, just watching. But you know it isn't the job and so on, it's you.	TR4 TM3
C2: Well, the job really is bad, what they're doing in that place isn't right, but other times I'd be able to do something with it, I know.	P2
T2: So it's true what you feel about them, but also, the way you're being inside you is not OK.	TR4 TM2
C3: Yes.	
T3: So we have to go see where your good energy went to. *(long silence)*	TR5 TM4
C4: I have lots of energy there, but it's tied up.	P5
T4: You can feel your energy right there, but it's tied up.	TR5 TM4
C5: Yes.	
T5: Can you sense what's tying it up? *(long silence)*	TR5 TM2
C6: It's like a heavy wall in front of it. It's behind that.	P5
T6: You can feel a heavy wall. *(long silence)*	TR5 TM4
C7: It's a whole part of me that I keep in. Yes, a whole part of me, like when I say it's OK when it's not. The way I hold everything in. *(long silence)* There's a part of me that's dead, and a part that isn't.	P6
T7: Two parts, one is dead, and one . . . ah	TR6 TM4
C8: Survived. *(silence)* It wants to scream, to live.	P6 (in context of C7)
T8: The dead part wants to scream and be let out. *(phrased tentatively)*	TR6 TM5
C9: And there's also something vague, I can't get what that is.	P5
T9: Make a space for that vague thing, you don't know what it is yet. There's something vague there, but it isn't clear what it is.	TR5 TM3
C10: I feel a lot of tension.	P5
T10: OK, take a break. Just step back a little	TR5

bit. There's the vague thing, and then also, there's the tension. Let's talk a little. You've come a lot of steps. [*C: relaxes, shifts in the chair*] Yes, that's right. Let the body get whole again, when we come a long way there have to be little breaks.	TM4
C11: It's hard to take a break.	P4
T11: That's why I'm talking, I'm just saying anything so you can have a break.	TR2 TR3
C12: Yes, I'm getting a break because I'm listening to what you're saying. (*shifts again*) Now I'm going back.	P4
T12: There was a vague thing, and tension.	TR5 TM4
C13: It's *like* I want to run.	P5
T13: Step back just a little step, and be next to the wanting to run. (*long silence*)	TR5 TM4
C14: Someone will be mad at me if I let that part live, and that's very uncomfortable.	P6 (the feeling has opened up)
T14: If you let that live, someone will be mad at you, and that's hard to stand.	TR4 TM4
C15: Yes. (*long silence*) I want to run and never look back, and just be free.	P6 (in context of C14)
T15: You want to run, just not look back, go free. (*silence*)	TR6 TM4
C16: Then that's sad.	P6 (still in context of C14 and 15)
T16: Somehow it feels sad, if you run and don't look back.	TR6 TM4
C17: Yes. Running from the vague thing is sad. Some of me wants to find out what the vague thing is. (*long silence*) Some of me doesn't.	P6
T17: You can feel a part of you that doesn't want to find out, and a part that does. [*C: looks angry*] Be friendly to this place, just step back a little bit, like, OK this could take a while, it's OK if it takes a week to find out, slowly. Make room for a part that doesn't want to find out, a part that does.	TR5 TM4
C18: I don't feel friendly. I want to jump on it.	P5
T18: Yes, that's what I thought. Well, make a space for the anger too. The anger gets to be here too. Just don't let it get on this thing. Let the anger flow through. (*long silence*)	TR5 TM4
C19: I'm very angry.	P6
T19: Lots of anger. (*long silence*)	TR6 TM4

C20: It's a big loss, something missing.   P6
That's what the vague thing was.

T20: A big loss. Something big missing.   TR6
(*long silence*)   TM4

C21: And my energy is right there too.   P6

T21: So that's also where your energy is. It   TR6
is there with the vague thing that turned out   TM4
to be a big loss of something big, missing.

C22: Yes, I feel lighter!   P6

T22: It feels better.   TR6
    TM4

C23: Yes, I don't know what that is yet,   P6
that's missing, but even though I don't know
what it is, I feel lighter. I feel all right inside
myself again.

The effect of these questions and restatements that point to the client's felt sense must be carefully validated by each further step the client takes. The felt sense that unfolds, is, by its very nature, shaky, vague, hard to hold and maybe rambling, not neat, unfinished, and unclear. The therapist must avoid the temptation to wrap up the issue and to complete conceptual pictures too fast. If the therapist's reflections have been on target, and on the potential for experiential opening, the patient will move along at his or her natural pace.

The Relational Encounter

The therapist's presence in the sessions has an important and inescapable experiential effect. Even when the therapist's reactions are not openly the subject of attention, the "client's present experiencing is always concretely with and toward that real other person" (Gendlin, 1968, p. 220). The potential for feedback from the therapist, for his or her feelings and reactions to emerge, is always there and can be made explicit.

Therapist experiencing may be especially useful in promoting a client's focusing when the client is having difficulty staying "on track" with felt referents. At such points the therapist may attend to his or her own responses to and feelings about the client and make them known. As in the following clinical example this may take the form of the therapist's "imaginatively sensing the client's felt meaning" (Gendlin, 1968, p. 221). This requires both openness and restraint. The therapist must be able "to confront [his or her] own feelings, reactions, fears, embarrassments, stuck points, angers, impatiences—whatever is focally felt, and must sense whether and how that is related to the present interaction with the client" (Gendlin, 1979, p. 338). However, these reactions are usually expressed *only* to make the client's experiencing more explicit. The therapist's feelings may become the focus if need be; when honestly and responsibly shared, the therapist's expression of feeling can signify the therapist's willingness to "risk" himself or herself with heightened living and also model the way in which blocks, stoppages, etc., can be moved through. "Such open responding is rare in ordinary society, but essential in psychotherapy" (Gendlin, 1979, p. 338). Even the direct expression of the therapist's negative feelings (e.g., frustration, anger, boredom) may be constructive when expressed with the specificity possible after focusing and in a "context of positive commitment" (Gendlin, 1979, p. 339). It is important that the therapist first be clear about personal reactions, know that they are relevant, and express them sparingly and briefly. Because therapist expression can have a powerful effect on the patient, the therapist must be very careful not to distract or overwhelm.

In the following example the therapist's interactive response is minimal, but the acknowledged reaction to just a part of the client's affect is enough to encourage the client's ownership of feeling.

	EXP STAGE
C1: It just, to watch, I—I'd see, know people I'd know in four years of high school just be programmed to be incompetent, and to be programmed to feel that they're, they're not worthy of anything because of the situation, that they could have—because of the way they took it and the way they couldn't stand up to it, and the way people are just shitting on them, and I just—I'm so alienated by that. When I saw it happening to me I just turned off.	P2
	P3
T1: Doesn't sound like you're turned off.	TR3
	TM2
C2: Like I what?	
T2: Doesn't sound like you're turned off.	
C3: Well, when I say turned off, I mean I—I was very—I was very angry about it. But I mean I didn't respond in the classroom, is what I'm saying oftentimes. And sometimes I'd just skip class, I just wouldn't bother going.	P4

A second example of therapist's experiential restatement makes clearer use of the therapist's presence in the interaction. This excerpt is a continuation of the excerpt that begins on p. 230.

	EXP STAGE
T1: Are you tapping it again? [Refers to a restless feeling the client has described]	TR4
	TM2

C1: What came to me right now was . . .   P3
like I know what it's about . . . because it
started when I was typing my dream, the one
I did with you the other day, and uh I did an
active daydream with images, and I cried all   P4
the way through it. I couldn't stop crying,
cause I really got into it . . . it was awful,
and since then I've been walking, and I
couldn't.

T2: It's where that went, that went real deep   TR5
and then it got stuck, is that right? And since   TM5
then it's been jumpy.

C2: The part where it really got stuck was   P5 (in context of C1)
. . . it was all OK about the people on the
platform. It felt like a grieving there and that
was OK, but the other part my father walking
out and that, I just wasn't ready to deal with
it.

T3: Mhm. Mhm. Wait. There was a part of   TR5
the active imagination you did that was all   TM3
right.

C3: Yea.

T4: But there was another part that had to   TR5
do with him walking out, that part. [C: Mhm]   TM3
Did you go a ways with it and then got stuck
in the middle of it being bad, or was it that
you could sense it was going to be that way?

C4: When I started out it was fine, then I   P6
really got into it . . . um . . . it was sad.
It was real different, trying to process it
alone. There's a change there, because I
could before. It felt real lonely it felt awful!

T5: (laughs) I have a part to play after all.   TR5
It's different being able to relate to people.   TM5
Used to be your way to do it was alone
(8-second silence) but you can do more with
other people, than you can do alone.

C5: Well, the desire is there now to be with   P5 (in context)
other people. It's different.

T6: Here we are!   TR4
     TM6

C6: I knew you would say that!   P3

T7: All four billions of us and me. *(25-second*   TR4
silence) Um. Where'd you go?   TM6

C7: What?   P2

T8: Did I interrupt? It's OK.   TR4
     TM4

C8: I just touched the pain. [T: Mhm] Then   P5
I started playing around again.

T9: So you know where it is, and you . . .   TR6
can touch it, but it's pretty bad. [C: Mhm]   TM4
(*10-second silence*) It's all right to just touch
it and then back away from it. Can you say
that's all right? . . . (*10-second silence*)
. . . then you don't have to play around,
you can just know you're doing that . . .
and take a break . . . (*10-second silence*)
that's a right way to do, just touch it, and
take a break . . . (*110-second silence*)

C9: I'd say that there is something in my   P5
way.

T10: Mhm. (*105-second silence*) There is   TR5
something in the way?   TM5

C10: Yes.

T11: At the painful spot? [C: yes] Between   TR5
you and it.   TM5

C11: Mhm. Like I'm trying to climb a   P5
mountain or something and, uh, can't crawl
and can't do it.

T12: Mhm. Mhm. Makes me think of climb-   TR5
ing the mountain with the truck. [C: Mhm]   TM5
You're trying to climb the mountain and you
can't do it. [C: Mhm] And do we know what
the mountain is?

C12: (104-second silence) Mhm. It's like   P5
. . . I want to get to the top of the mountain
so I can see everything clearly, but I don't
think I want to go through the pain of getting
there.

T13: Mhm. So from the top of *that* moun-   TR6
tain you'll be able to see it all clearly but there   TM5
is a lot of pain still . . . between you and
. . . seeing clearly something that feels like
it doesn't *want* the pain . . . Is that right?

C13: (*10-second silence*) Yea, I'm going to   P5
get hurt getting up there (*10-second silence*)
I think I'm still looking at the routes how to
get there.

REFERENT MOVEMENT, THE FELT SHIFT, RESOLUTION

In experiential therapy the felt shift, or referent movement, is the "peak" moment when change and growth are possible. The unfolding of new experiencing that is the result of the felt shift is accompanied by bodily relief, which is also a direct sense of the immediacy or "rightness" of words and referent. The referent is then easier to stay with and is experienced differently than before. Part of the client's new felt understanding is his or her grasp of positive tendencies and possibilities and appreciation of his or her own richness and authenticity. Even if the new experience does not "solve" anything for the client, the sense of authenticity and autonomy is gratifying. The newly found sense can be used to validate choice and take responsibility (Gendlin, 1979). As Gendlin (1979) states, "The recognition that values are real, frees the person for working with them, instead of remaining locked at some inchoate and mute point of conflict between so-called rational expedient living and subjectively felt unacceptables and unlived potentialities" (p. 342).

Some of these principles are shown in this excerpt, which is a further continuation of the excerpt from pp. 230–231 and 238–240.

	EXP STAGE
T1: (*after an interruption*) Are you tapping it again? [Note the similarity to T1 on p. 238.]	TR5 TM5
C1: Yes, it's restless again when I don't feel the pain.	P5*
T2: Maybe there is a place where you can be *closer* to the painful spot, but not be in it. (*minutes of silence*)	TR5 TM5
C2: It's OK now! I put the restlessness down, and I put the pain far away, and you know what made it OK? I was imagining *playing*!	P6
T3: Oh . . . yes . . . sure. That's neat!	TR6 TM6

These moments are the results, the endpoints of efforts at experiential focusing, where the effort involved in staying experientially with conflict, pain, confusion, and vagueness pays off. Because the emergent sense of the issue is somehow closer to the crux, the whole thing is a new, fresh experience, and further focusing steps and shifts continually change what is found. Even if the content is familiar, the grasp is different—more complete, more complex, more differentiated, with more awareness of the interaction with the environment, more bodily feeling, *and* with recognition of the potential for responsibility, choice, autonomy, and growth.

This felt shift is a culmination of focusing steps and is characterized by the two highest stages of the scale, 6 and 7. Gendlin (1979) describes this shift well:

> Although one may be unable to live freely, openly, and courageously in the world, one does live in this *manner* when one allows the coming of whatever feelings may come. Although one may not know how to change some narrowness or stoppage, in the very letting come and letting be, one is, just

*In context of the earlier shift at P4 on p. 239 this could be rated as P6.

then, living beyond exactly those limitations. One is living exactly the manner which, according to the content, one cannot. And, *therefore* the content soon changes. At the first step of letting come, what comes is some unlovely truth—but already a few minutes later at a second step, a felt shift, a further feeling emerges. The content then focused on arises from that first step of fuller process. One had lived beyond the seeming limitations of that content one focused upon, and one did that in the very act of focusing upon it, in letting it come and in letting it be. (p. 343)

The therapist's role in such moments may be, or seem to be, minimal. Some clients, especially after some experience, may be able to run through the cycle of experiential referent, focusing, and felt shift with little help from the therapist. When help is needed, the same principles described for focusing apply. To help someone "make a place" where some new experiencing can form, the therapist must, first and foremost, be very careful *not* to impose ideas, perceptions, or constructions. Openness, constant checking, and brief, gentle restatements can help to keep the client on the experiential track. The therapist can suggest that one need not "go in" nor "run away," but offer a third possibility: "Stay near it. Don't go in; back up and let all 'of it' be 'over there,' a little distance away." Then to help the development of a felt sense the therapist can refer to the quality of "all that" and ask the client to sense what the quality really is. To help a shift to happen the therapist can ask questions (e.g., "What is the worst of it?" or "What would it take to feel better?") and ask the client to refrain from answering too soon. The felt sense should be asked, and the client must wait for "it" to "answer."

The therapist at this point must also be personally focused on the emerging edge. This may take the form of paying attention to the authenticity of what the client has been struggling with. It requires that the therapist's experience shifts at or near the same time as the client's shifts occur, so that the process is modeled and genuinely shared. In such moments the client–therapist interaction is especially salient and close. In essence, the therapist's "set" and quality of involvement at this stage is *more critical* than any specific words or ideas. It is *essential* that he or she be experientially involved, attuned with immediacy, and responsive to positive, autonomous facets of the client's being. The interactive quality of this involvement is essential, for it is only through interaction with the environment (therapist) that the client's experiencing can authentically unfold. All of these points are illustrated in the therapy excerpts, except for the one on pp. 235–237.

In summary, "An experiential therapist is committed to aid the patient to articulate life, and thereby accords the patient full responsibility and validity for any choice, sense of significance, for the unique way of construing anything which is this person. This has a freeing effect which aids one to move on through false constraints, securities, and imposed values to which one fearfully clings. The validity and respect accorded the client's values and meanings . . . is a therapeutic agent" (Gendlin, 1979, p. 342).

PERSONALITY CHANGE AND A CONCEPT OF HEALTH WITHIN THE EXPERIENTIAL MODEL

Client-centered theory defines health as a process, not as a static set of value concepts or as an endpoint. In a 1950 article outlining his then current formulation of client-centered therapy, Rogers described the "phase" of therapy after the felt shift as a time when "the client is likely to experience a raw, newborn, uncertain, fluctuating quality about himself which puzzles him" (p. 448). As the reorganized self is in action, the individual's behavior changes, "not as a result of struggle but rather unconsciously and spontaneously" (p. 448), and there is a sense of assurance. As feelings are now experienced as real, the client is freed from other's perceptions and can depend on his or her own perceptions. All problems are by no means solved, but there is a new capacity to know and use one's own experience, directly faced, as a guide.

Gendlin (1967) has gone further to explain how this "experiential process" which gives rise to values is the key to responsible and healthy functioning and the desired outcome of good psychotherapy. The psychotherapy process determines values and health insofar as it promotes the kind of ongoing experiential living in which an individual can make choices and judgments and provide conceptual shape and form to life. To base values on experiencing is not to say that values are arbitrary or that the ideal person is in a constant state of flux; rather, values based on an experiential process (or "process values") are more likely to allow the person to discover and integrate his or her own "specific cultural, intellectual and individual training which can be experientially felt, differentiated, and resolved" (Gendlin, 1967, p. 200). In this sense, process values lead the individual toward universal values, culture, and intellect and are not individualistic, chaotic, or without form (Gendlin, 1967).

RESOLVING CLINICAL IMPASSES

In this discussion we have been mainly concerned with the facilitative role played by the therapist in his or her references to and reflections and restatements of the client's experiencing. In terms of the "two-channel" conception of the Therapist Experiencing Scale, we have thus put more emphasis on the client referent side. We have done this in the belief that while the client–therapist relationship is important, and while the therapist's feelings and personal involvement in the encounter are crucial, the referent channel is the primary mechanism for therapeutic influence. This is not to say that the manner (or more interactional) channel is not important; rather, it can substitute for the referent channel less frequently, or less extensively. High-quality therapist referring is essential over the long haul of therapy; high-quality manner (in the consistent absence of comparable referent involvement) cannot carry the day. Diverse therapeutic techniques and styles, if effective, can be found to share common levels on the referent dimension. Thus, good psychoanalysis, good client-centered therapy, good rational–emotive therapy, and so forth, all have in common the therapist's manifest concern with and encouragement of the client's experiencing. At the same time, therapists are likely to vary more with respect to manner. Some theories and schools openly encourage therapist expression of personal feeling and personal involvement (e.g., client centered); other schools downplay or even discourage such therapist expression and are predicated on a more intellectual engagement (e.g., strict psychoanalytic therapy and much of rational–emotive therapy is carried out at Stage 2 therapist manner).

Although therapist manner is in the background, it can exert a powerful influence on therapy, particularly when therapist referent efforts fail to produce client progress. One classic example can be found in a familiar and common clinical impasse: the dilemma provided by the client who has the facility to talk freely and fluently about feelings, but who does not use this facility to tackle important areas of conflict and/or ambiguity. Often characteristic of therapeutically experienced clients, people who habitually speak of feelings and relationships in an open, self-disclosing style, or persons who have become familiar with parts of themselves through repeated contact and display, this type of fluent, apparent self-revelation can nonetheless block and frustrate further advance. It is as if the capacity for experiential discourse, once tried and familiar, probably having been rewarded by the therapist's response in its more tentative beginnings, becomes a safe, familiar style, taking on a certain autistic quality. This glib style evades the central demand of therapy to probe deeper and reach beyond the familiar and safe to the more risky and unknown experiential edge.

This sort of impasse has already been described in the section on problematic focusing. Here, however, we have in mind those occasions when the therapist's repeated encouragements, support, or direct suggestions to make the transition to a more problematic focus (i.e., to Stage 5 on the Patient Experiencing Scale) may have failed to yield substantial progress. Such points of impasse, when appropriate referent probes have failed, may call for straightforward use of the principles implicit in therapist manner. Greater influence may come from the therapist's genuine but deliberate acknowledgment of the effect of the impasse on the client–therapist relationship. This might take the form of the therapist's sharing of his or her frustration or puzzlement. Such a tactic could make the issue of blocked exploration and resistance to change more immediate, real, and concrete than any further repetition of the experiential content. This suggestion is, of course, consistent with the core tenet of experiential theory that experiencing is carried forward and open to change when in interaction with the immediate environment.

A second clinical problem occurs when a client experiences felt shifts in therapy and yet cannot seem to initiate a consequent behavioral change outside of therapy. In other words, a client does not seem to be making use of the insights gained during therapy to improve his or her "real-life" situation. Theoretically, any client could present this problem; however, persons who have had extensive exposure to therapy seem particularly likely to develop this difficulty. Several factors appear responsible for this finding: First, a client who has experienced a positive and personal interaction with a therapist has probably found the relationship to be comfortable and thus may be reluctant to give it up. Second, the client may savor the regard that the therapist communicates when shifts are occurring and believe (in spite of anything the therapist might indicate to the contrary) that the regard would be in jeopardy if the client were to share or admit fear or apprehension about putting the changes into practice. Third, the client may have become a "hothouse" experiencer: he or she may have been encouraged, in previous therapeutic circumstances, to progress in terms of keener self-understanding but with no specific attention paid to carrying forth these learnings into his or her life outside of therapy. For whichever of these reasons, the client actually experiences a felt shift or a new aspect of the self but does not choose to integrate that view of the self with the "outside" world. In failing to do this the client does not get needed feedback on the new, experienced self, and thus the new sense of awareness does not get external validation.

The therapist will know that this problem is developing as he or she monitors the discrepancy between cycles of experiencing levels that run from Stages 4–6 within the therapy hour in contrast with lower levels apparent in the client's reports of what is happening outside of therapy. When confronted with this "stoppage," the therapist should make it the focus of his or her attention. The following program of interventions should prove helpful:

1. Develop, in collaboration with the client, specific tasks ("homework") aimed at providing the client with means by which to implement new learnings about the self. Great pains should be taken to make sure that the task is clearly understood and that

potential difficulties are honestly acknowledged and dealt with during the therapy session, before the client attempts to carry out the task in a real-life situation.

2. The therapist should assume the responsiblity for maintaining continuity of focus in subsequent sessions. The client who tends not to bring the new self into contact with the world outside presents a therapeutic issue which should take priority until such times as the client provides evidence that he or she has become accustomed to generalizing from the therapy experiences. During this period the therapist should expect lower levels of experiencing to occur more frequently than in the recent past, as the client reports on what has happened to him or her in a behavioral sense since their last meeting, in other words, as the client brings in the "homework." Such a temporary drop to the lower levels of experiencing is theoretically coherent and appropriate for a therapeutic focus of this type.

REFERENCES

Bergin, A. E., & Lambert, M. J. The evaluation of therapeutic outcomes. In S. L. Garfield & A. E. Bergin (Eds.), *Handbook of psychotherapy and behavior change* (2nd ed.). New York: Wiley, 1978.

Gendlin, E. T. *The function of experiencing in symbolization.* Unpublished doctoral dissertation, University of Chicago, 1958.

Gendlin, E. T. Client-centered developments and work with schizophrenics. *Journal of Counseling Psychology*, 1962, *9*, 205–212. (a)

Gendlin, E. T. *Experiencing and the creation of meaning.* New York: Free Press of Glencoe, 1962. (b)

Gendlin, E. T. A theory of personality change. In P. Worchel & D. Byrne (Eds.), *Personality change.* New York: Wiley, 1964.

Gendlin, E. T. Values and the process of experiencing. In A. R. Mahrer (Ed.), *The goals of psychotherapy.* New York: Appleton-Century-Crofts, 1967.

Gendlin, E. T. The experiential response. In E. F. Hammer (Ed.), *Use of interpretation in treatment: Technique and art.* New York: Grune & Stratton, 1968.

Gendlin, E. T. Focusing. *Psychotherapy: Theory, Research and Practice*, 1969, *6*, 4–15.

Gendlin, E. T. Client-centered and experiential psychotherapy. In D. A. Wexler, & L. N. Rice (Eds.), *Innovations in client-centered therapy.* New York: Wiley, 1974. (a)

Gendlin, E. T. The role of knowledge in practice. In G. F. Farwell, N. R. Gamsky, & P. Mathieu-Coughlan (Eds.), *The counselor's handbook.* New York: Intext Educational Publishers, 1974. (b)

Gendlin, E. T. Experiential psychotherapy. In R. Corsini (Ed.), *Current psychotherapies* (Revised ed.). Itasca, Ill.: F. E. Peacock, 1979.

Gendlin, E. T. *Focusing.* New York: Bantam, 1981.

Gendlin, E. T. *Experiential psychotherapy.* Unpublished manuscript, 1982.

Gendlin, E. T., Beebe, J., Cassens, J., Klein, M., & Oberlander, M. Focusing ability in psychotherapy, personality, and creativity. In J. M. Shlein (Ed.), *Research in Psychotherapy* (Vol. 3). Washington, D.C.: American Psychological Association, 1968.

Gendlin, E. T., Jenney, R., & Shlien, J. M. Counselor ratings of process and outcome in client-centered therapy. *Journal of Clinical Psychology*, 1960, *16*, 210–213.

Gendlin, E. T., & Tomlinson, T. M. *Experiencing scale*. Unpublished manuscript, Wisconsin Psychiatric Institute, 1962.

Gendlin, E. T., & Zimring, F. M. *The qualities or dimensions of experiencing and their change*. Counseling Center Discussion Papers, Vol. 1 (No. 3), University of Chicago Library, 1955.

Gorney, J. E. *Experiencing and age: Patterns of reminiscence among the elderly*. Unpublished doctoral dissertation, University of Chicago, 1968.

Greenberg, L. S. The intensive analysis of recurring events from the practice of Gestalt therapy. *Psychotherapy: Theory, Research and Practice*, 1980, *17*, 143–152.

Gruver, G. G. *The use of a process measure in student development groups*. Unpublished doctoral dissertation, University of Arizona, 1971.

Karon, B. P., & VandenBos, G. R. Experience, medication and the effectiveness of psychotherapy with schizophrenics. *British Journal of Psychiatry*, 1970, *116*, 427–428.

Kiesler, D. J. *Refinement of the experiencing scale as a counseling tool* (Contract No. OEC 3-7-061329-2835). Report to U.S. Department of Health, Education and Welfare, Office of Education, Bureau of Research, 1969.

Kiesler, D. J. Comparison of Experiencing Scale ratings of naive versus clinically sophisticated judges. *Journal of Consulting and Clinical Psychology*, 1970, *35*, 134.

Kiesler, D. J., Klein, M. H., & Mathieu, P. L. Sampling from the recorded therapy interview: The problem of segment location. *Journal of Consulting Psychology*, 1965, *29*, 337–344.

Kiesler, D. J., Mathieu, P. L., & Klein, M. H. Sampling from the recorded therapy interview: A comparative study of different segment lengths. *Journal of Consulting Psychology*, 1964, *28*, 439–357.

Kiesler, D. J., Mathieu, P. L., & Klein, M. H. Patient experiencing level and interaction-chronograph variables in therapy interview segments. *Journal of Consulting Psychology*, 1967, *31*, 224.

Klein, M. H. *Overview of rating methodology*. Paper presented at the meeting of the American Psychological Association, Washington, D.C., September 1971.

Klein, M. H., & Mathieu-Coughlan, P. The Patient and Therapist Experiencing Scales. In L. Greenberg & W. Pinsoff (Eds.), *The psychotherapeutic process: A research handbook*. New York: Guilford, in press.

Klein, M. H., Mathieu, P. L., Gendlin, E. T., & Kiesler, D. J. *The experiencing scale: A research and training manual*. Madison: University of Wisconsin Extension Bureau of Audiovisual Instruction, 1969.

Lewis, C. M., & Beck, A. *An application of the experiencing scale to the analysis of group development*. Paper presented at the meeting of the Society for Psychotherapy Research, Asilomar, Calif., June 1980.

Mitchell, K. M., Bozarth, J. D., & Krauft, C. D. A reappraisal of the therapeutic effectiveness of accurate empathy, nonpossessive warmth and genuineness. In A. S. Gurman & A. M. Razin (Eds.), *Effective psychotherapy: A handbook of research*. Elmsford, N.Y.: Pergamon Press, 1977.

Rogers, C. R. A current formulation of client-centered therapy. *Social Science Review*, 1950, *24*, 4.

Rogers, C. R. The necessary and sufficient conditions of therapeutic personality change. *Journal of Consulting Psychology*, 1957, *21*, 95–103.

Rogers, C. R. A process conception of psychotherapy. *American Psychologist*, 1958, *13*, 142–149.

Rogers, C. R. A tentative scale for the measurement of process in psychotherapy. In E. A. Rubenstein & M. B. Parloff (Eds.), *Research in psychotherapy* (Vol. 1). Washington, D.C.: American Psychological Association, 1959. (a)

Rogers, C. R. A theory of therapy, personality, and interpersonal relationships, as developed by the client-centered framework. In S. Koch (Ed.), *Psychology: A study of a science: Formulations of the person and the social context* (Vol. 3). New York: McGraw-Hill, 1959. (b)

Rogers, C. R., Gendlin, E. T., Kiesler, D. J., & Truax, C. B. (Eds.). *The therapeutic relationship and its impact: A study of psychotherapy with schizophrenics.* Madison: University of Wisconsin Press, 1967.

Ryan, R. P. *The role of the experiencing variable in the psychotherapeutic process* (Doctoral dissertation, University of Illinois, 1966). (University Microfilms No. 66-785)

Schoeninger, D. W. *Client experiencing as a function of therapist self-disclosure and pretherapy training in experiencing* (Doctoral dissertation, University of Wisconsin, 1965). (University Microfilms No. 65-14,929)

Schoeninger, D. W., Klein, M. H., & Mathieu, P. L. Sampling from the recorded therapy interview: Patient experiencing ratings made with and without therapist speech cues. *Psychological Reports*, 1967, *20*, 250.

Schoeninger, D. W., Klein, M. H., & Mathieu, P. L. Comparison of two methods for training judges to rate psychotherapy recordings. *Journal of Consulting and Clinical Psychology*, 1968, *32*, 499-500. (a)

Stiles, W. B., McDaniel, S. H., & McGaughey, K. *Verbal response mode correlates of "experiencing." Journal of Consulting and Clinical Psychology*, 1979, *47*, 795-797.

Truax, C. B., & Mitchell, K. M. Research on certain therapist interpersonal skills in relation to process and outcome. In S. L. Garfield & A. E. Bergin (Eds.), *Handbook of psychotherapy and behavior change.* New York: Wiley, 1971.

Walker, A., Rablen, R. W., & Rogers, C. R. Development of a scale to measure process change in psychotherapy. *Journal of Clinical Psychology*, 1960, *16*, 79-85.

Wexler, D. A. *Depth of experiencing of emotion and the elaboration of meaning.* Paper presented at the meeting of the Western Psychological Association, San Francisco, April 1974.

8

A Discovery-Oriented Approach
to Significant Change Events
in Psychotherapy: Interpersonal
Process Recall and
Comprehensive Process Analysis

ROBERT ELLIOTT
University of Toledo

The research strategy described in this chapter is analogous to exploring new, uncharted territory without the benefit of a map or a theory about the terrain. In such a case, the practical thing to do is to hire local guides, both to keep one from getting lost and to help one find the significant features of the new land—mountains, swamps, resources, and safe routes. The discovery-oriented research strategy assumes that psychotherapy process is such an uncharted territory and that the theory-maps currently available are akin to the fantastic cartographic inventions of 16th-century maps of the New World. If this is the case, a highly useful approach would be to enlist the guidance of local inhabitants, keeping in mind the need to corroborate such information with more systematic measurement.

In more specific terms, the discovery-oriented approach to significant change events in psychotherapy asks a number of basic questions: What would we find out if we asked clients and therapists to point to significant moments of psychological change in psychotherapy? What would they tell us if we provided them with the means of describing in close detail just what was happening during particular moments of significant change? How could we combine this kind of information with other sorts of information on change episodes, in order to tell therapists how to conduct psychotherapy more effectively?

This chapter has four major goals: The first goal is to spell out the key ideas and rationale underlying this discovery-oriented approach. The second goal is to present the procedures utilized in the discovery-oriented approach: interpersonal process recall and comprehensive process analysis. The third goal is to demonstrate how the discovery-oriented approach works by applying it to a collection of four "insight events." The final goal is to integrate the comparative analysis of insight events in order to develop a tentative model of the change process in psychotherapy and to suggest therapist intervention tactics.

PRINCIPLES OF A DISCOVERY-ORIENTED APPROACH TO CHANGE EPISODES

The discovery-oriented approach rests on four general or operating assumptions. These assumptions have been discussed in more detail elsewhere (Rice & Greenberg, Chapter 1; Elliott, 1983a, 1983b) and are for the most part shared by the process researchers represented in this volume. The assumptions are as follows:

1. An important place to begin research on psychotherapeutic processes is with the experiences and perceptions of the participating clients and therapists. There are two critical choices to be made when one is conducting research on the process of psychotherapy (Elliott, 1979b). The first choice is which perspective of observation to make use of— phenomenological (i.e., client, therapist) or behavioral (i.e., trained raters). In this approach, one begins with phenomenological data and adds behavioral data later. The idea here is that clients and therapists are "expert witnesses" to the process of their interactions, although, like all witnesses, their testimony must be combined with other sorts of evidence. In particular, clients occupy a privileged position, since they are the "consumers" of the offered psychological help. Whether "true" or "false," their views matter and have consequences.

2. Phenomenological data can be made more useful by anchoring them in specific behavioral events. The second critical methodological choice in process research has to do with level of analysis—whether to consider therapy sessions or relationships as global entities or to examine specific events within sessions. This choice is usually made in tandem with the first choice of perspective of measurement, resulting in one of the two most common measurement strategies used in psychotherapy process research: The first is the global–phenomenological approach, in which questionnaires are filled out by clients and therapists (e.g., Barrett-Lennard, 1962; Orlinsky & Howard, 1975); the second is the event-based behavioral–objective approach, in which therapy process measures are rated by outside observers working from transcripts or tapes of therapy sessions (e.g., Hill, 1978; Rice & Wagstaff, 1967). Global questionnaire methods have shown limited utility for guiding clinical decision-making at particular moments within therapy sessions because they do not translate readily into concrete strategies for therapists; behavioral process systems have often suffered because of the difficulty in demonstrating relevance to client and therapist experiences. However, there is a third method which combines the advantages of both approaches: This is the event-based phenomenological approach in which client or therapist experiences and perceptions can be anchored to particular observable events (client or therapist verbal or nonverbal behaviors) by means of the method of interpersonal process recall, pioneered by N. Kagan (1975).

3. *Psychotherapy research can be made more useful by focusing on significant change events.* As stated in other chapters in this book, previous research on therapy has, with few exceptions, assumed that all events are equally important. In addition to a number of methodological defects such as sampling, directionality, and construct validity problems (cf. Fiske, 1977; Gottman & Markman, 1978), the usual approaches of sampling and averaging ignore the existence of clinically significant events (Greenberg, 1977; Lambert, DeJulio, & Stein, 1978). These "critical incidents" or "turning points" are episodes in which something changes for the client, "for better or for worse." They have been reported sporadically in the literature (e.g., Kelman, 1969; Standahl & Corsini, 1959; Strupp, Hadley, & Gomes-Schwartz, 1977).

4. *Since significant events are both infrequent and highly complex, they should be studied closely and comprehensively when they are encountered.* When it comes to significant change events, the usual psychotherapy research methods of group clinical-trials designs and univariate quantitative process measurement are inappropriate, or at least premature. Instead, what may be needed is something closer in spirit to the work of naturalistic clinical observers (e.g., Scheflen, 1973). Further, in order to correct for possible limitations and idiosyncrasies, such qualitative observations can be corroborated by including data from other viewpoints. In particular, the views of raters using standard therapy process measures and the reports of the involved client and therapist can be incorporated. Previous analyses of psychotherapy events by Pittenger, Hockett, and Danehy (1960) and Labov and Fanshel (1977) have come close to this degree of comprehensiveness. However, these investigators did not focus on therapeutically significant events, nor did they make use of phenomenological data. These limitations attenuate the clinical usefulness of the earlier studies for guiding the conduct of actual psychotherapy sessions, in the course of which therapists seek to maximize significantly helpful events while minimizing events that hinder client change.

Thus, the discovery-oriented approach to studying change episodes in psychotherapy rests on phenomenological observation linked to specific therapy events, focused on significant moments of change, and analyzed in as comprehensive a fashion as possible. These methodological principles are embodied in two distinct (but related) research procedures: interpersonal process recall and comprehensive process analysis.

INTERPERSONAL PROCESS RECALL
FOR PSYCHOTHERAPY PROCESS RESEARCH

The first of the two procedures, interpersonal process recall (IPR), was developed by Norman Kagan (1975) as a technique for training psychological helpers. IPR is a special interview procedure in which a helping session is taped and immediately played back for the client or therapist. The person is asked to remember and describe the momentary experiences and perceptions associated with particular events in the session. IPR makes it possible for participants to recapture fleeting impressions and reactions which would ordinarily be forgotten or merged into more global perceptions.

As originally presented by Kagan (1975), IPR was quite unstructured, with virtually complete control accorded to the respondent. However, since its original use as an educational technique, IPR has been adapted as a research tool for the systematic study of interpersonal processes in psychotherapy and counseling (Elliott, 1979b; Elliott, Barker, Caskey, & Pistrang, 1981; Young, 1980). In these initial studies, IPR was used to capture information about the subjective meaning and impact of specific therapist interventions. Subsequent to these original studies, the research applications of IPR have been developed for a variety of purposes (Elliott, in press). The purposes most relevant here are identification of significant events and qualitative description of significant events.

IDENTIFICATION OF SIGNIFICANT CHANGE EVENTS

One of the simplest uses of IPR is as a measure of the "suboutcome" (Rice & Saperia, Chapter 2) of the impact of particular therapist responses. Most commonly, therapist responses are rated by clients on a 9-point "helpfulness" scale (1 = extremely hindering, 5 = neutral, 9 = extremely helpful). These ratings have been used as part of more traditional process research designs to examine the differential effectiveness of types of therapist behavior (e.g., interpretation vs. question, Elliott, Barker, Caskey, & Pistrang, 1982). However, such ratings also lend themselves to use in identifying significant change events.

The current procedure (Elliott, in press) is as follows: Client and therapist separately review the videotape of the entire session, rating the helpfulness of each therapist response, using the 9-point helpfulness scale.

A recall consultant records these ratings. After the informants have rated all therapist interventions, each selects the two *most* significantly helpful and hindering interventions. This procedure results in two sets of significant events, those identified by the client and those identified by the therapist.

QUALITATIVE DESCRIPTION OF SIGNIFICANT CHANGE EVENTS

The other use of IPR which is relevant here is providing qualitative information on how a significant event unfolded. After a significant event has been identified, the recall consultant replays the tape of the significant event and encourages the informant to talk about it. The recall consultant follows a standard schedule of questions designed to cover three important aspects of the significant event:

1. The informant describes in as much detail as possible what was going on before the event: For clients, the focus is on intentions and covert experiences; for therapists, the focus is on cues provided by the client to which the therapist responded and the covert decision process which led to the subsequent significant intervention.
2. The informant is asked, first, to explain in more detail what made the event significantly helpful or hindering; second, to describe the speaker's intention; and, third, to describe the immediate overt or covert impact of the event on the client.
3. The informant describes what happened following the event, in particular, the further covert or overt impact of the event on the client. Finally, the informant summarizes by describing the nature of the change involved in the event.

As the examples to be presented in the third section of this chapter will show, this qualitative descriptive use of IPR is capable of picking up surprisingly rich and detailed information about therapeutic process. These data are probably most useful within a discovery-oriented research strategy. However, to the extent that theories of the change process exist for a particular approach, IPR can be used as a verification procedure. For example, Gestalt two-chair experiment, the theoretically specified processes (e.g., heightening) can be compared to the processes actually found to be operating at significant moments within that therapy.

In conclusion, IPR provides a rich vein of information about significant change events in psychotherapy. It lends itself to the discovery of basic types of significant change events. However, because IPR is a recent development in process research there remain a number of questions about its reliability, validity, and practicality: For example, to what extent do clients and therapists consciously or unconsciously distort or reconstruct their original experiences during the recall process? How much does the identification method limit the selection of significant nonverbal behavior or client responses? Preliminary answers to many of these questions are becoming available (see Elliott, in press). However, more research on the strengths and limitations of the IPR method is needed.

COMPREHENSIVE PROCESS ANALYSIS

The second major procedure in this discovery-oriented approach to studying psychotherapy is comprehensive process analysis. Comprehensive process analysis is a procedure for describing significant change events systematically on a battery of process measures. The comprehensive process analysis method and framework are an integration of the methodological and conceptual work of Horowitz (1979), Kiesler (1973), Labov and Fanshel (1977), Orlinsky and Howard (1978), and Russell and Stiles (1979). The idea of a battery of process measures being applied to the same segments of significant psychotherapy process is analogous to the proposed psychotherapy outcome battery (Waskow & Parloff, 1975) and derives from the work of Rice and colleagues (Rice, Klein, Beck, & Greenberg, 1977; Rice, Klein, Hill, Greenberg, Elliott, Whiteside, & Benjamin, 1978). The psychotherapy process battery used in this paper is organized by a framework of three sets of variables: person (client or therapist), aspect of process (content, action, style, state-experience, and quality) and perspective (client, therapist, observer), as shown in Table 8-1.

There are five steps to comprehensive process analysis (Elliott, 1983b):

1. *Identification of significant event.* In the analysis to be presented shortly, events were identified by use of IPR; however, other methods could be used, including high scores on third-party rating scales such as Patient Experiencing Scale (Klein, Mathieu, Gendlin, & Kiesler, 1969).

2. *Definition of interaction episode.* All responses are embedded within interaction episodes that provide the immediately surrounding context for the event. The second step in comprehensive process analysis is defining this episode. Two criteria can be used for defining episodes: First, there must be enough client speech preceding and following the significant event to allow meaningful

TABLE 8-1. COMPREHENSIVE PROCESS ANALYSIS FRAMEWORK

			ASPECT		
PERSON	CONTENT	ACTION	STYLE	STATE-EXPERIENCE	QUALITY
Client	Person Action Time Clinical Issue	Help-seeking mode Conversational mode	Voice quality Expressiveness Nonfluencies Speech rate Nonverbal behaviors	Client state Recall data	Experiencing Working Recall data
Therapist	Person Action Time Clinical Issue	Helping Response mode Conversational mode Recall data	Expressiveness Nonfluencies Speech rate Nonverbal behaviors	Friendly Critical Recall data	Experiencing Helpfulness Empathy

Note. See Tables 8-2 and 8-3 for information on measures. The third dimension of the model, Perspective, refers to the source of the process ratings—client, therapist, observer.

"before–after" comparisons of client process. Second, the episode should provide enough context to make references clear and enough postevent material to display the impact of the event adequately. Pre- and postsegments satisfying these criteria are usually each about 2 minutes in length.

3. *Transcription.* The next step in comprehensive process analysis is the transcription of the episode and any data obtained by IPR. The transcript of the significant event episode must be as accurate and detailed as possible. In addition, client and therapist remarks during tape-assisted recall should also be transcribed.

4. *Measurement of process variables.* The crucial step is the assessment of the episode using a battery of quantitative and qualitative process analysis measures. Wherever good quantitative measures are available, these should be used. However, there are many areas of therapy process defined by the comprehensive process analysis framework for which there are as yet no definite measures (e.g., nonverbal behavior); in these cases, qualitative analyses should be used to fill in the gaps. Finally, much of the information provided by clients and therapists by means of IPR will be in narrative descriptive form; some sort of content analysis is needed to organize these data. A suggested battery for assessing significant change events is presented and will be used for analyzing a collection of four insight events.

5. *Integration of analyses.* The last step in the analysis is to weave all the information together. This can be done as a narrative or in the form of a table (cf. Elliott, 1983b). However, when a collection of significant events of a particular type (e.g., insight events) is available, analyses of common characteristics and themes become possible. These analyses of commonalities constitute a valuable stage in generating models of therapeutic process; they will be used for this purpose in this chapter.

In summary, comprehensive process analysis is a broad-band procedure for understanding the nature of significant change events and for discovering basic change processes. Comprehensive process analysis systematically considers both persons involved in the therapeutic process (client and therapist) in terms of five aspects of process (content, action, style, state-experience, and quality) and draws on three points of view for doing so (observer, client, and therapist). Comprehensive process analysis proceeds in five steps: identification of significant event, definition of relevant interaction episode, transcription of episode, measurement of process variables using quantitative and qualitative methods, and integration of information in the form of summary tables, narratives, or comparative analyses.

AN ANALYSIS OF CLIENT INSIGHT EVENTS

The remainder of this chapter will demonstrate the usefulness of the discovery-oriented approach for exploring a class of significant psychotherapy change events—events in which the client arrives at a new understanding or awareness of self.

Many kinds of change occur in psychotherapy. The question is which of the multitude of events that occur in therapy should be chosen for study? In this case, the choice of insight events can be justified for several reasons: (1) They are relatively common (Elliott, Barker, Caskey, & Pistrang, 1982). (2) Some are very clearly marked, so that they are readily apparent to client, therapist, and outside observers. This mutual recognizability suggests the presence of a relatively accessible and regular set of features. (3) They have been referred to often in the psychotherapy literature (see review by Roback, 1974). In other words, insight events fit two criteria (Greenberg, 1977; Rice & Greenberg, 1974) for selecting psychotherapy events for study: They are potent and recurrent.

In the presentation to follow, the procedures for selecting the four events studied will be described briefly; then the process battery will be described; the next, the four examples of change events will be given, which will prepare the way for a search for common themes and recurring patterns in the events; this search for commonalities will give rise to a tentative model of insight events, followed, finally, by a discussion of implications for research and practice in therapy.

Data Collection

The four events come from four different therapy and quasi-therapy dyads in a research project on significant change events in psychotherapy. The therapies and one-session quasi-therapy interviews examined were broadly psychodynamic or insight-oriented; altogether, 20 sessions were represented. Each session was audio- or videotaped. After the session IPR was used to allow client and therapist each to identify and describe the significantly helpful and hindering events in the session. Early analyses of these data uncovered the present collection of four insight events, whose members share the following two definitional features: (1) All were identified as significantly helpful by both client and therapist; and (2) all were clearly described by both client and therapist as involving the client coming to some new understanding of self. As described in the discussion of Comprehensive Process Analysis, each of the insight events was then located within an episode (average length of episodes was 3:12 minutes), and these episodes were transcribed, along with the information supplied by clients and therapists in recall.

MEASUREMENT OF PROCESS VARIABLES

The four insight events were then rated on a battery of process measures. The battery followed the framework presented in Table 8-1. That is, client and therapist behavior was assessed in terms of five aspects of process (content, action, style, state-experience, and quality). In addition, wherever possible, client, therapist, and observer perspectives were used to provide the information that each one is best suited to provide; for example, clients were asked to describe their subjective experience. Finally, client measures were used for rating the segments preceding and following target therapist interventions; therapist measures were used for rating the target interventions themselves.

Information on the actual instruments used, including sources, categories, rating procedures, and reliabilities is given in Tables 8-2 and 8-3.

THE FOUR INSIGHT EVENTS

In order to allow the reader to get a feeling for the events under analysis, brief descriptions of each of the four insight events will be presented here along with transcripts and client and therapist descriptions of what made the events significantly helpful. Each of the events is identified by the code number of the client (e.g., P203). This number will be used throughout to reference the event. Videorecordings were available for all but the first event.

Event P203

This event came from a one-session quasi-therapy interview. The therapist was a female clinical psychologist operating in an eclectic psychodynamic mode. The client was an undergraduate male in his late 20s; he volunteered for an insight–exploratory-type helping interview focused on something he did not understand about himself—in this case, the reasons for a recurring nightmare about being pulled into a piece of heavy machinery. The event occurred about 40 minutes into the 50-minute hour. The segment begins with the client restating his presenting concern in a revised form: He says that what he doesn't understand is the timing of the dream.

The special symbols shown on the transcript are used in accordance with the Jefferson Transcription system.*

---

*In the Jefferson transcription system (Schenkein, 1978), the following special symbols and conventions are used: "H" and "h" are out-breaths of varying loudness; "'h" is an in-breath. ":" means that the preceding sound is drawn out. "°" means oversoft. "=" means no interturn latency. "//" stands for the point at which an interruption begins. Square brackets are used to indicate the end (and occasionally the beginning) of the simultaneous

C1: . . . I mean, it never really (2.0), I, like I've said, it, the dream has never really worried me as much as, as the timing of it h (2.4) because =

T1: $\frac{(or)}{(hu)}$ Why it happened after =

C2: Yeah, because, see, d(h)uring the time I was working there, was when there was a lot of stress in the family, (1.0) a lot of stress at the work, you know, personal stress, (1.5) why, why, is it coming back, though, after the, I quit working, (1.2) is, you know, I could understand why the dream and the tension and the stress and °(everything)° (1.0) but why is it coming out, why did it come out later, after I quit working? (1.0)

➤ *T2.1:* From what you're telling me, I'm, I'm getting the (1.0) image of a, of a man, who for, for many years has felt, (1.0) like ya had to be stro:ng, like ya had to be:, you were taking care of your *fa*mily, you're taking care of your*se*lf, (1.0) uh even at work ya had to take care of: the other people in case of an emergency you had to be the strong one to get the thing open. (1.5) And you even said and it didn't seem right, that you were allowed to have any kind of anxiety, (C: Uh-huh) or any kind of: fears, you weren't supposed to, y-you said like the masculine thing there for a minute, uh didn't go with the image (1.0).

➤ *T2.2:* And I'm kinda wondering uh (1.5) is it, does it seem possible in any way that, the dream could be: or could—could have been a wa:y of expressing the anxiety that was inside that was causing the ulcer, that was there, that we all have, like you say you know now that everybody has the anxiety, (1.0) but it was also, the one thing in your life, the job where there was real danger, so (C: Mhm) it was OK even for a man maybe (1.0) to be afraid of of a machine like that, cause that'ss (1.0) so there was no: (1.0) t sounds like there was something that, *anybody* would be afraid of so (C: Mhm) you didn't have to think, "Gee, I'm not much of a man if I'm afraid of that." I'm just wondering if some of the other kinds of anxiety (1.0) were being expressed (C: At, through the dream) = through the dream, cause that was one way you let yourself perhaps (1.0)//[°be anxious°]

C3: But (w-)] and then why it's been (1.0) lessening in frequency then is cause I don't have as much stress, perhaps (2.0) uh—I never thought of it th—you know in that h in that way I:—(1.0) I thought it like as a (1.0) I tried to like think of stressful things that had happened before (2.0) and I couldn't really remember any, happen(ing), you know, right before the,

---

speech episodes. Target events are indicated by arrows at the left. Single parentheses serve a variety of purposes: When they enclose numbers, they refer to pauses in excess of 1 second; when they enclose speaker identifications and brief comments (e.g., T: Yeah), they refer to backchannel behaviors by the other party; otherwise, they are used to indicate alternative or uncertain hearings. Double parentheses are used for descriptions of speech and nonverbal behavior.

Some therapist speaking turns have been divided into parts (e.g., T1.1, T1.2) by clients or therapists, and occasionally backchannels have been numbered (e.g., C2.1: Yeah).

TABLE 8-2. CLIENT PROCESS MEASURES

ASPECT: VARIABLE	FORM	SOURCE	RATERS	RELIABILITY
A. *Content* Person Activity Time Clinical Issue	Qualitative (e.g., self) (e.g., feeling) (e.g., present session) (e.g., core interpersonal conflict)	Elliott (1983b)	Author	—
B. *Interpersonal Action* 1. *Client Help-Seeking Mode* Self-disclosure Narrative Request for help Agreement Disagreement Self-help Attending	Seven 4-point anchored rating scales	Videorating Scale: Elliott & Shulman (1981)	Author and two trained graduate student raters	.98[a] .83 .65 .87 .88 .54 .49
2. *Client Conversational Mode*	Qualitative microanalysis	Labov & Fanshel (1977) Schenkein (1978)	Author	—
C. *Style* 1. *Client Vocal Quality* Focused Externalized Limited Emotional	Four mutually exclusive categories	Rice, Koke, Greenberg, & Wagstaff (1979)	Author	
2. *Client Expressiveness*	5-point anchored rating scale	Videorating Scales: Elliott & Shulman (1981)	Author and two graduate student raters	.80[a]

260

3. *Nonfluencies and Speech Rate*	Qualitative	Mahl (1956)	Author	—
4. *Nonverbal Behavior*	Qualitative	Ekman & Friesen (1969)	Author	—
Emblems				
Illustrators				
Regulators				
Adaptors				
Facial affect				
Body position				
D. *State-Experience*				
1. *Client State*	Five 5-point rating scales	Videorating Scales: Elliott & Shulman (1981); cf. Horowitz (1979)	Author and two graduate student raters	
Depressed				.89[a]
Optimistic				.63
Anxious				.77
Positive				.47
Negative				.51
2. *Client–Therapist Recall*	Free-response descriptions of client	Elliott (in press)	Client, therapist content analyzed by author	—
E. *Quality*				
1. *Client experiencing*	7-point anchored scale	Klein, Mathieu, Gendlin, & Kiesler (1969)	Klein	—
2. *Client working*	5-point rating scale	cf. Horowitz (1979)	Author and two graduate student raters	.83[a]

[a]Cronbach α values for the two graduate student raters for a larger data set.

TABLE 8-3. THERAPIST PROCESS MEASURES

ASPECT : VARIABLE	FORM	SOURCE	RATERS	RELIABILITY
A. *Content*	Qualitative	Elliott (1983b)	Author	—
Person	(e.g., self)			
Activity	(e.g., feeling)			
Time	(e.g., present session)			
Clinical Issue	(e.g., core interpersonal conflict)			
B. *Interpersonal Action*				
1. *Therapist Response Mode*	Ten 4-point anchored rating scales	Elliott (1979a); cf. Goodman & Dooley (1976)	Author	—
Open question				
Closed question				
Process advisement				
General advisement				
Reflection				
Interpretation				
Reassurance				
Disagreement				
Self-disclosure				
General information				
2. *Therapist Conversational Mode*	Qualitative microanalysis	Labov & Fanshel (1977) Schenkein (1978)	Author	—
3. *Client–Therapist Recall*	Free response descriptions of therapist' intention	Elliott (in press)	Client, therapist	—
C. *Style*				
1. *Therapist Expressiveness*	5-point rating scale	Elliott & Shulman (1981)	Author and two graduate student raters	.76[a]
2. *Nonfluencies and Speech Rate*	Qualitative	Mahl (1956)	Author	—

	Qualitative		Author	
3. *Nonverbal Behavior*		Ekman & Friesen (1969)		—
Emblems				
Illustrators				
Regulators				
Adaptors				
Facial affect				
Body position				
D. *State-Experience*				
1. *Therapist State*	Two 5-point rating scales	Videorating scales: Elliott & Shulman (1981)	Author and graduate student raters	
Positive				.63[a]
Negative				.65
E. *Quality*				
1. *Therapist Experiencing*	Two 7-point anchored rating scales	Klein & Mathieu-Coughlin (in press)	Klein	—
Manner				
Response				
2. *Generic Helpfulness*	9-point adjective anchored rating scale	Elliott (in press)	Five trained undergraduate raters	.87[b]
3. *Response Empathy*	Eight 5-point anchored scales	Elliott, Zapadka, Harrigan, Gaynor, Filipovich, & Reimschuessel (1980)	Five trained undergraduate raters	
Components				
Feeling reference				.93[b]
Inference				.90
Centrality				.93
Expressiveness				.74
Collaboration				.76
Verbal allowing				.85
Exploration				.80
Impact of exploration				.80

[a] Cronbach α values for the two raters for a larger data set.
[b] Cronbach α values for the five raters for a larger data set.

263

the dream came, especially (1.0) uhh (1.5) maybe it's just you know like a: suppressed stress that comes out later when there's a, relaxing period (T: Mhm) u:h (1.5) maybe that I feel that you know I don't wanna s—hh (1.5) burden myself with it while I'm at a very stressful point, where I need all my energy °but° when it slacks off, is when it comes back out (2.5) I—I never thought of it that way (1.5)

The segment ends with the client stating the content of his insight, which is that he now understands the dream to have been a delayed reaction to stress in an earlier period of his life, a reaction which had originally been suppressed. In recall, client and therapist described what made the event significantly helpful:

> *Client:* It seemed to be a big change point in the session. Things started to mesh together. I could see where things fit. Stuff I hadn't thought about . . . it [therapist's response] showed me a new perspective of the problem. . . . I felt more sure of her, less nervous. I continued to think about the new perspective. . . . My confidence level rose.

> *Therapist:* [It was] the major interpretation of the session. It put the elements of the session together. . . . He [the client] accepted the interpretation. The light went on. . . . He was definitely with me and finished the interpretation. He took over for me. [It was] an example of self-interpretation. The client tied it all together, making this the high point of the session.

Event 300-1

The second insight event came from the initial session of a short-term therapy case. The client was a female undergraduate in her early 20s who sought treatment for problems involving low self-esteem, interpersonal anxiety, and unresolved anger toward her alcoholic mother. During the time of treatment she was single and living alone. The therapist was a male clinical psychologist with 6 years' experience; the approach taken with this client was eclectic and broadly psychodynamic. The segment comes from very near the end of the hour. The segment begins with the therapist announcing that the end of the session is approaching, which stimulates the client to state a problem (C1): It is the end of the first session and she doesn't know what to focus on in therapy. This is the signal for the therapist to do a summarizing intervention (T3.1–T3.5). The rest of the segment is taken up with the client's reaction to this intervention, centering around the insight that her dependency feelings, which are frightening to her, are what she needs to focus on in therapy.

T1: We *have* to stop in about five minutes, so=
C1: °I know° (.8) (T: °Mh°) So I guess that just makes it harder for me to know where to be(he)gin I guess, you know, because I don't feel

particularly threatened (1.0) 'h °Huhh° (0.8) Hehh, so to speak= I know that fear——= you know, I don't know, °exactly but° you know like *what* events to st(h)a(h)rt with er, you know, whatever °you know, but I guess(it happened a(h)r(h)ady) so°=

T2: Pardon? (.5)

C2: But I guess it's already ha—you know, like things have come out °already so I don't know° (1.0)

➤ *T3.1:* I think so (C: °Uhuh°) I've got some, there's some big themes I've seen today, I mean, your sort of *struggle* where you want to be indepe:ndent, you have—a tre*men*dous conflict between (1.0) wanting other people, especially female-type people, and wanting to be independent and do it for yourself, like you said, be your own mother (1.0) A::nd you've—gone, you've swung back and forth, you were really independent and you were making it and you felt *really* good about it, now you've (1.0) you've swung the other di—other di*rec*tion.

T3.2: You know, you've got yourself in a situation where you('re) gonna (be) you know, like a relationship with a mentor as I understand it, they—well, maybe that's the old-fashioned version from (C: Hehe) three centu(h)ries ago, but n they tell you what to do:, the:y (1.0) You really subjugate your will to them (.8) Is that? (1.2) (C2.1: Yeah, I mean//it's—)

T3.3: Something like that, where it's, it's, a real almost like a parent-child kind of relationship, where that's very similar to that (1.5) A::nd that's,

T3.4: Ok, well, my main point was that's a big theme for you, that struggle.

➤ *T3.5:* Wanting other people, wanting to do it yourself (1.0) (C: °yeah°) Being, maybe being scared of how much you want other people (0.6)

C3: °Mhm° (1.7) °(yeah, I guess it's heh)° 'hh (2.0) °hm° (5.5) 'hh (2.0) ((raises hand to forehead, hitting coffee mug in process))

T4: What are ya feelin' right now? (.5)

C4: Supr*i*(hhed)ed(h) 'hh I feel real good, I mean I—(2.0) I didn't see that before, you know, just the way you were saying heh h were saying it (T: Hm) you know (2.0) and it's helpful to me to think of it that way= I mean I guess I have a lot of fears, you know hh, like especially you know depen— you know the depending on people thing, it (T: Mhm) would scare the hell out of me (T: Mhm) and I think (T: Mhm) it's it's always been a woman, and that scares the hell out of me, it's never, 'h °and uh° °You know,° that is a a real struggle, you know, for me and// like

T5: It scares the hell out of you that it's a *woman*? (.5)

C5: Yeah, I mean I— why, you know, w- why feeling that, you know, feeling that need for intimacy or something like that, you know 'n *mo*thering or whatever, 'h a:nd (2.0) you know and just the way you said it, "indep—" you know wh- when you said that "independent" like I- I saw that part of it, and I didn't see how really dependent I'm feeling right now (T: Mhm) h until, you said that.

In recall, client and therapist described the event as follows:

Client: Because he really put together all the different pieces that I was talking about and it made sense to me, it helped me to see it in a different way. . . . Putting it that way made it where I could understand it, made me see that I have tremendous conflict there. . . . My response was [that] that was something for me to think about, it was a new idea that I hadn't had before. It was something I could take home. . . . It made me feel good about the session and about doing it, [that] there was a purpose. I felt relieved.

Therapist: I knew it was helpful because of what she said immediately afterward. [I was] summarizing what the major themes were. The summary reflection was news to her . . . The therapy starts here. She realizes that things have already started happening . . . this is a junction point. . . . She was picking up where I left off; she wanted to go on with it.

Event P208

The third insight event also came from a one-session quasi-interview. The therapist was a female graduate student in clinical psychology who had 5 years of previous practice as a master's level clinical psychologist. The client was a 19-year-old female undergraduate volunteer whose problem was that she couldn't understand why she was so disturbed by her boyfriend's use of marijuana. The event occurred about 8 minutes into the hour. The segment begins with a small sidetrack, which the therapist terminates with a premature version of the significant intervention; this leads the client to restate her presenting concern; the significant intervention is then restated and elaborated. However, the therapist truncates the client's exploration of the event by moving immediately to a new issue, which occupies the remainder of the segment. Nevertheless, the significance of the event was recognized by both client and therapist.

Cl: I think, we:ll, not to, get on to him, but um, I think that he's not, he is very immature (T: Mhm) in some ways, in some ways he's very mature, but (1.4) he can face responsi*bil*ity, but, he(s) doesn't, he doesn't wanna face um (2.0) other things like uhh (1.6) well, ((louder)) *some* responsibilities he can face and some (them) (T: Mhm) and some he can't. You know like, car payments and things like that he can handle just fine, being to work, 'hh but, when it comes to, the things like uhm telling me where he's going to go or, er something like that, he wants his *own*, own freedom, his way of doing things. (1.5)

➤ *T1.1:* 'h I'm thinking that this thing about you being important and not being put second, is kind of getting acted out, in your, you know, in your (1.0) objection, to his smoking pot=

T1.2: Because actually you don't seem to be saying that the pot is all that awful to you. You just don't like the fact that he does it (1.0) when you object (1.0) (C: Mm) in spite of your objections. But you're not saying that, you know, like, that the effects of pot or any of that sort of stuff, umh is what it is, (1.0) //that bugs you.

C2: Uh, I don't really think it] *could* be the effect of what it does= because I don't really *know* what it does (T: Mhm, yeah) I really, I don't know *why* it bothers me, maybe— (.5)

➤ *T2:* So it seems to *symbolize* something, that somehow his //(C: Ye:ah, that could be) smoking pot has some] kind of symbolic meaningfulness in terms of the relationship in general. (.8)

C3: (That) could be=

➤ *T3.1:* OK, if that were true, assuming that's true (C: Mhm ((done as quick aside:)) and we might be off on a, bad tangent here (C: laughs) ((T laughs through:)) but, assuming that then it's true. 'Hhh u:m (2.0) then, then you're saying that you, you know, you wind up having feelings yourself of, you know, not feeling terribly important, and needing k someone else to treat you as important in order to *feel* it (C3.1: Right, ex*act*ly) about yourself]=

T3.2: OK 'h u::m. where does that come from, where—how— you know eh I'm assuming maybe family or something of that nature? (.5)

C4: The—what? that I don't feel important?=

T4: Uhuh, how does that go in the family? you know=

C5: I don't know, I think, my family's always made me (1.0) ((as an aside:)) don't know if important 'h ((louder)) I've never—they *treat* me like a *chi:ld*, but um, 'h they've—they make me feel important, you know like when I go to do something °you know° "I'm sure you can *do* that"= they always give me *con*fidence that I'm *cap*able (T: Mhm) but then at the same time in other things they treat me like, you know like I'm not—I don't have enough responsibility to do anything. They force me, but then they hold me back.

In recall, clients and therapists described the event as follows:

Client: She [therapist] told me something I never expected. It was just something that I never thought of that she presented. . . . During the response I was sort of amazed. [I thought] Wow! maybe that has some connection. It was kind of a relief, too. . . . Maybe later that would lead to more confusion, but for right now it was something to think about instead of my own vicious circle. . . . My expectations were growing because she got things right. I was on the edge of my seat waiting for what happens next.

Therapist: I think that's important. . . . I was trying to clarify what I meant . . . I remember the smile and her face. The eyes got a little bit bigger and she had a slight smile on her face as if it was dawning on her— that sense of "Oh, yeah." So at that point I felt confirmed.

Event 401

The fourth insight event comes from the 20th session of a continuing therapy. The client was a female undergraduate student in her mid-20s, seen by a male therapist. Issues of depression, self-esteem, and social anxiety appeared to be central in the therapy. The therapist was a counseling psychologist with 5 years' experience; he described his approach with this client as "cognitive–supportive." The target segment comes from about 40 minutes into the hour. The topic of discussion is the client's weight and body image. The segment begins with a presequence that introduces an exploration of what it felt like for the client to be thin. The client's concern that being thin is scary to her triggers the target therapist intervention. The segment concludes with the client exploring the insight that body fat and bulky clothes both serve the same purpose for her—namely, protection.

T1: 'Hh Have ya ever bee:n (1.6) thin? ((moves to more open body position, C oriented away)) I know you say (you) never really felt good about ya body= but have you ever been to the point where you say 'hh "Yeah, I'm thin"=I mean after high school, (wh)ere you know you—=
  C1: After high school=
  T2: Yeah (.8)
  C2: O:h uh, ye:ah (a) couple times (.7) ((C eye contact; T nods))
  T3: What happened? (2.0) ((nonchalantly; C looks away))
  C3: I=don't=know—(h) it do (he)esn't las(he)st ve(he)ry lo(he)ng.
'hh U:m (.5) ((bites lip; smiling; T smiles also, conveys nonchalance))
  T4: Short spells, huh?—
  C4: Szh(Heh) 'hh uh=ye:ah=I:: I (d)on't know=I-I ge— I guess it just (3.0) felt um (1.8) (a) little sca:red (2.8) ((looks to T for reassurance)) and=um (2.5) (T: Hm) (6.0) ((C goes into "introspective" position)) I-I mean I (1.0) I could *feel* th(h)ings 'h and=uh, and that, felt funny °somehow I° (1.4)
  T5: Could feel thin=
  C5: I mean I could f:eel, you know it's felt different=I could feel my *m*:uscles ((illustrates by touching arms, legs)) and that you know (1.0) and (2.0) (it) somehow that, felt, scary=to=me (.6)
  T6: Hm (1.6) Being thin (.5)
  C6: Mhm (3.5) ((T nods))
  T7: Uh=t=did it affect the people *around* you or the way they related to you at all? (2.6) ((C nods))

C7: Well, I felt better pro— I think w— felt better about myself, so I think that people would react to that, just I don't think the thinness had anything to do with it really (.5) ((hand to ear-preening or protection))

➡ *T8:* °Hm° (2.0) Hh hm I just had this flash=it's almost like 'h the— the more weight ya lose, the more people get to see *you* 'hh 'cuz the covering kind of goes away (C: Hh) and now here's the real (C's first name) 'hh and that's not real comfortable (1.0)

C8: Nope, because see then, then I can dress the way I- I feel like I want to, (they can) people will see, ((eye brows raised briefly)) that and I don't think I want them to see that (.5)

➡ *T9:* M 'hh *That*'s something about your dress. I've always— (1.5) Now I got it (.5) (C: (What?)) (1.0) Your clothes (1.0) you always wear clothes, that hide you (2.0) (C: Hm) N They're al:ways um a:— they're nice, I may steal that coat the(he)re(h) t(h)oo 'hh (C: long laugh) but they're always rea:l loose-fitting=// (C: Oh, yeah) n kind] of *la:rge* u:hm (C: Mhm) and I know they're not from when you were, //(C: burst of laughter) big and large] (C: Uh yeah) you probably buy 'em that way (C: Uhuh) Uhhm (1.3) They all hide you, they don't allow any of *you* to kind of come out at all ((studying C's wardrobe; one hand on chin, other pointing)) Y'know, 'hh jeans that are mmaybe a size too la:rge 'h mm, loose shirt, stylish, but again, kind of large 'h boots, um, *fine* but (1.3) I know there's a foot in there somewhere (.5) ((C bites lip)) (C: 'hh Yeah, uhuh) (.5) And then the coat, y'know (.5)

C9: Mhm (1.0) Yeah, I— *Ye:ah*, I never thought of that (1.0) And, and I get real sca:red see, Spring is always real scary to me 'cuz "Oh my god, I can't do this now (T: Uhuh)=I can't wear a coat anymore (("trying on" gesture with shoulders)) (T: Right) What am I going to do=I can't wear boots anymore" (.5)

T10: N God forbid I, try an look a little bit alluring like some of the young women do, t and wear something that's tight (1.0) or slightly revealing, because it is warm (C: Mhm) Can't wear sweaters (C: ((laugh)) Mhm) and you wore a *lot* of sweaters (C: Mhm) (1.5) *Prac*tical but, (1.0) (a) certain style about it all (4.0)

C10: Yeah, and say if: if I lose weight then, I (1.5) I don't know, I guess I can't hide anymore=I mean I guess I could still wear clothes too big and everything=(T: Mhm, sure) But I guess if I feel like I'm thin I— can't do that anymore// (T: Yeah, the protection's gone) I'm not sup*pos*ed to *do*] that er something. (T: Mhm) (6.0)

In recall, this event was described as follows:

Client: It was real perceptive and it was like he was catching me on something. I felt he was noticing something that I hadn't really thought about before. . . . It was real important . . . I think. I kind of think about that sometimes, but I didn't think it was that—obvious?—maybe; I didn't think that people would be aware of that . . . [It was] a whole new insight. . . .

Pressure was taken off . . . he understood. . . . [Afterwards] I was taking it further and saying what was happening now. . . . It also made me feel grateful that he did point that out. . . . I felt a kind of closeness, some kind of neat camaraderie.

Therapist: [First part] A significant issue for her. I gave it the rating I did because I got the insight. . . . I always kind of wondered where that fit in for her. . . . It was kind of an interpretation, but a lot of it was just re-stating what she knew, just a step or two [behind me]. It hit, it made sense to her, she took it that extra step further. . . . [Second part] I think it gave her something more concrete, maybe a little easier to deal with [her clothes instead of her weight]. . . . Effect: an awareness now [of] what she's doing.

ANALYSIS OF COMMONALITIES

The point of this section is to rise above the forest of details inherent in each event in order to detect common elements or themes. In other words, given a collection of events identified phenomenologically (in recall) as involving a similar type of change (client insight), what other behavioral and phenomenological similarities will be found? In addition, will these further similarities add to our understanding of the phenomenology of insight or of the behavioral correlates or sources of insight? The comparative analysis presented here follows the comprehensive process analysis framework: To begin with, each event is broken into three temporal phases: client presegment; therapist target intervention; client postsegment. Then each phase-unit is described in terms of each of the five aspects of process (content, action, style, state-experience, and quality). Finally, within each phase–aspect combination (e.g., presegment–action), information from all available sources is integrated, including, wherever possible, data drawn from client, therapist, and observer perspectives.

Client Presegment or Context

Content
The content of the client presegments was assessed qualitatively by the author. The one common element in the content of all four events was the statement of some problem. In two of the events (P203, P208), a problem of understanding was stated explicitly (e.g., "Like I've said, the dream has never really worried me as much as the timing of it"—P203). In addition, the problems stated in the other two events contained implicit problems of self-understanding. For example, in event 300-1 the client's problem can be restated thus: "I know I'm in therapy for a reason; but I don't exactly know (in the sense of being able to put into words) what that reason is." In fact, these problem statements resemble Rice & Saperia's

(Chapter 2) problematic reaction points; following the language of task analysis (Greenberg, Chapters 3 and 4), they constitute understanding tasks.

Action

Client action was measured by video ratings and qualitatively. The fact that the content of the insight events involved problem statements has implications for the action which was taking place in them: Stating a problem is one way of performing an indirect request (Labov & Fanshel, 1977; Searle, 1975). In fact, the video ratings (by author and colleagues) identified mild requests for help in three of the presegments (in 401 self-disclosure and agreement were present without request for help). One therapist commented on this in recall ("He set it up by asking indirect questions"—P203). In events where indirect request was present, there was also mention of the failure of a current or obvious approach or view of the problem. In fact, the statements of problems made all presegments "occasions" for help: In other words, the clients presented situations in which help could be offered and was likely to be well received. In addition, video ratings indicated that client self-disclosure was generally present.

Style

Client style or manner was assessed by three observer methods: Client Vocal Quality, video ratings of client expressiveness, and qualitative analyses of verbal and nonverbal manner. In three of the events the client used predominantly externalized vocal quality, meaning that the client's speech had a lecturing or preplanned feeling to it. In all four presegments the client was rated as "somewhat" expressive. The combination of these two sets of ratings suggested that the client's energy was generally focused on how he or she was communicating with the therapist. Finally, for the three events which were recorded in videotape, several nonverbal patterns were consistent across events: The client offered little if any eye contact; the client illustrated his or her speech with gestures; the client emitted numerous adaptors (small nervous movements, e.g., biting lip, playing with microphone cable).

State-Experience

Client psychological state preceding insight events was measured descriptively by means of video ratings and client recall information. Video ratings of client state indicated some degree of anxiety in three of the events; more striking were the clients' descriptions of what was going on with them prior to the significant events. In three cases clients explicitly reported some sort of momentary subjective distress: "[There] was confusion. I also felt defeated, because I didn't know what to do about it."—

(P208). "I still didn't feel like I had resolved anything. [I felt] hurt, groping, and put off, but trying to act like things were OK"—(300). "I was feeling kind of nervous or embarrassed, almost like I didn't really want to talk about it"—(401). In the fourth case, P203, the client implied that he had been nervous, tense, and uncomfortable by commenting on the fact that these lessened after the insight event. Thus, all clients described or implied some sort of subjective distress. In two cases (P208, 300-1) the major affect seems to have been hopelessness (cf. Luborsky, Singer, Hartke, Crits-Christoph, & Cohen, Chapter 5); in the other two cases (P203, 401), the emotion was anxiety. These state ratings and client reports are consistent with the qualitative observations of client style, which suggested the presence of various anxiety indicators (speech non-fluencies and nonverbal adaptors).

Quality

Moving to evaluative measures of what Greenberg (Chapter 3) refers to as client "task performance," four sources of information became available: the Patient Experiencing Scale (Klein *et al.*, 1969); video ratings of client "working"; recall data from therapist; and qualitative observations by the author. Client experiencing ratings were generally in the 2–3 range; the clients were, for the most part, reporting their behaviors or describing situationally restricted feelings or reactions. Similarly, video ratings of client working at therapeutic tasks were in the slight to moderate range (i.e., averaging about half a standard deviation above the mean). These ratings, along with the externalized vocal quality, suggest that the clients were not resisting or avoiding working at their self-understanding task, but neither were they performing particularly well. The therapists' descriptions of what they noticed prior to the target interventions shed some light on what was going on. Two themes emerged:

1. Client readiness for intervention: In all four cases therapists observed in their clients some form of readiness for the intervention. Because these descriptions may be useful for defining intervention markers (cf. Greenberg, 1977) for insight events, they are cited here: "He set it up by asking indirect questions" (P203); "She has some inkling of that not being it" (P208); "She realizes that [in answer to her question] things have already started happening [in the therapy]" (300-1); "She's such a good client" [commenting on client's disclosure of her fear of being thin, (401)]. In describing the context of the second parts of their multipart interventions, two therapists remarked: "He was ready for a deeper integration" (P203); "She had already got hold of that idea" [i.e., the subject of the following interpretation, (401)].

2. Problems necessitate intervention at that moment: If clients were

engaging in somewhat productive process before the therapist intervention, one may question why the therapists choose to intervene at that point rather than letting their clients arrive at their own insights. The answer to this question is that the therapists all perceived some sort of trouble or limitation which required them to act. Two therapists reported limitations in the client: "He was still not able to connect the elements" (P203); "It was just a little bit fuzzy for her. If I hadn't responded, we would have just buzzed right by and not really paid much attention to it" (401, second part). On the other hand, all four therapists described problems or limitations external to the client: "Time was running out in our session" (P203); "We were going off on a tangent" (P208); "Because of the time in the session [i.e., near the end], this was a juncture point" (300-1); "I got off again, it wasn't following her at all" (401).

What is distinctive about the therapists' descriptions of the context is the combination of potential for insight with trouble that might have blocked this potential. Therapists' perceptions therefore corroborate both observers' descriptions of mildly favorable process and clients' reports that they were experiencing difficulty.

In sum, then, prior to the target intervention, clients were disclosing a problem which was distressing to them; this disclosure was also a signal of the clients' openness to receive help. Similarly, the clients appeared to be working at the tasks of therapy but having their task performance impaired by difficulties. In other words, clients (1) were working moderately well at the current therapeutic task, but (2) were encountering some sort of difficulty in doing so; furthermore, they (3) were experiencing momentary distress and (4) were indirectly requesting therapist intervention.

Target Intervention

Content
As assessed qualitatively, a common theme was found to run through the content of the four significant therapist interventions: In all cases, the topic of the intervention was some core issue for the client, either some basic conflict (P203, 300-1; e.g., being the strong one vs. being afraid) or some basic aspect of how the client regards other people (P208, 401; e.g., "needing someone to treat you as important"; cf. Luborsky, 1977).

Action
The nature of the interpersonal action accomplished by the target therapist interventions was measured from all three perspectives: Clients and therapists described the intervention, while the author rated the intervention

for therapist response mode and decribed it qualitatively. These analyses revealed three commonalities among the events:

1. The three perspectives were unequivocal in describing these events as involving therapist interpretation, although various other types of response mode also played supportive roles. Response mode ratings showed interpretation to be present in all four events. All four clients described some form of interpretative intention on the part of the therapist, such as looking for deeper or broader meanings or increasing awareness. Finally, three of the therapists explicitly described their interventions as interpretations. (In 300, the therapist said he was summarizing the session, which does not rule out interpretation.) Qualitative analyses suggested that the specific nature of the interpretive activity varied both across and within interventions. Most common were causal or functional analyses of the client's problem (three out of four cases; e.g., "Does it seem possible that the dream could be a way of expressing the anxiety?", P203) and attribution of unexpressed feelings to the client (three out of four cases; e.g., "being scared of how much you want other people," 300-1). A third type of interpretive activity was the use of an integrative summary of content previously presented in the session (two out of four cases; e.g., "There's some big themes I've seen today: you have a tremendous conflict between wanting other people . . . and wanting to be independent," 300-1). By engaging in these interpretive activities, the therapists clearly addressed the clients' problems of understanding and responded to the indirect requests for help commonly found in the presegments.

2. A second commonality emerged from qualitative analyses: In all four cases the therapist intervention was a complex, multipart utterance. To begin with, all cases involved a combination of two different types of interpretive activity (e.g., causal analysis and attribution of feelings). In addition, all interventions involved some form of redundancy, either a straightforward repetition of the key point after some elaboration or a simplified, less technical version of the key point. Finally, the four interventions were interactive. Their multipart structure allowed feedback, which influenced the remainder of the intervention. In the cases under study here, the intervention was cumulative: The client agreed with the first part of the intervention, then the therapist went on to add further inferences or to extend the topic (e.g., in P203, the client response was nonverbal agreement, signaling the therapist to move from integrative summary to causal analysis). The complexity of these interventions, especially their interactive nature, makes it virtually impos-

sible to fit these events into simple cause–effect explanations or easy-to-analyze "before–after" designs. In other words, the client insights that occur cannot be simply attributed to one person or the other; neither can one neatly contrast client process variables before and after the pivotal intervention. Client and therapist response interpenetrate, forming "joint events" which are cooperatively produced.

3. Finally, in all four cases, the therapist's message was framed in such a way as to attenuate or soften its potential directiveness. Three types of softening were used in these instances: self-disclosure framing (four out of four cases; e.g., "I get the image", "I just had this flash," 401), humor (two out of four cases, e.g., "I may steal that coat there," 401), and reflection (two out of four cases; e.g., "And you even said that it didn't seem right", P203). This softening personalizes the interpretation and provides a balance for the "weight" of the interpretive activities. Two therapists also reported trying to make the client feel less nervous or feel better about the therapeutic relation. In addition, the tentativeness of interpretations also gave interventions an explanatory quality which may have provided a model for clients' self-exploration.

Style

Video ratings of expressiveness indicated all therapist interventions to be in the somewhat to moderately expressive range (i.e., about a standard deviation above the mean). At least part of this expressiveness was carried out nonverbally: All three of the events for which there are video recordings feature strong illustrative gestures. Qualitative analyses also revealed frequent nonverbal affiliative behaviors (e.g., Knapp, 1978): Eye contact was generally maintained throughout the intervention; smiling or laughter was present (P208, 401); and in event 300-1 the therapist leaned forward. This latter pattern is consistent with the report by two therapists (300-1, 401) that they had an ancillary intention of enhancing the therapeutic relation or making their client feel less nervous.

State-Experience

Video ratings of therapist warmth indicate the therapists to have been in the range of somewhat to moderately warm in responding to the client at this point (i.e., about a standard deviation above the mean). Thus, these ratings are consistent with qualitative observations of nonverbal approach behaviors.

Quality

The quality of the key therapist interventions was assessed by a number of methods:

1. Observer *helpfulness* ratings were generally around 7 (moderately helpful), which is high for these ratings (about two standard deviations above the mean).
2. For observer ratings of *therapist experiencing* level, there were two consistent patterns: First, Peak ratings for the content of the response were in the 4–5 range, indicating "high points" of hypothesizing or describing client feelings (cf. interpretation and feeling attribution, p. 274). Second, Mode ratings for therapist manner were in the 2–3 range, suggesting that therapists were interested but not particularly involved with the client (cf. warmth ratings).
3. *Empathy* ratings varied, but analysis of the profiles of subscales suggests that all four therapist interventions were high on reference to issues probably central to the client (cf. analyses of content, p. 273), level of inference (cf. interpretation, p. 274), and reference to client feelings.
4. Finally, all of the interventions contain some sort of *imperfection*. Specific flaws included providing an "answer" largely irrelevant to the client's request for help (P203); premature, overtechnical interpretation (P208); and, most commonly, muddying the waters by introducing irrelevant and distracting new topics (P208, 300-1, 401). Nevertheless, these interventions were significantly helpful to clients in spite of their sloppiness, which the clients generally noticed and chose to ignore. (This may be reassuring to some less-than-perfect therapists.)

Summary of Interventions

Thus, the information on therapist target interventions can be summarized as follows: These insight events involve therapist interpretations which address the clients' requests for help. The interpretations have the following features: (1) They speak to some core interpersonal issue of the client; (2) they have a complex structure involving a variety of interpretive and other secondary activities, as well as some redundancy; (3) they have a multipart structure which allows and builds on client feedback; and (4) their interpretive force is softened by various verbal framing and softening devices and by nonverbal affiliative manner (warmth). Finally, these interventions possess noticeable imperfections, which clients choose to overlook.

Client Postsegment or Impact

Content

Qualitative comparisons of the content of pre- and postsegments suggest that the client postsegment reflects the addition of new topics not present in the presegment but carried over from the therapist intervention (e.g., dependency relationships in 300-1).

Action

Three sources provide information about the nature of the clients' interpersonal action in the postsegment: To begin with, video ratings indicate that (1) self-disclosure is present, at about the same level as in the presegment; (2) agreement has increased slightly; (3) self-help (e.g., self-interpretation) has increased (two out of four cases vs. none in the presegment); and (4) requests for help have disappeared completely.

However, qualitative microanalyses of client behavior in the postsegment allow a more fine-grained picture of the impact of the therapist intervention. These microanalyses suggest that, following the end of the therapist's interpretation, the insight event unfolds in three steps. Each of these steps consists of a set of functionally equivalent activities from which the client chooses in forming his or her response:

1. *Mild agreement:* All clients began by providing either some form of mild agreement (e.g., "Yeah, that could be") or by engaging in a collaborative response. Collaborative responses continue what the therapist has been saying, as if picking up in the middle of a sentence (e.g., "And then why . . .", P203). Both mild agreements and collaboratives appear to communicate that the client has received the information and is continuing to process it.

2. *Insight marker:* Next, there followed an insight marker or a strong agreement. Insight markers are reports of insight which has occurred either at the time or very shortly before the marker: "I never thought of it that way" (P203); "I didn't see that before . . . I didn't see it until you said that" (300-1); "I never thought of that" (401). Strong agreements can be thought of as functionally equivalent to insight markers; both provide the therapist with an index that something has "struck" the client: "Right, exactly" (P208); "Yeah, *yeah!*" (401).

   Insight markers and strong agreement were also reflected in what three of the therapists had to say about the impact of the event: "The light went on" (P203); "I remember the smile and her face. The eyes got a little bit wider and she had a slight smile on her face, as if it was dawning on her"; (P208); "It hit, it made sense to her" (401). These descriptions use tactile or visual metaphors that highlight the suddenness of the event. In addition, the terms used make it clear that the therapists were relying partly on nonverbal cues.

3. *Unfolding:* Finally, one of three things happened: (a) the client explored further, expanding or providing new information about

himself or herself; (b) the client provided a self-interpretation; or (c) the client's response was truncated by the therapist going off in a new direction. These three possibilities all involve the unfolding of the insight event in terms of new exploration or self-understandings. In P208, the behavioral unfolding was truncated: However, the recall data provided by the client indicate that the client later continued the process of exploration; it can be assumed that the exploration would have taken place publicly if the therapist had not interrupted. The existence of this unfolding step was corroborated by recall data from three therapists: "He finished the interpretation and took over for me" (P203); ". . . picking up where I left off" (300); "She took it a step further" (401).

The three steps described above provide the basis for a tentative microanalytic model of one aspect of these insightful events, the process by which the insight event is manifested behaviorally in the client's subsequent task performance. This model runs as follows:

simple agreement → insight marker → unfolding
 (processing)   (if not truncated)

Style

Observer ratings of client vocal quality, video-ratings of expressiveness, and qualitative descriptions of verbal and nonverbal manner provided a complex pattern of information about client communicational style in the postsegments. To begin with, three of the four events produced at least some focused voice in the postsegment. (In contrast, focused voice was found in only one of the presegments.) According to Rice, Koke, Greenberg, & Wagstaff (1979), focused voice indicates a turning of attention inward, as if "to grope one's way through new territory" (Vol. 1, p. 5) Consistent with this, qualitative analyses of nonverbal behavior suggested that clients were in a "thinking" posture, marked by little eye contact and by a move in two events to a more closed, self-focused position (e.g., in 300-1 the client raised her hand to her head at what may have been the "moment of insight").

On the other hand, qualitative observations of speech rate and level of nonfluencies suggests that, if anything, clients became more fluent in postsegments. Finally, level of nonverbal adaptors (signs of nervousness) and illustrators remained about the same, and client expressiveness ratings (video rating scale) were at about the same moderate level in the postsegments as in the presegments. Thus, the pattern that emerges seems to be one involving increased inwardly focused cognitive activity which is manifested verbally, although not necessarily in externally directed communicative activity.

State-Experience

Video ratings of client state following the target interventions indicated a change of psychological state (cf. Horowitz, 1979): clients were rated as more friendly and more optimistic. However, these ratings are somewhat inconsistent with the nonverbal behaviors (especially the trend toward more closed positions).

The most detailed and rich source of information about client state following the target interventions is the client recall data. Client descriptions of the impact of insight events evidenced a variety of common themes.

1. All clients reported a sense of *newness*: "Stuff I hadn't thought about" (P203); "Something I never expected, connected, or thought of" (P208); "It was exactly what I had been saying, but in a way I had never thought of before" (300-1); "A whole new insight" (401).

2. All clients experienced a sense of *relief*: "My confidence level rose . . . I felt less nervous, tense" (P203); "Relief—it was something else to think about" (P208); "Relieved—like the pressure was off me to talk; there had been things resolved" (300-1); "It made me feel that the pressure was taken off because he was saying what I was trying to say" (401).

3. All clients provided evidence that the therapeutic *alliance* had been enhanced: "I felt more sure of her" (P203); "My expectations were growing" (P208); "It made me feel good about the session and about doing it, that there was a purpose" (300-1); "I felt a kind of closeness, some kind of neat camaraderie" (401).

4. All clients described having been *cognitively stimulated*: "Her saying 'I wonder' made me think 'I wonder' and I started to think" (P203); "Trying to visualize it in my mind . . . to see if that was true" (P208); "I just wanted to settle back at that point and really think about that" (300-1); "I was taking what he said and going a little further with it" (401).

5. All clients experienced the therapist's intervention as *important*: "It was a big change point in the session" (P203); "I was sort of amazed" (P208); "An important statement for me; I could see that as a really big thing, Just wow!" (300-1); "It was real important" (401).

6. Three clients reported a sense of *connection*: "I could see where things fit; things started to mesh together" (P203); "Wow, maybe that has some connection" (P208); "He put together all the different pieces that I was talking about, where before it was just a lot of isolated events" (300-1).

7. Three clients described a sense of accuracy in the therapist's intervention: "She got things right" (P208); "That was really true, that

was really how I was feeling" (300-1); "It made me think 'Ahah, yeah, that's right, what he's saying is true'" (401).

The consistency of descriptions among the four cases is striking, and offers the best support for treating these cases as members of a class of significant psychotherapy events.

Quality

Both of the scales used to evaluate quality of client task performance provided evidence for a positive shift in client process accompanying the insight event: Scores on the Patient Experiencing Scale shifted an average of 1.5 points for both mode and peak ratings, to 4.0 and 4.5, respectively. This means that in general clients were at least providing detailed descriptions of their experiences. In fact, there were two cases of experiencing ratings of 5 or higher in the postsegments, as contrasted with the presegments, in which there were no ratings higher than 4. Finally, the positive shift in client experiencing was consistent across all four events. Video ratings of client working also shifted positively in three cases. These two sets of quality ratings suggest that, with the insight event, clients moved more firmly into a working state (cf. Horowitz, 1979).

Summary of Postsegment

The postsegment in these insight events involves a tandem experiential–behavioral process: On the one hand, the insight event unfolds in the client's experience. Thus, the client's energy is turned inward (focused voice, posture) towards the experience of newness, relief and cognitive stimulation–connection. At the same time, however, this experience "spills over" behaviorally and becomes manifest both in the characteristic sequence of agreement–insight marker–unfolding and in enhanced task performance (experiencing and working). Thus, shifts in experience and behavior occur together. In addition, the client experiences help as coming from the therapist (which results in a strengthening of the therapeutic alliance) and reveals that help has occurred (which is interpreted by observers as increased friendliness and optimism). In terms of a state analysis (cf. Horowitz, 1979), one could say the client has moved from a distressed, help-seeking state to a more ideal state which combines working at the therapeutic task with interpersonal engagement.

TENTATIVE MODEL OF INSIGHT EVENTS

The analyses of commonalities in the four insight events have turned up numerous themes and clues for how the change process is operating in these examples. These findings can be woven into a tentative model which is consistent with the task analytic approach (Greenberg, 1977; also

Greenberg, Chapters 3 and 4; Rice & Saperia, Chapter 2). Such a model is diagrammed in Table 8-4 and summarized here.

CONTEXT (PRESEGMENT)

Client and therapist are engaged in a self-understanding task (cf. Greenberg, 1977) in the context of an insight-oriented approach. Shortly before the target therapist intervention, the client moves into a state in which he or she is working toward task resolution while experiencing distress at not being able to attain it. This client state produces an indirect request for help (a statement of the problem accompanied by evidence of not being able to resolve it). This is the behavioral marker (Greenberg, 1977) for the target intervention. In addition, there is a more situational marker: The therapist becomes aware that there is some difficulty in the immediate therapy process which is blocking the client's task performance. These situational markers include therapist errors and time limitations.

INTERVENTION

The contextual factors of task, client state, and markers lead the therapist to perform a major interpretation. This interpretation addresses some core interpersonal issue, allows for feedback from the client, contains redundancy and softening, and is delivered in a friendly manner. In spite

TABLE 8-4. TENTATIVE MODEL OF INSIGHT EVENTS

CONTEXT (PRESEGMENT)	TARGET INTERVENTION	IMPACT (POSTSEGMENT TASK PERFORMANCE)
Task: Self-understanding	*Aspects*	*Stage 1: Processing*
State: Distressed and working	• Content: Core interpersonal issue	• Experience: Thinking, energy inward
Markers	• Action: Interpretation (multipart, redundant, interactive, softened)	• Behavior: Agreement, focused voice, closed posture
• Indirect request for help (statement of problem)	• Style, State: Affiliative, warm	*Stage 2: Insight*
• Difficulty in task environment	• Quality (Imperfections)	• Experience: Newness, accuracy, relief, alliance with therapist
		• Behavior: Insight marker, friendly, optimistic
		Stage 3: Unfolding
		• Experience: Cognitive stimulation, connection
		• Behavior: Increased exploration, self-help
		• State: Friendly and working

of this, it may contain substantial imperfections, which are overlooked by the client.

The actual insight event occurs following the target intervention and can be described as a felt shift (Gendlin, 1978) which is manifested immediately in the client's task performance. The insight event runs through three phases, which may be described as processing, insight, and unfolding: (1) The client immediately (probably during the target intervention) begins processing the new information offered in the interpretation. As the interpretation concludes the client turns his or her attention inward to continue processing. This is communicated behaviorally by mild agreement, focused voice, or closed posture. (2) Next, the insight occurs: the client experiences a sense of newness, accuracy, relief, and helpfulness from the therapist. This is manifested by the insight marker, and by not entirely well-understood behaviors which give a global impression of increased friendliness and optimism on the part of the client. (3) Finally, the client experiences further cognitive stimulation and connection; this is indicated by enhanced task performance in the form of increased self-exploration and self-interpretation.

It should be pointed out that this exact model does not apply to all insight events. Indeed, an analysis of a larger collection of significant events drawn from client 300-1 (Elliott, James, Shulman, & Clines, 1981) suggests that these insight events are unusual in their clarity; most client insight events are probably not so clearly manifested. In these other cases, the felt shift is not manifested immediately or marked as clearly; thus, most appear to go unnoticed by the therapist. In some cases, the insight occurs only later in the session or afterwards. Unsurprisingly, most of these events are not accompanied by process shifts of the type found here. In fact, the chief value of the present collection is precisely their public nature, which makes it possible to trace their unfolding and to add the therapist's perceptions to those of the client and observers. This, in turn, makes them useful for model-building, as "ideal cases."

CONCLUSIONS: IMPLICATIONS FOR RESEARCH AND PRACTICE

RESEARCH

The central purpose of this chapter has been to describe and illustrate the use of a discovery-oriented approach in exploring psychotherapeutic change episodes. The methods described earlier were applied for the purpose of shedding light on one type of significant event in psychotherapy. Interpersonal process recall made it possible to locate a set of four insight events. Once these events had been located, it was possible to analyze them using comprehensive process analysis.

However, interpersonal process recall proved useful for more than locating these events—it was also used to enable clients and therapists to describe what was occurring in these events. In particular, the method opened the door for phenomenological analyses of the events, most strikingly exemplified by the rich detail of client descriptions of the impact phases of these episodes and therapist descriptions of the context of the intervention. Analyzing a set of these insight events for common themes proved to be valuable. This, in combination with the comprehensive process analysis, allowed the generation of a tentative model of client insight events.

This tentative model draws strength and richness from corroboration among observer, client, and therapist perspectives. It is, of course, highly tentative, but has provided a set of hypotheses to be tested on larger sets of insight events. Thus, the example provided an illustration of the stages in the discovery-oriented approach advocated in this chapter: (1) identification of a category of significant change events; (2) location of a set of events exemplifying this category; (3) comprehensive process analysis of each event separately; (4) analysis of the commonalities in the set of events to discover common features or themes; and (5) derivation of a tentative model from the analyses. As developed here, this discovery-oriented approach has much in common with Greenberg's (1977) task analytic approach, in that it selects specific therapeutic events for study on the basis of potency and recurrence, subjects them to analyses whose result is the identification of common features, and uses these common features as the basis for constructing models of the change process in psychotherapy.

PSYCHOTHERAPY PRACTICE

What are the possible practical uses of a discovery-oriented approach to significant psychotherapy events? The following suggestions drawn from the present work are offered largely to illustrate the kinds of conclusions that may be produced by further research along this line.

1. Within self-understanding tasks, clients' indirect requests for help may provide signals of client readiness for major interpretations, particularly if there is other evidence of readiness, such as when the client is working but is distressed and momentarily blocked by some problem in the immediate therapeutic process.
2. Interpretive interventions may have great value in self-under-

standing tasks, especially when they are framed in a tentative manner, delivered in a friendly manner, and structured so as to allow for client feedback and correction or extension along the way.

3. It is important for therapists to be sensitive to insight markers, which signal that an insight event has occurred, and to allow their clients to engage in further self-exporation or self-interpretation.

4. The alliance-building function of insight events suggests that this type of event may have additional value as a predictor of positive psychotherapy outcome.

5. The approach described in this chapter also has some broader implications for the practice of psychotherapy: It clearly illustrates the interactive nature of significant therapeutic events. It suggests an image of clients as highly perceptive, yet forgiving, observers of therapeutic process, particularly of the impact of significant events. It offers the possibility that therapists as well as researchers might benefit from greater use of clients as guides in the discovery and mapping of new territories of therapeutic process.

ACKNOWLEDGMENTS

I am deeply grateful to the clients and therapists who provided and described the four therapy events used in this paper. I am also indebted to Laura Rice and Les Greenberg for the invaluable intellectual stimulation and encouragement they have given me in the development of the work described in this chapter. The example P203 was originally presented at meetings of the Society for Psychotherapy Research, Oxford, England, July, 1979, as part of a workshop to which Marjorie Klein, Les Greenberg, and Germain Lietaer also contributed both ratings and ideas. Cher Morrow-Bradley, Rich Shulman, and Susan Rubenstein helped with the data collection; Howard Filipovich and Tammy Linhart helped with transcription; additional ratings were contributed by Marjorie Klein, Wendy Schwartz, Sue Smitley, Cora Reimschuessel, Linda Harrigan, Judy Zapadka, and James Gaynor. This research was supported in part by grants from the Graduate School of the University of Toledo and National Institute of Mental Health Grant 1 RO-MH35468-01.

REFERENCES

Barrett-Lennard, G. T. Dimensions of therapist response as causal factors in therapeutic change. *Psychological Monographs*, 1962, *76*, (43, Whole No. 562).

Ekman P., & Friesen, W. V. The repertoire of nonverbal behavior: Categories, origins, usage, and coding. *Semiotica*, 1969, *1*, 49–98.

Elliott, R. *Helper behavior rating system, 1979 version.* Unpublished manuscript, University of Toledo, 1979. (a)

Elliott, R. How clients perceive helper behaviors. *Journal of Counseling Psychology*, 1979, *26*, 285–294. (b)

Elliott, R. Fitting process research to the practicing psychotherapist. *Psychotherapy: Theory, Research & Practice,* 1983, *20,* 47–55. (a)

Elliott, R. *"That in your hands . . .": A comprehensive process analysis of a significant event in psychotherapy.* Psychiatry, 1983, *46,* 113–129. (b)

Elliott, R. Interpersonal process recall (IPR) as a process research method. In L. Greenberg & W. Pinsof (Eds.), *The psychotherapeutic process.* New York: Guilford, in press.

Elliott, R., Barker, C., Caskey, N., & Pistrang, N. Differential helpfulness of counselor verbal response modes. *Journal of Counseling Psychology,* 1982, *29,* 354–361.

Elliott, R., James, E., Shulman, R., & Cline, J. Significant events in psychotherapy: A systematic case study. Presented at meetings of the Society for Psychotherapy Research, Aspen, Colorado, June 1981.

Elliott, R., & Shulman, R. *Videorating scale: 1981 version.* Unpublished manuscript, University of Toledo, 1981.

Elliott, R., Zapadka, J., Harrigan, L., Gaynor, J., Filipovich, H., & Reimschuessel, C. *Response empathy rating scale.* Unpublished manuscript, University of Toledo, 1980.

Fiske, D. W. Methodological issues in research on the psychotherapist. A. S. Gurman & A. M. Razin (Eds.), *Effective psychotherapy: A handbook of research.* New York: Pergamon, 1977.

Gendlin, E. T. *Focusing.* New York: Everest House, 1978.

Goodman, G., & Dooley, D. A framework for help-intended communication. *Psychotherapy: Theory, Research and Practice,* 1976, *13,* 106–117.

Gottman, J. M., & Markman, H. J. Experimental designs in psychotherapy research. S. L. Garfield & A. E. Bergin (Eds.), *Handbook of psychotherapy and behavior change: An empirical analysis* (2nd ed.). New York: Wiley, 1978.

Greenberg, L. S. A task analytic approach to the events of psychotherapy (Dissertation, York University, 1975). *Dissertation Abstracts International,* 1977, *37,* 4647B. (Available from National Library of Canada, Ottawa K1A OBA; Order no. 26, 630.)

Hill, C. E. The development of a system for classifying counselor responses. *Journal of Counseling Psychology,* 1978, *25,* 461–468.

Horowitz, M. J. *States of mind: Analysis of change in psychotherapy.* New York: Plenum Press, 1979.

Kagan, N. *Interpersonal process recall: A method of influencing human interaction.* Unpublished manuscript, 1975. (Available from N. Kagan, 434 Erickson Hall, College of Education, Michigan State University, East Lansing, Michigan 48824.)

Kelman, H. Kairos: The auspicious moment. *American Journal of Psychoanalysis,* 1969, *29,* 59–83.

Kiesler, D. J. *The process of psychotherapy.* Chicago: Aldine, 1973.

Klein, M., & Mathieu-Coughlan, P. The Patient and Therapist Experiencing Scales. In L. Greenberg & W. Pinsof (Eds.), *The psychotherapeutic process.* New York: Guilford, in press.

Klein, M., Mathieu, P., Gendlin, E., & Kiesler, D. *The experiencing scale: A research and training manual* (Vol. 1). Madison: Wisconsin Psychiatric Institute, 1969.

Knapp, M. L. *Nonverbal communication in human interaction* (2nd ed.). New York: Holt, 1978.

Labov, W., & Fanshel, D. *Therapeutic discourse.* New York: Academic Press, 1977.

Lambert, M. J., DeJulio, S. J., & Stein, D. M. Therapist interpersonal skills: Process, outcome, methodological considerations, and recommendations for future research. *Psychological Bulletin,* 1978, *85,* 467–489.

Luborsky, L. Measuring a pervasive psychic structure in psychotherapy: The core conflictual relationship theme. In N. Freedman (Ed.). *Communicative structures and psychic structures.* New York: Plenum Press, 1977.

Mahl, G. F. Disturbances and silences in the patients' speech in psychotherapy. *Journal of Abnormal and Social Psychology*, 1956, *53*, 1–15.

Orlinsky, D. E., & Howard, K. I. *Varieties of psychotherapeutic experience.* New York: Teachers College Press, 1975.

Orlinsky, D. E., & Howard, K. I. The relation of process to outcome in psychotherapy. In S. L. Garfield & A. E. Bergin (Eds.), *Handbook of psychotherapy and behavior change: An empirical analysis* (2nd ed.). New York: Wiley, 1978.

Pittenger, R. E., Hockett, C. F., & Danehy, J. J. *The first five minutes.* Ithaca, New York: Martineau, 1960.

Rice, L. N., & Greenberg, L. *A method for studying the active ingredients in psychotherapy: Application to client-centered and Gestalt therapy.* Paper presented at a meeting of the Society for Psychotherapy Research, Denver, 1974.

Rice, L. N., Klein, M., Beck, A., & Greenberg, L. *Development and use of process rating systems in psychotherapy research.* Workshop presented at the eighth meeting of the Society for Psychotherapy Research, Madison, Wisconsin, June 1977.

Rice, L. N., Klein, M., Hill, C. E., Greenberg, L., Elliott, R., Whiteside, J., & Benjamin, L. S. *Comparison of process systems as descriptors of productive interactions in psychotherapy.* Workshop presented at the ninth meeting of the Society for Psychotherapy Research, Toronto, June 1978.

Rice, L. N., Koke, C. J., Greenberg, L. S., & Wagstaff, A. K. *Manual for client vocal quality* (Vols. 1, 2). Toronto: Counseling Development Centre, York University, 1979.

Rice, L. N., & Wagstaff, A. K. Client voice quality and expressive style as indexes of productive psychotherapy. *Journal of Consulting Psychology*, 1967, *31*, 557–563.

Roback, H. B. Insight: A bridging of the theoretical and research literatures. *The Canadian Psychologist*, 1974, *15*, 61–88.

Russell, R. L., & Stiles, W. B. Categories for classifying language in psychotherapy. *Psychological Bulletin*, 1979, *86*, 404–419.

Scheflen, A. E. *Communicational structure: Analysis of a psychotherapy transaction.* Bloomington: Indiana University Press, 1973.

Schenkein, J. (Ed.). *Studies in the organization of conversational interaction.* New York: Academic Press, 1978.

Searle, J. R. Indirect speech acts. In P. Cole & J. L. Morgan (Eds.), *Syntax and semantics, Vol. 3: Speech acts.* New York: Academic Press, 1975.

Standahl, S. W., & Corsini, R. J. *Critical incidents in psychotherapy.* Englewood Cliffs, N.J.: Prentice-Hall, 1959.

Strupp, H. H., Hadley, S. W., & Gomes-Schwartz, B. *Psychotherapy for better or worse: An analysis of the problem of negative effects.* New York: Aronson, 1977.

Waskow, I. E., & Parloff, M. B. (Eds.) *Psychotherapy change measures.* Rockville, Md: National Institute of Mental Health, 1975.

Young, D. W. Meanings of counselor nonverbal gestures: Fixed or interpretive? *Journal of Counseling Psychology*, 1980, *27*, 447–452.

SECTION FOUR

CONCLUSION

9

Future Research Directions

LAURA N. RICE
York University

LESLIE S. GREENBERG
University of British Columbia

INTRODUCTION

In this final chapter we would like to suggest an outline for research programs that might be undertaken by investigators interested in the intensive analysis of change patterns. The core of the program would be the intensive analysis of different classes of recurrent change episodes in order to discover the client mechanisms that make these changes possible. The building up of a collection of well-understood client change mechanisms, together with a knowledge of some of the therapist interventions that can stimulate and shape their emergence, is an urgently needed step in the field. Whether one wishes to develop an informed eclecticism or use a single orientation knowledgeably and flexibly, such a collection would enable one to recognize a variety of markers of opportunities for client change and some of the ways in which change could be implemented.

Even a casual look at different orientations suggests a number of possible change episodes that could be analyzed in order to understand the moment-by-moment processes and the internal client mechanisms involved in the change. Such therapeutic events as the restructuring of irrational beliefs, the redirection of causal attributions, the emergence of warded-off content, or the resolution of "push–pull" ambivalence concerning closeness, described in object-relations formulations, could be analyzed in detail. Each of these can be "explained" within the structure of some theoretical system, but at the level of client mechanisms they are not clearly understood: This is the great gap between theory and practice.

Even more interesting, perhaps, would be explicating and analyzing some of the change episodes observed by expert therapists but still only vaguely and implicitly understood. The study of expert therapists has been suggested for some years as a promising research direction (Bergin & Strupp, 1972), but without the structure of an actual research strategy the task has perhaps seemed too diffuse to undertake. In our suggestions we will pay particular attention to the application of a discovery-oriented approach to identifying and understanding new change episodes.

289

Building up a collection of well-understood client change episodes and an understanding of the client mechanisms involved could be a collaborative effort involving both researchers and clinicians. This would be much like the process in other disciplines of building a cumulative body of knowledge. Over time, shared descriptions of basic change mechanisms would be constructed. Much of the work could be done by separate research teams, thus avoiding many of the problems of collaborative research, yet the separate teams could build toward a shared goal. Eventually it would be possible to recognize that certain client mechanisms are important in a variety of orientations, thereby suggesting a variety of alternative therapist interventions that could be used to stimulate and shape the occurrence of these mechanisms. In addition to the more general mechanisms, a number of others would be found to be unique to particular approaches and could therefore broaden the scope of our understanding.

STAGES OF THE SUGGESTED RESEARCH PROGRAM

We envision a research program that proceeds in three stages. The emphasis of the first two stages would be on discovery and understanding, though each stage would contain some verification designs. The emphasis of the last stage would be on formal designs for testing the discoveries of the first two stages. Stage 1 involves constructing client performance models for one or more classes of change episodes. The research team, working within a particular setting and orientation, identifies and intensively analyzes some class or classes of recurrent change phenomena in order to discern performance patterns and thereby understand the essential client mechanisms of change and the therapist interventions that characterize this class of change events. The team would also verify in a preliminary way the effectiveness of the event in leading to positive change. Stage 2 involves defining the range of application of the models built in Stage 1. In collaboration with clinicians in settings with a broader range of therapeutic approaches and populations, the researcher would investigate some of the variables that limit the applicability of the model. Stage 3 involves verification of the efficacy of the therapist interventions and client mechanisms, making use of more conventional group designs.

The research program suggested here applies specifically to the approach described in Section II, the analysis of change events that involve the resolution of affective tasks. In this approach change events are defined as having a "marker" of an opportunity for change, a series of therapist interventions hypothesized to be optimal for promoting change at this marker, and an ensuing series of client process steps culminating in the resolution of an affective problem. Each of the other four approaches, described in Section III, involves somewhat different definitions of a change episode and each envisions a somewhat different research program. But all of the approaches in this volume have in common the assumption that a detailed understanding of the context of the emergence of certain classes of therapeutic change episodes will point to and illuminate some basic human change mechanisms and that this basic understanding can be integrated into a broad range of therapeutic approaches.

CONSTRUCTING THE PERFORMANCE MODEL

The first stage would focus on the discovery and understanding of different classes of change episodes, drawing heavily on what we consider to be essentially task analytic procedures in order to construct models of recurrent client change events. One could begin with some therapeutic episode already identified as significant by clinicians or assumed to be important within some theoretical system. Or one could function as both investigator and clinician, as in most of the research programs reported in previous chapters.

An especially interesting approach would be an exploratory form of task analysis designed to explicate the implicit maps of expert clinicians not normally involved in research. The investigator would locate one or more expert clinicians regarded by colleagues, trainees, and clients as being instrumental in facilitating substantial amounts of positive client change. The clinician might have an explicit theoretical rationale for his or her interventions or might be guided mainly by an implicit feel for what to do next; for most clinicians it would be some combination of the two. One would select taped or videotaped interviews that both therapist and client regarded as highly productive. The investigator and therapist would listen together to the potent episodes in these interviews, with the investigator asking such questions as "What happened there?", "What made you respond that way?" or "What were you observing in the client's process that suggested that that would be a useful intervention?" Both questions and answers should be at a searching, almost naive level, at which no clinical assumptions are taken for granted. The questioning and discussion should be continued until both participants get a sense of three things:

1. What were the client markers that signaled that there was something that the client needed to tackle and was at that moment ready to work on?
2. Why did those therapist interventions seem appropriate to that moment? In other words, what processes was one trying to stimulate and shape in the client?
3. What would be a successful resolution of the issue, that is, a successful in-session suboutcome of therapy?

At this stage one could also use with the therapists some of the interpersonal process recall (IPR) procedures discussed by Elliott in Chapter 8 or the Tester's Training method described by Greenberg in Chapter 4. This first step may be very time consuming, but in our experience it has proved to be extremely stimulating for the therapist and his or her trainees or students.

Once a recurrent and seemingly potent event—consisting of a marker of an opportunity for change, a client performance, and relevant therapist interventions—is selected, the questioning and the "thought experiment" continue in order to push the clinician to explicate further his or her implicit cognitive map of events of this kind. The goal of this aspect of the investigation is the preliminary description of some possible performance patterns that could appear in successful events. The investigator draws on at least three sources to make these preliminary descriptions: (1) the body of theory relevant to the class of change phenomena selected for study; (2) the explication of the clinician's map; and (3) some informal but intensive study of tapes, videotapes, or transcripts of episodes of the kind selected for anaysis. The preliminary descriptions obtained by these means specify the probable components of the client performance and the possible sequences in which these components might appear. At this beginning stage of the analysis, these descriptions constitute a very tentative and groping understanding of the way in which the phenomena may unfold. The more clearly the possible client performances are spelled out, the more the data-collecting stage will illuminate similarities and differences between the actual therapeutic phenomena and the preliminary description of them.

The generation of the preliminary descriptions of client performance begins a process of looping back and forth between rigorous observations of actual performance and the emerging performance model. This involves the next two aspects of model construction, establishing the reliability and relevance of observational categories and discerning patterns of client performance by means of rigorous observation. During this process of looping the investigator selects or develops several descriptive process rating systems that might serve as indices of underlying client mechanisms taking place. After establishing the relevance and reliability of these systems, the investigator uses them to check whether or not the expected patterns of client performance are actually appearing.

The establishment of the reliability and relevance of observational categories is essentially a measurement construction step in which one asks two related questions. First one asks, "How will we recognize in the performance of the actual clients the elements that make up the preliminary description?" In other words, the investigator attempts to translate the expected performance sequences of the preliminary description as unequivocally as possible into recognizable behaviors. Second, one asks whether or not these client behavior classes can be reliably classified by raters who are blind to the expectations of the investigator.

Without adequate classification systems for assessing and quantifying client performance, the preliminary description can never be adequately corrected and elaborated. The anchoring of theoretical constructs to observables is, of course, a required step in conventional research paradigms, though often this forms the weakest link in the chain. However, the essence of the present approach is a fine-grained description of the actual client process during the event. It is from this that the investigator successively corrects and elaborates the performance descriptions and begins to construct models of some of the mechanisms of change.

Once the investigator has a set of measuring instruments that will capture the phenomena of interest, a series of new examples of the class of phenomena under study are systematically examined. The actual client behavior is rated by means of the descriptive process systems. Comparison of a series of actual client performances with the expected performance of the preliminary description enables one to establish with a large degree of certainty whether or not the expected performance sequences in fact took place. Nevertheless, this procedure is primarily a creative–inductive one in which the tentative description is corrected, enriched, and rethought: Some behaviors that are expected are not found to occur, other performance aspects that have not been thought about are found to occur, and new ideas about processes of change come into focus.

As the investigator's understanding grows and the preliminary description becomes less tentative and more refined and is more or less confirmed by each new series of segments analyzed, a clearer model of expected client performances begins to develop. It is this specific model, relevant to a more general theory of human functioning, yet at the same time testing and extending it, that is an important yield of this investigative strategy.

One further step of the intensive analysis would be the writing of a therapist manual which would guide the therapist in shaping the performances specified in the model. This first manual would be revised and improved as more data were gathered on the effects of different therapist interventions on the appearance of the necessary client performance steps. The manual would be used in later stages of the research in training therapists to facilitate this class of change events.

In this first stage of the research program, two kinds of verification studies are appropriate, one before and one after the model construction. Initially one needs to verify the uniqueness and potency of the change episode by comparing the productivity of sessions in which the marker is followed by the prescribed therapist interventions with the productivity of sessions in which the therapist has been instructed to use a different form of intervention which induces a different client performance at that marker. This design was used in Chapters 2 and 3, and seems essential to ensure that the event to be investigated intensively does contain some active ingredients of change.

The second kind of design, used after the client performance model has been constructed, involves using a new sample of similar characteristics to validate the components of the model assumed to be essential for change. For instance, in Chapter 3, Greenberg used two types of designs to investigate whether clients whose performances contained the key process components had better outcomes than those for whom some of these components were missing.

DEFINING THE RANGE OF APPLICATION OF THE PERFORMANCE MODEL

The goal of the first stage is to understand one or more classes of change events in as pure a form as possible and to construct a reasonably satisfactory model of the essential client performances, together with the appropriate therapist interventions. The goal of the second stage is to move this change event into the field in order to define the individual difference, relationship, and setting variables that limit its applicability. This is done by broadening the range of clients, therapists, and target problems under investigation and identifying the instances in which the expected client performance does not seem to occur. The procedure is essentially one of looking for exceptions to the general rule embodied in the client performance model, in order to understand more fully the phenomena under investigation.

This search for anomalies would proceed by approaching clinicians in settings that use rather different approaches to therapy from the one in which the event was originally studied and that work with somewhat different populations of clients. This extension into the field would not only yield more varied samples, but would also encourage a broad range of practicing clinicians to become more involved in trying out new interventions and studying their effects (Barlow, 1981). Clinicians would be engaged in research at a level of interest to them, while the investigators would profit from the feedback they would receive from the clinicians on how the interventions applied in broader contexts. This is precisely the kind of productive two-way information flow between clinician and researcher that is needed.

Clinicians agreeing to participate would be shown the models of the essential client mechanisms and taught how to recognize the relevant client markers and use the kinds of therapist interventions considered optimal at various points. They would be asked to incorporate these procedures into their approach at times when a suitable client marker appeared. One advantage of using these brief, relatively self-contained treatment units would be that they could be discontinued after a few trials if they seemed clearly unsuitable for the client involved, thus not conflicting with the therapist's responsibility to the client. The clinicians would be asked to use repeated postsession outcome measures as well as final outcome measures. They would also be asked to keep detailed case notes concerning both unsuccessful and successful change episodes.

These broader samples could be used to replicate studies done in the first stage, in order to check the essential components of the model with larger numbers and a broader range of therapists and clients. The most important goal of Stage 2, however, would be the intensive scrutiny of the clients for whom the target change events were not successfully completed. When a client seemed unable to carry out some of the processes necessary for successful completion of the event, the researchers would look for potential variables to explain the anomaly. Was the original marker poorly chosen? Were the therapist interventions not facilitative? Was the nature of the ongoing therapeutic alliance incompatible with therapist interventions required for this event? Or was it a matter of some client characteristics, such as habitual processing styles, that seemed to make particular client operations difficult or impossible? Using detailed process ratings of the relevant sections of the interviews, the case notes of the therapists, and the postsession outcome measures, one could explore each of these questions, teasing out clues to be investigated more systematically. This would be similar to some of the procedures recently advocated by Barlow (1981) for studying psychotherapy, but would have a more specific focus.

The great advantage of this approach would be its application to the study of change episodes in which essential client processes had already been identified. This type of study of targeted change mechanisms where presence or absence could be reliably measured would make possible a more focused search for factors affecting change than would be possible with a general examination of case notes and postsession ratings from the field. Once one is aware of the necessary component client mechanisms, together with the process indicators by which they can be recognized, one can begin to pinpoint what is *not* happening and why it isn't, and thereby increase immensely one's knowledge of factors affecting change.

From Stage 2 one would emerge with some interesting hypotheses in at least three areas: First, one would have a clear and more detailed understanding of the way different therapist interventions could be used to stimulate and shape the necessary client mechanisms at different points during the event. Second, one would have formed a judgment about the kinds of therapeutic alliances in different orientations with which the interventions required by the target event would or would not be compatible. The third and most interesting kind of hypothesis would concern the particular client characteristics that seem to make one or more steps in the change event difficult to achieve. For example, the therapist's case notes might have mentioned a literal quality in the client's thinking or an inability to focus inward, or there might have been comments on an extremely high level of anxiety or rigidity. If such clues were present in the case notes, one could check them further with the detailed process ratings and the therapy session ratings. From such explorations one would identify a limited number of relevant individual difference variables and some possible ways of assessing them.

This discovery-oriented approach to identifying individual difference variables that may affect client performance in particular events is important in at least two ways. In the first place, one would be viewing individual differences in performance in terms of a specific person–situation interaction. In other words, the individual difference variable would be defined in relation to a particular kind of situation which would be objectively similar for all clients. The situation would also be subjectively similar for clients, since the presence of the marker would indicate clients' construal of the situation as one in which they were ready to work on that specific affective problem. An individual difference variable defined in this way would be a differential predictor for a specific class of event rather than for a general therapeutic approach. In the second place, the individual difference variable would be measured at a process or performance level, rather than using global, paper and pencil types of personality measures. This use of a stylistic measure of the client's way of engaging in the situation under study would help to control client performance variance.

VERIFICATION DESIGNS

The task of the third stage is to conduct verification studies using more conventional group designs, from which one could draw causal inferences concerning the discoveries made in the first two steps. A number of different studies could be done in this stage, depending on the investigator's goal. Two such designs are briefly discussed here.

EFFECTS OF SPECIFIED THERAPIST INTERVENTIONS ON KEY CLIENT STEPS: SEQUENTIAL DESIGNS

One type of study made possible by the detailed understanding of client performance would involve testing the efficacy of specified therapist interventions in facilitating the emergence of the client processes found in the previous studies to be essential for change. With the larger numbers available in a group design one could use sequential analysis to establish the effects of particular kinds of therapist interventions on client processes at important transition points.

Although sequential designs have great potential value for understanding the interactions of therapy, there have been basic problems with most such studies using this approach. In the first place, the value of the findings from sequential analysis is limited by the value of the categories used. These categories are often oversimplified and are seldom generated from a study of the actual phenomena themselves. Furthermore, sequential designs, although attending to immediate sequence, make no provision for therapist or client behaviors that may have different meanings in different contexts. Sequential analyses of long interactional sequences require that all behaviors of a certain class be treated in the same way, without regard to the broader context in which they appear. This is one more example of the uniformity myth that the same process in different contexts has the same meaning.

These problems usually arise because investigators employ a purely empirical approach to finding sequential patterns, which only allows the use of a limited number of all-purpose categories. They have no way of specifying in advance important client transition points and the related therapist interventions on which to focus. The great advantage in using sequential designs *after* the key client change points are identified is that more appropriate categories can be used in a focused and context-sensitive manner. Although sequential designs are most often used as pattern-finding devices, they are, in our opinion, more appropriate for verifying patterns that have been discerned and understood by means of intensive analysis.

A form of multivariate uncertainty analysis could be used in studying the effects of therapist interventions on client transitions hypothesized to be important (Garner, 1962; Hayes-Roth & Longabaugh, 1972). An especially useful approach to studying the effects of specific therapist interventions in stimulating the key client transitions was suggested by Bakeman & Dabbs (1976). In this design the probability of the client moving from state C_1 to state C_2 when the specified intervention is used (the conditional probability) is compared with the probability of this same transition occurring in the therapy as a whole without regard to the therapist intervention used (the unconditional probability). If the conditional probability of the transition is significantly greater than the unconditional probability, evidence has been found for the effect of the intervention in producing the transition regarded as important to change.

INTERACTION EFFECTS OF CLIENT STYLE VARIABLES AND TYPE OF INTERVENTION ON OUTCOME

A second kind of study that would become possible at this stage would be a differential intervention design using client style and therapist intervention type as the independent variables. In this design two or more groups of clients, varying on several individual difference variables, would be randomly assigned to two or more "treatment" groups in which a specified series of interventions would be applied at a specified marker. The individual style variables tentatively identified in the previous stage as relevant to the essential client mechanisms could be assessed by means of process ratings in intake interviews, using measures shown in previous studies to be sensitive indicators of essential client processes. Other individual difference variables could be assessed by pretherapy measures. One could aim for a cluster of personality descriptions, with at least one performance level measure.

Clearly, one would still be grouping together clients heterogeneous on some individual difference variables and therefore building-in some of the problems of most individual difference research. But the advantage here would be that one would be classifying clients on the basis of variables assumed to be relevant to particular client mechanisms, rather than on more general "personality" or diagnostic variables. Thus, two usual sources of uncontrolled variance are reduced, at least partially. First, the individual difference variable is a person–situation interaction variable specific to a particular therapeutic event and therefore likely to be more predictive of client performance in that event. Second, it is a variable indicative of the client's ability to engage in the type of client mechanisms that are required for change in that event, for example, the capacity to focus on inner referents, rationally analyze, or free associate.

The following design is intended only as an illustration of this type of study; a variety of different events and task-relevant individual difference variables could be used. The therapists for the first treatment condition would be instructed to listen for markers of intrapersonal conflict of the kind described by Greenberg and to use the two-chair interventions for conflict resolution described in Chapter 3. At all other times the therapists' usual style of intervention would be used. Therapists for the second treatment condition would listen for the same conflict marker, but would respond with cognitive–behavioral problem-solving interventions, such as those specified by D'Zurilla and Goldfried (1971). All the therapists involved could have a basically cognitive orientation or could have as their basic approach one that was neither cognitive nor Gestalt.

Clients would be assigned to one of two groups on the basis of task-relevant individual difference variables, such as vocal quality, and then randomly assigned to one of the two treatment groups. The study would be most effective if the therapy was short-term and if the problems for which therapy was sought had some common focus that was likely to yield relevant intrapersonal conflict markers (e.g., decisional conflicts or interpersonal relationships). Such homogeneity of problem area would reduce another source of uncontrolled variance. As dependent variables one could use both postinterview productivity measures for the particular interviews in which the target events occurred, and pre, post, and final outcome measures.

Clearly, the interaction effects would be of most interest here. One would have a good chance of detecting such effects, if indeed they were present, because the knowledge gained from the first two stages of the research program would enable one to control some of the usual sources of uncontrolled variance. If significant interactions were found between different therapist interventions and task-relevant individual difference variables, there would be immediate implications for differential treatment decisions. A number of such studies, involving different events made up of different client markers and client performances shaped by different therapist interventions, all specified in the intensive analyses of Stages 1 and 2, would enable us to make differential treatment decisions from a knowledgeable position.

An additional study of great interest would be a large-scale study relating process to outcome. With a detailed knowledge of the type of clients and therapeutic environment variables that affect client performance, one could perform studies to experimentally induce the process regarded as crucial to resolution and relate the occurrence of this process to change. The type of design issues involved in uncovering the links between therapist intervention, client process, and outcome would be greatly simplified by the increased understanding and control of the phenomena under study. Initial experimental studies could be done demonstrating that in specified populations, particular therapist interventions led to particular client resolution performances. These would be followed by field experiments linking both therapist interventions and client resolution performances to specific outcomes.

CONCLUSION

In Chapter 1 we pointed to the problems inherent in the two kinds of designs most prevalent in psychotherapy research. The first design involved the use of aggregate process scores, summed without regard for context or pattern, and correlated with some other aggregate process measure or some external variable such as outcome. The second design criticized was the comparative outcome design in which it is assumed that groups of clients homogeneous on some diagnostic or individual difference variable will respond in a homogeneous fashion to some specified "treatment." In each case these studies are not able to provide the answers needed in the field because the questions they are testing cannot be answered in the form in which they are being asked. Thus, too many sources of variance are confounded to be able to provide any clear answers. What is needed is greater clarity in the questions being asked.

The remedy we have suggested is to focus first on understanding, in as pure a form as possible, the series of client mechanisms by which people are able to change in some class of therapeutic event, together with some of the therapist interventions that are effective at different points in the series. The first step in achieving clarity is to identify a client "marker" indicating a client's readiness to tackle a kind of issue. To use an analogy from task analysis, one might say that all clients exhibiting this marker may be seen as being in the same "problem space" at that time, rather than as struggling with very different kinds of issues. A second step toward clarity involves seeing the therapist as a task facilitator who can be instrumental in stimulating and shaping a particular kind of performance strategy in the client. Of the many ways a client might tackle this kind of task, the therapist interventions will shape certain strategies rather than others, especially if the therapist has a "road map" based on a knowledge of the kinds of interventions that are likely to stimulate the essential client mechanisms at different stages.

Once the pattern of task resolution is discerned and understood in this relatively pure form, then it will be possible to broaden out one's research, studying the pattern in groups of clients varying on some task-relevant individual difference variables, in different relationship contexts, or even with different kinds of therapist interventions. With specific patterns of client performance designated as significant change phenomena, we will be able to set up designs that will use these performance patterns as dependent or independent variables to give us much greater experimental control.

The new research paradigm, involving a rigorous but creative approach to the discovery and understanding of client mechanisms of change in a variety of events from different therapeutic orientations, is needed to bridge the gap between research hypotheses and clinically usable findings.

REFERENCES

Bakeman, R., & Dabbs, J. M. Social interaction observed: Some approaches to the analysis of behavior streams. *Personality and Social Psychology Bulletin*, 1976, *2*, 335–345.
Barlow, D. On the relation of clinical research to clinical practice: Current issues, new directions. *Journal of Consulting and Clinical Psychology*, 1981, *49*, 147–155.
Bergin, A., & Strupp, H. *Changing frontiers in the science of psychotherapy*. Chicago: Aldine-Atherton, 1972.
D'Zurilla, T., & Goldfried, M. Problem solving and behavior modification. *Journal of Abnormal Psychology*, 1971, *78*, 107–126.
Garner, W. *Uncertainty and structure as psychological concepts*. New York: Wiley, 1962.
Hayes-Roth, F., & Longabaugh, R. REACT: A tool for the analysis of complex transitional behavior matrices. *Behavioral Science*, 1972, *17*, 384–394.

AUTHOR INDEX

SUBJECT INDEX

Italicized page numbers indicate figures or tables.